MADE IN ARGENTINA MASTERED IN MADRID

MADE IN ARGENTINA MASTERED IN MADRID

How Diego Simeone Awakened a Sleeping Giant

ASHWIN REUBEN BALLAL

pitch

First published by Pitch Publishing, 2022

Pitch Publishing
9 Donnington Park,
85 Birdham Road,
Chichester,
West Sussex,
PO20 7AJ
www.pitchpublishing.co.uk
info@pitchpublishing.co.uk

A CIP catalogue record is available for this book from the British Library.

ISBN 978 1 80150 162 0

Typesetting and origination by Pitch Publishing

Printed and bound in Great Britain by TJ Books, Padstow

Contents

Acknowledgements

MADE IN Argentina, Mastered in Madrid: How Diego Simeone Awakened a Sleeping Giant originated with an idea in December 2020, when Atlético Madrid were top of the league after an excellent start to the 2020/21 season. Diego Simeone had recently done something thought to be impossible, changing his tactics and opting for a new formation altogether, but the shift seemed to work and Atlético found themselves in a position that they were perhaps not supposed to be in. Indeed, with the likes of Real Madrid and Barcelona always being favourites for the title, Spain's La Liga had long been a two-horse race and, at most, the honour of 'best of the rest' was at stake for the remaining 18 sides.

Yet, this was something that Atlético had done before and, in ten full seasons, not only have they firmly established themselves as the 'best of the rest' in Spain, but they have shown that they have what it takes to blow the race for top spot wide open, punching above their weight and winning the league twice while also making their presence felt in Europe's premier club competitions. It was not too long ago that Atlético found themselves well off the dizzying heights that they are at now, but in his trademark counter-attacking style, Simeone has taken them forwards in the blink of an eye, propelling them to unprecedented success.

Despite coming under fire for his often conservative approach, he has shown the world that success can be achieved in many different ways, and not only has the charismatic manager inspired an entire club to achieve success but he has also been a primary source of inspiration for this book. If anything, he has shown the world that as long as you give it your all, you can achieve whatever you set out to do and that with consistent effort you might even surprise yourself with the results. So, thank you, Diego Simeone.

The next big thank you goes out to Pitch Publishing, for believing in my idea and giving me the platform to turn it into reality. As a child, reading was one of my favourite pastimes and, though my passion for writing would develop only later on, I had always wondered how cool it must be for someone to purchase a few pages containing words that you had written. Thanks to Jane Camillin for allowing me to experience this, and special thanks to Duncan Olner, of Olner Pro Sports Media, for giving my dream an identity with his wonderful cover design. I know that I had a lot of worries and concerns with this being my very first book, but thanks to all of them for putting up with me and ensuring that this turned out in the best way possible. It truly was a pleasure working with you.

To Sam Leveridge, for without his valuable feedback and insights this book would never have gotten past the first few drafts. His knowledge and affection for Atlético Madrid and football in general knows no bounds and I will always be grateful for his contribution, shuffling between his media duties to read my work while covering a La Liga game somewhere. I certainly have not made your life easy, Sam, but I can never thank you enough for this massive favour. Hope you enjoyed working on this as much as I did.

Credit also to some of the other brilliant journalists, and outlets such as *These Football Times*, *Into The Calderon* and *La Liga Lowdown*, which have covered both Atlético Madrid and Diego Simeone extensively, providing excellent reference points for some of my work. Euan McTear's *Hijacking La Liga: How Atlético Madrid Broke Barcelona and Real Madrid's Duopoly* was one of the first books that I came across regarding the club, and its excellent narrative on the first title win under Simeone is well worth a read, as is Euan's other work on Spanish football. The same goes for *The Guardian*'s Sid Lowe and *FourFourTwo*'s Andy Mitten, both of whom have consistently displayed top-class journalism extending beyond the topics I have covered, and whose articles I have diligently followed long before the conception of this book. Special thanks to you all.

Big shout-out to Chris Darwen and Total Football Analysis for giving me the space to publish my first football-related article, effectively starting this journey when they took me in and gave me the support and development that I needed to grow. It was here that I first started paying greater attention to the intricacies of tactics and data in football, and without them I might never have wandered this deep into the sport. Chris especially has opened so many doors for me in the football industry and I would not be able to do the work I do today if not for his faith and trust. What started as a hobby has now sparked into a career, giving me the chance to work for clubs and clients across the globe and for all of this, I am truly grateful to you, Chris, and the rest of the Total Football Analysis community as well.

I would also like to thank the four Atlético Madrid fans who very kindly allowed me to pepper them with questions, giving me valuable insights. Their passion for the colours of red and white is evident, and they truly are a fair reflection of the greater Atlético faithful. In no particular order (and with their Twitter handles), they are Ayush (@parteyismo), Emmanuel Lavogez (@captainkoke), Carla Fernández (@cxrlxandone) and Amer Al-Hashimi (@HashimiATM), who also happens to run Atletico Universe (@atletiuniverse), a popular page for any and all content regarding the club. All of them are well worth a follow if you would like to stay in touch with Atlético and learn more, and I really appreciate their contribution to this book.

This brings me to the most important people in my life, my family, to whom I owe everything. Rajini and Sudhindra, my mum and dad, have been constant pillars of support for me all through my life and without their effort and endless sacrifices I could never even imagine writing a single word of this book. Even when I doubted myself, they pushed me to take the leap of faith and gave me all the space I needed to focus on this book, and I only hope that I have made them proud. Not to forget my younger brother, Vinay, who keeps me company for every single game across all the sports that we watch together, and whose jokes and jibes never fail to make my day. I would also like to thank my grandparents, who have loved, supported and pampered me no end, and especially my Joe Thatha, with whom I have shared many books and stories and though he may not be here today to see this, I hope that he is smiling down at me from up above. To them, and all my other extended family and friends, thank you very much for all your love and support, and for making my life that much better.

Finally, I would like to thank you, dear reader, for picking up this book and supporting my work. For so long Atlético Madrid and Diego Simeone have been unjustly cast in a negative light by the footballing world, and my main aim when I took on this project was to convey the true beauty of both club and coach to whoever was willing to listen. Thank you for lending me your ears. Just knowing that this book is in your hands makes all the countless hours of effort worth it, and I only hope that you enjoy reading this as much as I enjoyed writing it.

Ashwin Reuben Ballal

Before We Get Started

BEFORE WE dive in, just a quick note to explain the overall structure and introduce some illustrations and terms that you will come across in order to help you better navigate through the story.

This book actually starts about six months prior to Diego Simeone's arrival as a coach, looking into some of the problems, mainly tactical, that plagued Atlético immediately before his appointment. This should give you some idea of the urgent issues that needed fixing and, considering the fact that Simeone joined Atlético in the middle of the 2011/12 season, it would give you some insight into the tools that he had to work with since he would not be in a position to instantly make drastic changes.

Following this, we will look into the changes that he has been able to make later on relating to personnel, studying the recruitment pattern of Atlético through Simeone's tenure in order to understand how they have managed to assemble a squad boasting top talents in spite of a budget that pales in comparison to some of their bigger rivals.

While also including anecdotes and story elements, this book is primarily a tactical walkthrough of Simeone's Atlético, detailing the various patterns of play that are evident in his teams and highlighting key elements of his overall footballing philosophy. Rather than simply go through each variation as a whole, we will look into the specific roles of individual player positions across these different tactics hence it has been split into different chapters that look into each position separately.

A few definitions to note:

Black circles – highlighted Atlético Madrid players (according to position being discussed)

Grey circles – other Atlético Madrid players

White circles – opposition players

CB – centre-back

FB – full-back (right-back or left-back)

WB – wing-back (right wing-back or left wing-back)

CM – central midfielder

W – winger

F – forward

CAM – central attacking midfielder (not shown opposite)

GK – goalkeeper (not shown opposite)

- - - → *indicates the direction/path of movement of a player*

——→ *indicates the direction /path of a pass made by a player*

In order to help you visualise the tactics and sequences in question, we will be making use of figures, or tactics boards, like this one:

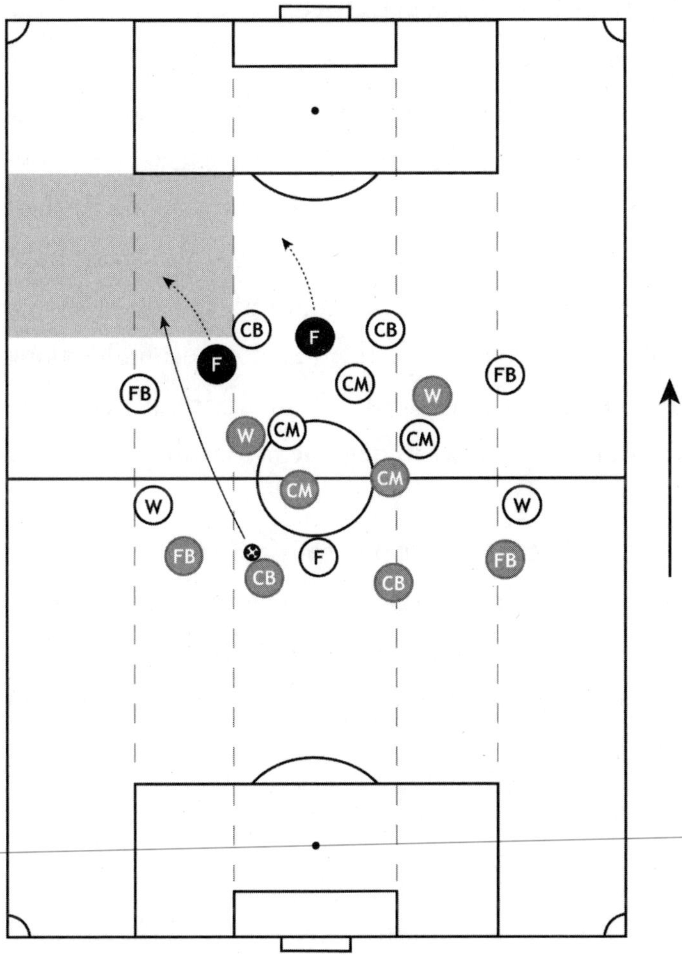

Sample Figure

Greyed-out spaces of the pitch indicate regions that have been highlighted in the current description

The vertical arrow along the side of the pitch indicates the direction of attack for Atlético Madrid

Dotted lines on the pitch are used to segregate the field into the wide areas, central areas and the half-spaces. The half-spaces, often referred to as the channels, are the spaces between the wide and central areas and are believed to be more advantageous positions of the pitch especially in attack, often owing to their accessibility. In our book, we will use the terms half-space and channels interchangeably, but do note that 'half-space' refers to the fixed narrow rectangles along the pitch, while the term 'channels' usually refers to vertical spaces between defenders, meaning they could vary in size.

Any other terms or phrases used will be explained as and when they appear in the course of this book.

Now that you are familiar with the general outline and what to expect in each chapter, let us get straight into it.

1
Introduction

'BUT, DAD, if you do well, you won't come back.'

Diego Simeone finds himself in Mar del Plata, a beach town in Argentina, sipping his coffee and munching on some croissants with his youngest son, Giuliano. He has just come off the phone and, having filled his eight-year-old in on the conversation, he awaits the child's response. For a few moments there is silence, before Giuliano finally speaks.

'Are you going to manage Falcao?'

'Yes.'

'Are you going to play against Messi?'

'Yes.'

'And Ronaldo?'

'Yes.'

'But, Dad, if you do well, you won't come back.'

This last line momentarily catches Simeone Sr off guard, not because his son has put an 'if' in that statement, but because it is perhaps the only thing about the phone call that required some thought. After all, it was a call that he had seen coming for some time now, and he knew that there was always going to be another chapter in his affiliation with Atlético Madrid. In truth, it had only been about six and a half years since the previous one had closed, when Simeone left Madrid for the second time and returned to Argentina to see out his playing career, but right from then he had been patiently planning his homecoming.

Simeone and Atlético go way back, but while he has largely remained the same over the years, the same cannot be said about the club that he had twice played for. Once firmly Spain's third-biggest club, Atlético looked nothing like that when the call went out to Simeone in December 2011 and frankly, there was no telling if they would ever get there again. They had not done enough on the pitch to suggest as much for quite some time and this was only made worse by the complete lack of structure and stability off it. It had all gone wrong for a club that is so rich in history, though some may argue that it was not even their fault. To understand why, let us first go all the way back to the beginning.

Founded in 1903 as Athletic Bilbao Sucursal de Madrid by three Basque students living in Madrid,

Club Atlético de Madrid was initially a branch of Athletic Bilbao (Bilbao), the team that the students had supported. Adopting the blue and white halved tops of Athletic, it was not until 1911 that they donned the now famous red and white stripes when their parent club switched over, hence earning them the nickname of *Los Rojiblancos*, or 'The Red and Whites', and since the pattern resembled the cloth used to make mattresses at the time they would also come to be known as *Los Colchoneros*, or 'The Mattress Makers'. While one of the explanations for this change of colours attributes it to the cost-effectiveness of printing the same combination as those on the mattresses, another rather interesting one suggests that the original blue and white kits had been linked to Blackburn Rovers in England, with the clubs sending someone to buy their kits from there. It is said that on one such visit, the delegate failed to find a Blackburn kit, instead purchasing the red and white tops of Southampton who happened to be the club from the port city they were in and the rest is history.

Later on, in 1921, they would split from their parent club and come to be known simply as Athletic Madrid, going on to win most of the important competitions at the time over the next decade. Their successes then warranted an invitation for the inaugural La Liga season in 1929, but just two seasons later they would suffer their first relegation to the second division, though they would return again in 1934. They should have been relegated once again after a couple of years, but the Spanish Civil War would postpone this, and with Real Oviedo unable to play owing to the destruction of their stadium, Athletic Madrid would win a play-off against second division champions Osasuna to stay in the top flight.

However, the club had lost eight of its players in the war, and hence it would merge with Aviación Nacional, a side founded by the Spanish Air Force that had been denied a place in the top flight at the last minute, to form Athletic Aviación de Madrid in 1939. The merger would prove to be successful and the club would win its first La Liga title that season, before retaining it in 1941, and with a decree that year from dictator General Francisco Franco banning teams from using foreign names, the name was changed to Atlético Aviación de Madrid. Eventually, they would drop the military association in 1947 and settle on Club Atlético de Madrid, or simply Atlético Madrid.

From then on though, city rivals Real Madrid established themselves as the dominant force in Spain, and with 14 league titles between 1961 and 1980 they were clearly the team to beat. This is not to say that Atlético were without their own successes, and in the next 40 years up to 1987 they would win the league six times along with six Copa del Rey triumphs and one each of the European Cup Winners' Cup, Intercontinental Cup and Supercopa de España. They would also make the final of the European Cup in 1974, a tie which is now infamous for the manner in which Atlético suffered defeat.

With just a minute to play and Atlético in the lead thanks to a curling free kick from the legendary Luis Aragonés in extra time, the story goes that goalkeeper Miguel Reina, father of Pepe Reina, turned to hand over his gloves to a photographer only to be caught out by a long-range effort from Bayern Munich defender Hans-Georg Schwarzenbeck. Of course, there is no conclusive evidence to verify this incident and Miguel Reina would deny this, but in an age without penalty shoot-outs the game would be replayed (the only time in the competition's history), only for Atlético to lose 4-0, now earning them the name of *El Pupas*, 'The Jinxed Ones'. There would be some sort of redemption though when, after Bayern refused to participate in the Intercontinental Cup the following season owing to fixture congestion, Atlético, now with Aragonés as manager, would take their place and lift the trophy.

'*Ganar, ganar, y volver a ganar*' was Aragonés's famous principle – win, win, and win again, and

Atlético's top scorer would go on to become their most successful manager across four different stints between 1974 and 2003, even going on to manage the national team and bringing them their first international trophy in 44 years when they triumphed at Euro 2008. It is fascinating that most of Atlético's dogged style and Spain's neat tiki-taka football can be attributed to the same person, but such was the legacy of Aragonés that his importance to both club and country cannot be understated, though the end of his first stint at Atlético would signal a turn for the worse for the side he once described as his life.

In 1969, a newly constructed building near the Spanish city of Segovia collapsed, killing 58 people and leaving many more injured. It was revealed that the structure had been opened even before the cement had dried, and that it had been erected without any plans or even consultation with a surveyor or architect. The man responsible? A certain property tycoon by the name of Gregorio Jesús Gil y Gil. A wildly extravagant character, Jesús Gil was everything that you would associate with an eccentric and rich bad guy and more, a man who had grown up in a brothel and later on starred in his own television series where he answered phone calls in a jacuzzi surrounded by women in bikinis. He would even be slapped with a five-year jail sentence for the building collapse, only to be released after 18 months following a pardon from General Franco himself. Why he is relevant to our story, though, is because in 1987, Gil would become the president of Atlético Madrid.

Atlético's problems in the modern era can be traced back to that fateful day when, after promising the signing of star Portuguese winger Paolo Futre in a Madrid nightclub, Gil completed his heist and took over the club in what would become their last presidential elections to date. He had not even been in the running for long, but his explosive entrance at the end saw him win convincingly and, even though there were some initial successes with five consecutive top-four finishes in his first five seasons and two Copa del Rey titles in this timespan, the club were in for a massive shock.

In 1992, Gil would controversially convert Atlético into a Sociedad Anónima Deportiva, or a Public Limited Sports Company, and while the fans did not immediately realise it, they were having their club taken away from right under their noses. Gil and his partner, film producer and current president Enrique Cerezo, would illegally acquire the majority stake (95 per cent) and to make matters worse he would close the youth academy as a 'cost-saving measure', a move which allowed Raúl to move to Real Madrid and become one of the finest players of his generation. By this time, he had also founded his own right-wing political party, GIL, named after himself (Grupo Independiente Liberal), and he was elected as the mayor of Marbella in 1991.

He clearly knew how to get votes, but his discriminatory and often extreme comments and actions regularly made the headlines, and one thing he was never afraid of was sacking coaches. In 1993, he ended Aragonés's second managerial stint, before going through another four coaches by the end of the season, and when Atlético narrowly escaped relegation in 1995 yet another change occurred and Radomir Antić was brought in to lead the side. A shock title followed the next season, with Simeone playing a crucial role in midfield, and Atlético managed to secure a league and cup double by winning the Copa del Rey as well. Gil would famously parade through Madrid on an elephant to celebrate the championship and Antić would survive for three consecutive seasons, but when he too was dismissed, Gil's reputation for skimming through coaches came to the fore once again. In total, he ended up going through 39 in his 16 years in charge, the third-longest tenure only behind Cerezo and the legendary Vicente Calderón.

It was this recklessness that saw Atlético face their first relegation since 1934 when they went down to the second division in 2000, and they started the new millennium well away from their heights of just four years prior. There was no final-day escape this time, though Gil and Cerezo were carrying out escapes of their own, having been saved from prison for their illegal takeover of the club by a statute of limitations simply because too long had passed since the case was lodged. Gil, however, would still have to step down from his role as mayor in 2002, after being issued with a 28-year ban from holding public office for funnelling money from the city council into Atlético via a sham shirt sponsor.

At this point, Aragonés had just completed his fourth and final coaching stint at the club, bringing them back up at the second time of asking, with a 19-year-old by the name of Fernando Torres captaining the side. What should have been 'one little year in hell', according to Gil, ended up being two, though when he eventually handed over the reins to his son in 2003, a year before his passing, it can be said that Atlético had spent 16 years going to hell and back. Gil's reputation for violence, racism, corruption and sexism tarnished the club's image and left it almost irreparable and, even with his departure from the post of club president, there would only be a slight improvement.

Atlético were still far from competing for major trophies and, in truth, all that they had going for them was their world-class line of forwards that grabbed the spotlight year after year. Miguel Ángel Gil Marín, the son of Jesús Gil, and Cerezo never got along and there seemed to be a power struggle at the top, with each one trying to out-do the other. The only success they would have was a Europa League win in 2010, followed by a UEFA Super Cup triumph later that year, but the trophy cabinet had long been collecting dust. As a club, Atlético had become a shell of their former selves, and the only constant through all this would be their fans.

'*Papa, ¿Por qué Somos del Atleti?*' a child asks his father from the back seat of a car, just as they stop at the red light. 'Dad, why do we support Atleti?' The father is silent, appearing lost for words and fails to offer a response. Instead, words flash across the screen. 'It is not easy to explain. But it is something very, very big.' This was the advertisement that Atlético ran when they went down into the second division, appealing to the passion of the fans to get them through this period. The ad itself would garner so much attention, and become an infamous part of the club's history, because in those few seconds it paints a perfect picture of Atlético. There was no logical reason to support them and yet, even when they were faced with relegation in 2000, ticket sales skyrocketed beyond explanation.

Somehow, fans had embraced the suffering and heartbreak that had become associated with the club and the narrative of being jinxed or cursed only served to strengthen the bond. Interestingly, there were enough events to suggest that Atlético were indeed a lucky side as, after all, not many clubs can claim to have been spared from relegation owing to a civil war, only to then win the league upon its resumption, and again not many clubs can claim to have won a trophy, in this case the Intercontinental Cup, without even actually qualifying for it. Still, having been overshadowed by Real Madrid during their best years from the 1960s to the 1980s, and never being able to cross the final hurdle of the Champions League or its equivalent meant that somehow the description stuck and Atlético developed an underdog mentality, a feeling of 'us against the world' that created a strong sense of unity.

In fact, the only thing stronger than this was their feeling of hatred towards Real Madrid, and Atlético fans simply cannot stand the flashiness and seemingly materialistic nature of their city rivals. 'Our fans are prisoners of a feeling, theirs are prisoners of results,' Fernando Torres would say, clearly not afraid of stating where the loyalties of each club lay. Most in red and white would agree and naturally, as in all rivalries, those in pure white would disagree, but in truth there would be a long period of time where it felt like it was the Atlético fans themselves who were prisoners of their club's results. They never really had much to cheer about and, even if they did, it was only a matter of time before it all came crashing down only for them to dust themselves off and ride this emotional rollercoaster again. It was football masochism, if you wish, with an entire fanbase growing stronger through the suffering.

This loyalty in the stands is perhaps Atlético's biggest resource, and it is no coincidence that the club entered into its most unstable period the moment it was taken away from its fans. Jesús Gil, Cerezo and Gil Marín had let their financial motives blind them from seeing the importance of the fans, though in Gil Sr's case it was also probably his huge ego, and with their haphazard running of the club they failed to properly unite the fans to fuel success. Instead, they took advantage of the fact that the fanbase would get behind anyone that donned their colours, setting the precedent for a constant changing of cast in search of short-term success that never seemed to arrive. This is, of course, until that phone call went out in December 2011, to their 49th coach in 21 years.

Atlético were in yet another downward spiral, and for a side that had finally shown some promise after winning the Europa League and the Super Cup the year before, it was back to square one. They hovered dangerously above the relegation zone as the halfway point of the season was approaching and once again the manager bore the brunt of the criticism, but pressure was mounting on Gil Marín and Cerezo as well. Their plans to build on from those victories and develop the club internationally had come crashing down even before they even took off, and it was only a matter of time before their frontman, who they had conveniently hidden behind, needed replacing. In truth, this managerial choice had not been popular at all considering some of the other names that were available, meaning that the next one needed to be right, or at least good enough to deflect the blame for a bit longer.

The name pulled out of the hat this time? Diego Pablo Simeone. He was the perfect choice because his appointment would finally unite the fans behind the manager as, having twice played for the club and being adored by the masses, it was evident that he would not be heckled nearly as badly as some of his predecessors if things went wrong and this was really all that the board needed. In all fairness, Simeone's own managerial record until then had been as inconsistent as Atlético and there was no telling how long this arrangement would last, or how well it would go, but for the time being there was someone that could defuse the situation for a while. This was a man who had been a crucial part of the previous Atlético side to win the league and unlike Gil Marín and Cerezo even, this was a man who knew very well what the club was all about.

Born in Buenos Aires, Argentina, in 1970, Simone, it could be argued, was born to be an Atlético from the very first moment as, even though his upbringing was far more privileged than his exterior suggests, he would never compromise on his core values of discipline and determination. His father was a successful salesman and his mother a hairdresser, but the pair would raise young Simeone to 'play football like a soldier', instilling those core values that are still evident today. With Argentinian football going through some of its most successful years during his childhood, winning the World Cup on home soil in 1978 and then in Mexico eight years later led by Diego Maradona, Simeone soon became hooked and made his mind up very early on that this was what he wanted to do.

Like most, he would be laughed off in school when openly admitting his ambitions, but what always stood out was his ability to lead, and a maturity that was far beyond his age. When he was about nine or ten, his music teacher would ask him to play the role of conductor for the band and, even if Simeone did not really know why at the time, his natural ability to lead shone through despite having to deal with students that were older than him as well. This would carry over to the football pitch and, when he was old enough, he took his game from the streets to the youth ranks of Vélez Sarsfield, linking up with another seasoned leader in Victorio Spinetto.

Spinetto had been a no-nonsense centre-back who had both played for and coached the national team at different stages on either side of a 14-year period during which he was the coach of Vélez, and he was also one of the key figures during Argentina's drastic change in style, which saw them move from their beautiful, free-flowing football to a more rigid and hardcore approach. By the time Simeone was coming through the academy though, Spinetto was away from the spotlight and helping his club with their youth setup, and it was here that Simeone picked up some of his early footballing philosophy, which would revolve around effort and tenacity. In fact, this immediately became a part of Simeone's own game, earning him his infamous nickname of *El Cholo*, a term that can be associated with a street slur, but in this case, one that was passed on owing to a resemblance to former Boca Juniors defender Carmelo Simeone (no relation) who was known for his intensity and doggedness.

By 17, *Cholo* had made his debut for Vélez and he had already given his first motivational speech after reporting late for his very first Argentina Under-20 training session. Simeone and a team-mate, Antonio Mohamed, had the wrong time and, despite thinking that they were early, they soon realised that the rest of the squad were long gone. Public transport was all they had but a train journey and a bus ride later, the pair had no money and still needed to catch another bus to get to the training camp. 'Take a good look at this face. One day I will be a professional footballer. I will play for Argentina. I will be a star. Remember my name, and also his. Don't forget us. We need just a small favour,' he would say to the bus driver and the pair rode this last leg free of cost. They were still over five kilometres away when the bus reached its last stop though, but the ever-determined Simeone would urge his team-mate on and the pair would run the remaining distance to finally reach their destination.

Training was over by this time, but impressed by the attitude, first team coach Carlos Bilardo would give them a chance to train with the senior players instead, accelerating Simeone's international career. He would make his senior debut the following year in 1988 and, by 1991, both Simeone and Mohamed were making the starting XI for their country and would go on to win the Copa América that year, before repeating the feat in 1993. Simeone's stock had risen at club level as well, and by the time he tasted international success, he had already moved to Pisa in Italy in 1990, still only aged 20. They were by no means the most exciting club in Italy, let alone Europe, but when their under-pressure president was glancing through a dossier full of promising Argentinian players on deadline day, his eyes would settle on young Simeone. 'I like him, he has a determined face,' he would remark, and just like that, *Cholo* was off to Europe.

He was still relatively unknown, but once again his professionalism and ability would catch the eye and Pisa knew that they had a gem on their hands. This was a player who could tackle, pass and cover every inch of grass and even though the club faced relegation in their first season, Simeone was arguably their most valuable asset. He would stay on for another year and in spite of an injury-affected campaign, it was clear that Serie B was too small a pool for him to swim in and the biggest clubs in Europe had taken notice. At this time, Bilardo had joined Spanish side Sevilla and he would once again bring Simeone to the big leagues, seeing him link up with Maradona at club level now. Both Bilardo and Maradona would leave within a year though, but Simeone would stay on under the new manager, none other than Aragonés himself, before moving to Atlético at the end of his second season in Seville.

It was 1994 and *Cholo* donned the red and white colours of *Los Colchoneros* for the first time, though his first season there could not have gone much worse. Four different managers would take charge of the side that year and Atlético would escape relegation by a single point after a final-day draw, and Simeone would have been forgiven for thinking that this was all a big mistake. He stayed on though, thankfully, and with Antić taking charge as coach he would be unleashed in his most forward role yet, scoring 12 times that season and finishing as the club's second-highest scorer en route to a league and cup double. It was Simeone who scored the opening goal in a final-day victory that sealed the title, Atlético's first in 19 years, and he was already a club legend. '*Olé, Olé, Olé, Cholo Simeone*' they chanted from the stands, and they would continue doing so even after he left the following season, in 1997.

Simeone returned to Italy, this time with Inter Milan, who boasted the likes of Javier Zanetti and Youri Djorkaeff, with a certain 20-year-old Brazilian by the name of Ronaldo leading the line. Luigi Simoni's side played a more counter-attacking style of play, originating from Italy's famous *catenaccio* and with Simeone playing regularly as a ball winner in midfield, Inter would finish second in the league and win the UEFA Cup in his first season. At the end of that campaign, *Cholo* would link up with his countrymen for the 1998 World Cup and despite some good performances in a run to the quarter-finals, he would make the headlines for a different reason. Facing England in a round of 16 tie, Simeone would go in hard for a challenge on David Beckham, prompting the Englishman to kick out at him as he walked away. The extent of the contact was visibly not much, but Simeone would go to ground and Beckham would be shown the red card, his side eventually losing on penalties. 'You take advantage of all the opportunities you find in your life,' Simeone would say in reference to the incident, delighted he had sent his side into the next round.

Their World Cup would end there though, and after another year at Inter, *Cholo* would move to join Sven-Göran Eriksson at Lazio, who had just narrowly missed out on the league title the year before. Simeone himself had little say on the deal, with Inter's president Massimo Moratti using him as part of a negotiation which brought Christian Vieri to the club. However, the move would work out exceedingly well and, with the attacking flair of Pavel Nedvěd, Juan Sebastián Verón and Hernán Crespo among the ranks, it was Simeone's signing that stabilised the midfield and helped deliver Lazio's second title in their history, before edging out former club Inter in the cup to secure his second double as a player, and the first since Atlético. In spite of this, Simeone insists to this day that Inter is where his heart lies in Italy, and after a couple of seasons more at Lazio, he would return to Spain and Atlético in 2003.

There were no heroics in the capital this time around and, aged 33, Simeone was winding down his playing career in a relatively mid-table Atlético side. It was only their second season back up in the top flight and, playing alongside Fernando Torres during Gregorio Manzano's first stint, he enjoyed an 18-month swansong in red and white, eventually departing in December 2004, stating that he would rather leave on a high than become a source for media speculation as a senior player and risk ruining his relationship with his favourite club. He would return to Argentina with Racing Club for the final year of his playing career, holding the record for having the most appearances for the national side (the last of which came in 2002) at the time, but if you think that there would be a break at this point, then you are certainly in for a shock.

Simeone was about 27 or 28 when he decided to become a manager, going back home from training at Lazio to pick up a folder and pretend that he was taking a training session. Such was his attention to detail even then that, by the end of this make-believe session, he would find himself surrounded by notes and drawings, and many believed that it was only a matter of time before he took his place in the dugout. Little did they know how soon it would happen, though, because one day Simeone was a football player for Racing and the next day he was their manager, his team-mates now directly under him. He had politely declined the offer twice before, but at the third time of asking he accepted and duly positioned himself on the sidelines. Racing were in pretty bad shape at the time and fighting relegation, meaning that Simeone's managerial career got off to a rough start and it was not until his seventh game that he picked up his first victory, though he eventually got them over the line. The election of a new club president would see Simeone being replaced, however, and he would take over at Estudiantes the following season.

It was here that *Cholo* tasted his first success, winning his first league title as manager and Estudiantes's second in 23 years after an exciting campaign that needed a final play-off match to decide the champions. Estudiantes were not as competitive the next year though, and Simeone would leave to join River Plate in 2007, taking charge of a side with a young Radamel

Falcao and Alexis Sánchez in their ranks. Once again, he would finish with the championship, but Simeone's style of play was still far from the one we know today and it was truly all in or nothing. The following season would prove to be disastrous and, with the side languishing at the bottom of the table with six games to go, he would leave at the end of 2008 and take up his next role a few months later in April 2009, when he joined San Lorenzo. It was yet another club in disarray, but there would be no success here, and a rather quiet stint saw them finish 17th, with questions popping up about Simeone's true managerial ability.

Nevertheless, he would leave Argentina for Italy for the second time and sign on to manage Catania at the start of 2011. The Italian club had 12 Argentinian players and this made Simeone a natural choice, but it was yet another relegation battle that he had on his hands. This time, though, he had seemingly understood that the conservative approach was the way to go and he instilled defensive principles that would define his managerial style, achieving safety with a game to spare and ending the campaign ten points clear of the drop zone. However, despite having a year left on his contract, Simeone would return to Argentina after a job well done and once again become the manager of Racing, though his second stint would end after just 19 games. The call had come, and *Cholo* was on his way back to Atlético.

So much about his playing and managerial career until that point was distinctively Atlético, from his gritty, combative style of play to his rollercoaster and nomadic managerial career that mirrored the very club that he was going to join, and it was no wonder that the pair felt such a strong connection to each other. Knowingly or unknowingly, Simeone had lived and breathed like a *Colchonero* all his life, and knowingly or unknowingly, Gil Marín and Cerezo were renewing one of football's greatest love affairs with this incredible marriage of fire. For all we know, there might be an alternative universe where this particular homecoming may have proven to be too much for either party, combusting rather unceremoniously, but this would not happen here and Simeone would treat the love of his life with the greatest care possible.

He understood what this club represented and, right from day one, he would ensure that his side encapsulated everything that Atlético stood for. 'The people of Atlético always wanted a competitive team. A team that was strong in defence and a team that would play on the counter attack and be a nuisance for the super powerful sides. My objective was focussed on that,' he said, making his intentions very clear and to do this he knew that what they lacked in financial power had to be made up by sheer effort. This was not something Simeone could do on his own either, and he set about transforming the entire club to get behind the core values of Atlético, igniting a spark that would result in unprecedented success.

Two of the more famous men involved in this transition would be long-serving assistant Germán '*Mono*' (Monkey) Burgos and fitness coach Óscar '*Profe*' (Professor) Ortega, who would ensure that the squad were regularly kept in check. Burgos was an imposing figure who had apparently been denied a place at Real Madrid owing to his long-haired appearance, instead playing for Atlético as a goalkeeper from 2001 to 2004. Burgos has battled cancer, been the frontman of a rock band named The Garb after his full initials and even been a coach on a football reality show, but he would finally join Simeone at Catania and follow him to Racing and eventually Atlético. 'I'm not Tito, I'll rip your head off,' he would famously say in a touchline confrontation with José Mourinho during a Madrid derby, referencing the time the Portuguese had poked then Barcelona manager Tito Vilanova in the eye. Much like Simeone, Burgos knew this club inside out and, much like Simeone, he was an eccentric figure with a cold exterior.

As for Ortega, his partnership with Simeone had started in the 2003/04 season when the latter had returned to Atlético as a player, with Ortega the fitness coach of the side at the time. The Professor's methods impressed Simeone so much that, when he started his managerial career, he took Ortega on board and has retained him ever since, through all his clubs, before coming back to Atlético. Ortega had been a rugby coach in his early days, but as he shifted over to football he would retain his intensive methods to ensure that the players could be as fit and tough as their rugby counterparts. This was perfect for Simeone and for Atlético, where the philosophy was now to cover every single blade of grass if they had to in search of success and the 'living hell' that the players were put through before the season would pay dividends by the end of the campaign.

Just like that, Atlético went from being a side that looked completely defeated, a feeling that had become increasingly ingrained, to one that was good enough to challenge the big guns and Simeone had channelled all his principles, *Cholismo* as it would come to be known, into the entire club. These principles were born of Atlético tradition, and back to the club they would go.

To this day, you will find a bouquet of flowers carefully placed near the far-right corner flag (when looking out from the tunnel) for every single home game, a tradition that has been carried on since 1996 when Margarita Luengo first left her idol and the side's designated set-piece taker, Milinko Pantić, two red and two white carnations, claiming that Atlético would score four goals that day. As fate would have it, the side would run out 4-1 victors, with Pantić scoring once and assisting another two, and the tradition stuck. Margarita says that Pantić initially moved them out of the way, but after explaining it to him via a note during one game, the tradition continued and four carnations have now become 24, half red and half white.

Only once during a family emergency has this been missed, but even through a stadium change, Margarita's increasing age and even the Covid-19 pandemic, the carnations remain at the corner flag. Club captain Koke took on the responsibility of calling Margarita before the first behind-closed-doors game during the pandemic to ensure that the flowers were placed properly, saying, 'Let's hope this brings us a lot of luck, let's hope that we win and let's hope that we score from a set piece.' Prophetic words they would be, and Koke himself would take a corner from that very spot in the 81st minute to give Atlético victory. In fact, when Atlético had won the league in 1995/96, nearly half their league goals had been from set pieces and, following this, in

2013/14, they had the second-highest number of set-piece goals in the league as well. Somehow, even the smallest of traditions had been reflected in Simeone's philosophy.

At time of writing, he stands as Atlético's most successful manager ever, having won eight trophies in just over a decade. Two La Ligas, two Europa Leagues, two UEFA Super Cups, one Copa del Rey and one Supercopa de España make up his cabinet, with two Champions League final appearances being an achievement as well, though in typical Atlético fashion he is yet to cross this final hurdle. 'My personality as a manager is down to the essence of my family, and of being Argentinian. There are also shades of when I was a footballer in Italy and Spain,' he says, and for someone who described himself as playing with a 'knife between the teeth', this Atlético side is not just a modern portrayal of *Rojiblanco* tradition, but also an accurate reflection of their charismatic leader, *El Cholo.*

For, whatever that description meant, it paints the picture of an aggressive warrior ready for battle, and right from his upbringing on the streets of Buenos Aires to the pitches of Vélez, from Argentina to Italy to Spain and back, and from Argentina to Italy and then Spain once more, his is a style that fuses so many elements together, eventually arriving at a formula for success that fits like a glove at his beloved Atlético. '*Partido a partido*,' he always says, meaning to take everything 'game by game', and with each passing week, the legacy of *Cholo* grows.

Made in Argentina and mastered in Madrid, this is how Diego Simeone awakened a sleeping giant.

2

The Predecessor: Gregorio Manzano

'Atlético is going to be strong and powerful'

'*NO SOY un incapaz.*'

Roughly translating to 'I am not incompetent', these were the words that Gregorio Manzano uttered at his presentation as Atlético Madrid manager in June 2011.

'If I am here it is not because my agent is García Quilón. There is no strange situation. I am here because I am a professional and I believe in myself … Atlético is going to be strong and powerful.'

Manzano was not new to coaching, and furthermore not new to Atlético Madrid, when he signed on to lead *Los Rojiblancos* in June 2011. In fact, he was a well-respected professional who first began coaching back in 1983, at the age of 27, moving up the ladder and coaching sides in Spain's third and second divisions before arriving at the top flight with Real Valladolid in

1999. The journeyman coach swapped outfits regularly from then on, moving to Racing Santander (2000), Rayo Vallecano (2001) and Mallorca (2002) en route to Atlético Madrid in 2003.

His first stint was altogether not too bad either as he took the side, then in their second consecutive top-flight season since being promoted back, to a seventh-placed finish, just a point off the UEFA Cup (now Europa League) places, only missing out to sixth-placed Sevilla on goal difference. It was also the season where Fernando Torres was named captain at just 19 years of age, finishing as the joint third-highest goal scorer in the league, netting 19 times. The man who would eventually succeed Manzano after his second stint, Diego Simeone, would also play a key role, returning to the club and making 28 appearances in midfield.

Funnily enough, both would leave six months apart in 2004, only for them to arrive six months apart later in 2011. By this time, Manzano had spent a season at Málaga, four years back at Mallorca and led Sevilla to Europa League qualification in the 2010/11 season, maintaining his status as a true journeyman capable of coming in and doing a quick job to bump sides up the table more often than not. However, this Atlético Madrid side had won a Europa League just two seasons prior, meaning Manzano's appointment seemed like a step backwards and, as is evident from his opening quote, the Spaniard immediately found himself defending his ability as a coach.

With Quique Sánchez Flores's departure at the end of the 2010/11 having been announced as early as April 2011, there was much speculation over who would take over. The side had finished seventh in an average season, having been knocked out of the Europa League in the group stages even though they had won the same competition, along with the UEFA Super Cup, just the year before. There was perhaps no expectation to achieve this consistently, but the squad still had potential to regularly push for European places.

As the rumour mill spun, it became clearer that contact had been made with Rafa Benítez, Luis Enrique and Joaquín Caparrós, with some reports suggesting Unai Emery as well, understandably leaving a section of fans bemused when they found Manzano's name signed above the dotted lines. After all, with no disrespect to Manzano, the others had a certain pedigree, excitement and international reputation to them, the latter point being particularly important as Atlético Madrid wanted to develop into a respected and well-known team in Europe. Benítez was the last man to win the league managing a side other than Real

Madrid or Barcelona, when he did so with Valencia in 2004, and from 2008 to 2012, it was Emery who ensured that the same club consistently qualified for European competition, finishing third in three out of the four seasons.

Enrique had ended a stellar playing career in 2008 and looked a promising manager, having led Barcelona B back to the second tier after an 11-year absence and subsequently taking them to the play-offs for the top flight, despite their ineligibility for promotion. Caparrós was best known for his success with Sevilla, ending their four-year wait to return to the top flight in his very first season in charge, back in 2001. More recently, he had taken Athletic Bilbao to the finals of the Copa del Rey in 2010, unfortunately falling at the last hurdle. Manzano's CV, though impressive in its own right, paled in comparison to what the other four (at least) could offer, meaning the start to his second stint rightly made for mixed feelings among fans.

There was no time to take in any pleasantries either, with Manzano having to deal with the transfer situation of two of the club's most promising youngsters right away. Twenty-year-old David de Gea had already signed for Manchester United and clubs were circling for the signature of a certain 23-year-old forward by the name of Sergio Agüero. With the uncertainty surrounding the Argentinian, Manzano needed to find replacements for two key positions, right down the middle at either end. Within the squad, Joel Robles and Sergio Asenjo, who was then recovering from injury, were the only goalkeeping backups at 21 and 22 years of age respectively. The forward line looked bare as well, with 31-year-old Diego Forlán being the only other recognised frontman, but he too departed later in the window.

Manzano was already set on changing the system, from the 4-4-2 that Sánchez Flores had predominantly used to a 4-3-3, even stating in an interview with Spanish news outlet *MARCA* before the season, 'It's about giving the middle one more man, a 4-3-3, with players who provide quality and balance, so that the team does not split and become weak.' To put this into effect, he needed quality players to lead the line, control midfield and to take up the goalkeeping spot and, in hindsight, the recruitment in his tenure set the foundations of the club for the next few years. Whether this is down to him, though, is a whole different question, as this was a period where Atlético Madrid were changing and evolving as a club with the hope of achieving international acclaim, and they had just hired José Luis Caminero as the sporting director to drive the project forward. Nevertheless, they got down to business.

Thibaut Courtois, then a promising 19-year-old, was loaned in from Chelsea to take his place between the posts and €40m was spent to bring Radamel Falcao from Porto to lead the line. Adrián López, who went on to be an able forward himself, joined on a free, with Arda Turan coming in as a winger for €13m. Diego was loaned in from Wolfsburg, Tiago was signed on a free and Gabi returned to his boyhood club for €3m to strengthen the midfield. Priority was given to strengthening the defence as well, with Sílvio and Miranda coming in to occupy the right-back and centre-back positions respectively. 'It is the goal of a team like Atlético,' Manzano said of the aim of finishing in the top four and the Champions League qualification places, and despite a shaky reunion with the side, it seemed like he had taken the right steps to make his vision a reality.

With the off-field aspect relatively well managed, the Spaniard could now turn his focus to translating his work into results on the pitch. Because the club had reached the qualifying rounds of the Europa League by means of their seventh-placed finish the previous season, Manzano's opening game was the first part of a two-legged tie against Norwegian outfit Strømsgodset IF. José Antonio Reyes scored twice in the home leg and, despite a late red card for Miranda, Atlético saw off the visitors 2-1. In the away leg, newly signed forward López opened his account for *Los Rojiblancos* and a stoppage-time goal from Reyes again ensured that Manzano got off to a winning start back in the dugout. There was still another qualifying round to get through, but the team brushed aside Portuguese side Vitória Guimarães, winning 6-0 on aggregate to reach the group stages. Atlético had scored 12 goals and conceded just once in four games by the time the La Liga season began, and with the first matchday having to be postponed due to a strike called by the Association of Spanish Footballers over unpaid wages, Manzano's side kicked off the campaign at home to Osasuna.

The momentum did not carry over though, and the side were held to an anti-climactic 0-0 draw at home before losing away in the next game at Valencia. However, a return to Europa League action for the group stages rekindled some form, with a 2-0 win over Celtic followed up by consecutive 4-0 league scorelines at home to Racing and Sporting Gijón. With the two resounding victories, Atlético sat eighth in these standings, a good recovery after the opening two games. It was still only September and, with Manzano having lost just once with seven wins in nine games, the start was still a positive one.

Then came a visit to the Camp Nou. In a game that ended 5-0 to the home side, Barcelona found themselves three goals up within the first half hour and then proceeded to knock the ball around for the rest of the game, with Lionel Messi scoring two late on to seal a hat-trick. Pep Guardiola's side was one of the best in Europe, but the manner in which Atlético were dismantled made it nearly impossible to believe that the teams were playing in the same league, let alone separated by a solitary point heading into the game.

The gulf in quality was starkly apparent and the thrashing sent Manzano's side down a slippery slope from which he never seemed to recover. They went winless in the next six in all competitions, the last one being against Marcelo Bielsa's Athletic Bilbao, a game in which resolute defence eventually gave way to a glut of goals, with the Basque side scoring thrice in seven minutes without reply. This was also a game after which, crucially, the fracture between Manzano and the supporters intensified when fan-favourite Reyes, who swore at the coach after being substituted, would go on to be ostracised and left out of the line-up and squad.

Excuses were invented to cover up his absence, but it was evident that Manzano had not handled the situation well enough. The fans were turning on him and despite Europa League form improving from there on, with

Atlético winning their remaining three games, this did not carry this over into the league, where with three victories and four losses in the next seven games they found themselves just four points off relegation. Defeats to then bottom side Getafe and another mismatch with city rivals Real Madrid were the gravest results, but the nail in the coffin was struck by third-tier Albacete in the Copa del Rey.

In what was Atlético's first match in the competition that season, they travelled away for the first leg of the tie, only to lose 2-1 with a late López goal rescuing some hope for the return meeting. Unconvincing and crucial losses to Espanyol and Real Betis, who were a few points off Atlético above and below them at that point, meant that the second leg was all the more important with pressure mounting on Manzano with every passing game. Against Betis, Manzano was sat in the dugout for about an hour before venturing out after conceding the first goal, only to walk right into the view of the thousands of fans who had been waiting for such a moment. In a Europa League game the week before, they had chanted for him to come off the bench so they could hurl insults, only to abuse him anyway when he remained seated. Now that they had got what they wanted, they were sure to not miss. '*Manzano véte ya! Manzano véte ya!*' they chanted, meaning, 'Manzano go now!'

Manzano's titanic had hit its iceberg, slowly inching towards its eventual sinking. *The Guardian*'s Sid Lowe rightly called him 'Atlético's dead coach walking', and when Albacete rounded off a stunning performance with a 1-0 win at the Vicente Calderón, progressing 3-1 on aggregate, the axe swiftly came down the next day and ended the Spaniard's tenure.

When he joined, Manzano had mentioned that the defence was an area to improve, with the side having conceded the second-highest number of goals in the top half of the table the previous season. At the time of his dismissal, only two teams had let in more goals than Atlético, and they had failed to outscore opponents regularly either, having a goal difference of -4. 'Modern football has a balance between attack and defence,' he said, but what he seemed to understand by this failed to show itself in his tactics. Despite stating that a 4-3-3 would be his preferred formation, Manzano also used a 4-2-3-1 equally and to a much lesser extent, a 4-4-2. As you would expect from subsequent results, these setups had inherent flaws in them and this meant that, much as Manzano would have liked them to be, Atlético were neither solid at the back nor an attacking force to be reckoned with. What they were left with was a side that sparked at times, but never caught fire to burn as brightly or as consistently as they could have.

Twenty-one points off rivals and table-toppers Real Madrid, ten points off fourth place and a Champions League spot, five wins from 16 in the league, four points off relegation and knocked out of the Copa del Rey in the first round: this was where Atlético stood at the time, and not even topping the Europa League group with 13 points from a possible 18 was good enough to make up for it.

Dissecting Manzano's tactical setup, fundamental flaws, both in terms of instructions and execution, are apparent. By failing to rectify these faults, Atlético continued to be exposed regularly, largely depending on the individual quality of their players to mask some, if not all, of these errors on a game-by-game basis. While not only being vulnerable in the defensive phase and against transitions, an ineffective and poorly executed build-up was also a key feature of the side, all of which warrant a deeper look.

* * *

Poor defensive organisation

Out of possession, there are a few main things that a team must do consistently in order to maintain solidity. Firstly, they have to ensure that they are in position, which means that they have occupied the right areas of the pitch according to their tactical setup, ensuring that no area has been left vacant due to them not being positioned correctly. Secondly, they have to be certain that they are maintaining the right distances between team-mates and are shifting accordingly to ensure their shape off the ball is maintained. Thirdly, they should look to minimise the time and space that opponents have on the ball, while also cutting down their options.

This is usually known as pressing, where teams quickly move in to put opponents under pressure and force them into a bad pass or nick the ball off them to win back possession. An alternative means of doing this is to cut out the potential passes that an opponent has, basically allowing only the ball carrier enough time and space to play, but reducing their passing and shooting options by closing down team-mates or blocking their line to goal. Finally, a team must ensure that they have the concentration and communication to consistently carry out their role by anticipating and then effectively dealing with potential situations.

Unfortunately for Manzano, his Atlético side did not tick any of these boxes regularly.

Despite aiming for defensive solidity and ensuring that his midfielders remained deep enough to support his back line, his players were consistently dragged out of position by clever passing manoeuvres and combinations. Even when they looked to maintain their shape and defend deep, they were not able to effectively cut out any passing options and opened up wide areas of the pitch for multiple players, allowing easy passes and conceding possession in dangerous areas. Not to

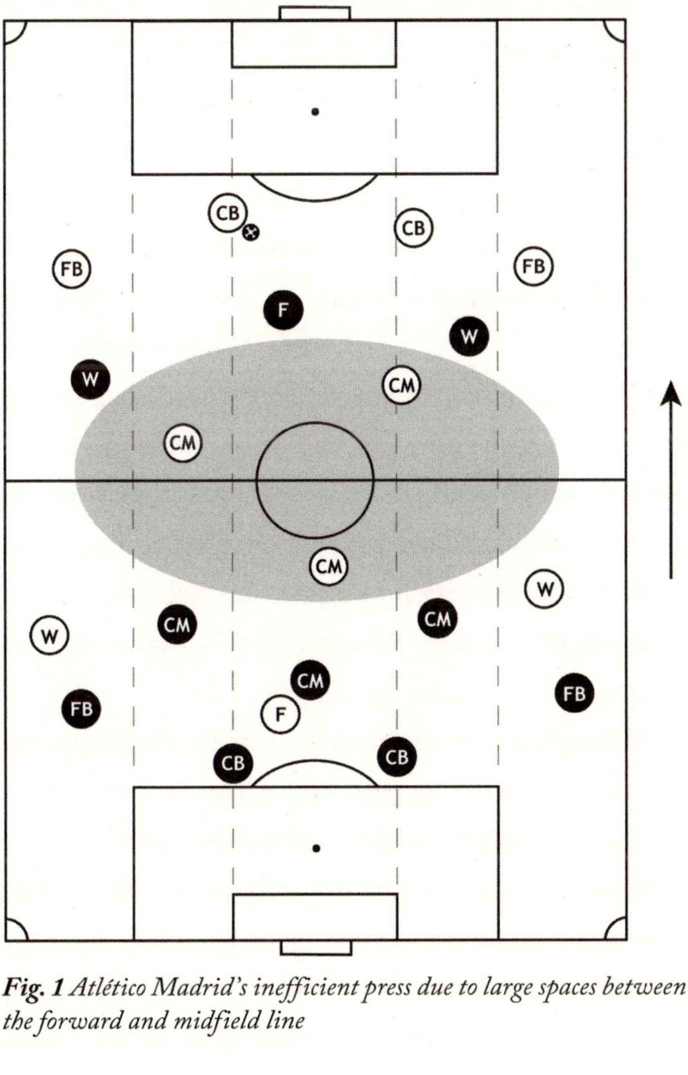

***Fig. 1** Atlético Madrid's inefficient press due to large spaces between the forward and midfield line*

mention that Atlético also found themselves vulnerable in transitions regularly, with poor concentration and communication, meaning that they did not consistently anticipate quick passes; nor did they track runners in behind consistently, leading to opponents exposing them on counter attacks regularly.

Visualising these errors, we shall start with the faults with the defensive shape.

As mentioned earlier, in order to provide additional support for the back line, Manzano ensured his midfield dropped deeper and closer to the defence, minimising the space between the two lines. The priority, at least initially, was to drop deep and take up positions closer to their own penalty area to ensure they could form a solid enough structure at the back to defend their goal. In such scenarios, a side needs to drop in synchronisation, with all the players looking to get behind the ball and not only ensure compactness horizontally, but also vertically. As for this Atlético Madrid side, the attacking line did not often do this regularly, staying higher up to press the opposition defenders instead.

It is important to understand that pressing is a tactic of a team and not just a few individuals, but in this case it was only the attacking line looking to apply pressure higher up in the hope of forcing a turnover. With no support from their midfielders or full-backs, the forward line could only cut out so many passes, having to prevent passes to the opposition full-backs, within the centre-backs and to their central midfielders as well. This, along with the fact that the attacking line was so detached from the rest of the side, allowed the opposition midfielders to then have loads of space to roam in the middle of the pitch. With simple movements, they could make themselves an easy passing option and a single pass to them would bypass an entire line of Atlético players, while also allowing them to receive with ample time and space.

The opposition midfield could then pass it among themselves or carry the ball forward to move quickly deeper into the Atlético half, where their own attacking line would already be present. In such a scenario, there are six opposition players compared to seven for Atlético, and should the opposition full-backs make quick supporting runs forward, Manzano's side would be outnumbered deep in their own half. Such a quick move forward by the opposition could then lead to the instance shown in the figure overleaf.

Here, we see that using their wingers, central midfielders and full-backs, opponents are able to exploit the wide areas of the pitch by creating triangles, and with Manzano's desire to stay compact centrally they cause overloads, which means that they have more

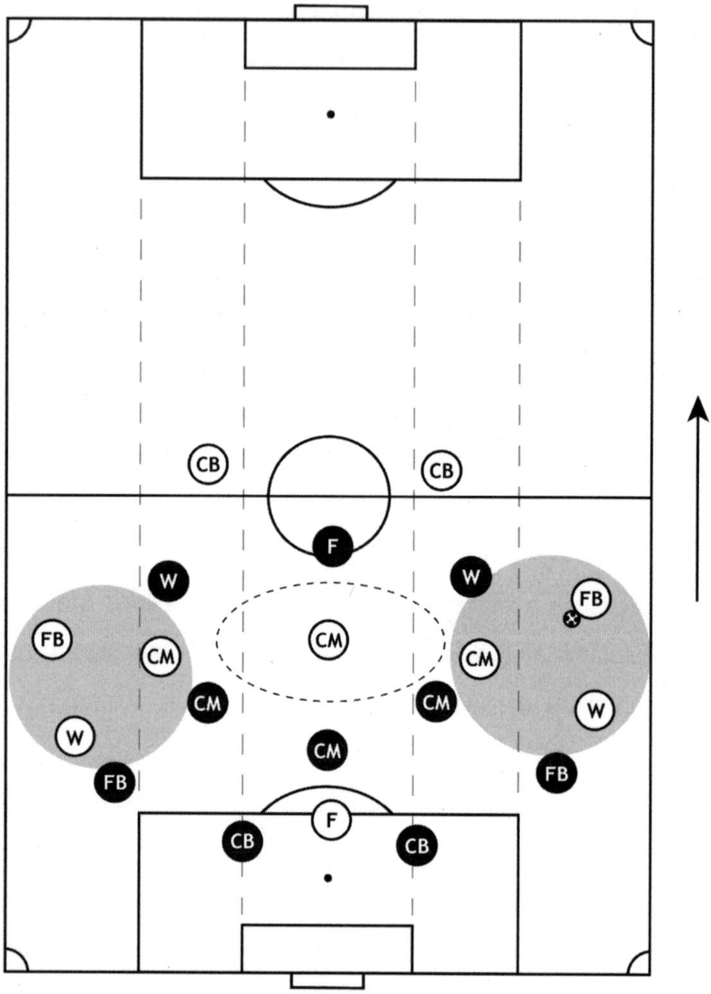

***Fig. 2** Opposition players using triangles and overloads to exploit the spaces out wide*

numbers in that particular area of the pitch. The gap between the forward and midfield line from earlier means that the front three of Atlético are slower to track back, meaning that they are not able to drop in and neutralise the numerical advantage regularly.

This also means that one of the opposition's central midfielders (the one in the middle) would be allowed ample space to dictate the play and control the flow of possession from his position, making it easy to switch flanks as well. The Atlético forward is unable to drop back in time to neutralise this player and their two central midfielders cannot risk stepping out for fear of leaving their man free down the flanks. Atlético's central midfielder and full-back have to be wary of committing in such scenarios, for fear of being dragged out of position, and if they are beaten, they risk allowing opponents considerable space in and around their box.

If we look more closely into the situation, we also see that due to the Atlético winger's higher position, it is often a three-v-two in favour of the opposition, hence why we have called it an overload. In this overload, we notice that it is usually the opposition full-back who finds himself free, while his central midfielder and winger have pinned (i.e. holding them to their position) the Atlético central midfielder and full-back respectively. In such scenarios, the full-back is allowed further freedom to get forward and make runs either down the outside, called overlaps, or down the inside of the winger, known as underlaps.

Such runs are crucial for a full-back to make as it usually means that they are able to attack spaces higher up the pitch, either wider or more centrally depending on the run, giving them time to pick out crosses and passes to team-mates. It is tough for the defending full-back to deal with such a situation on their own since they would already be occupied with a winger, and hence they would require support either from a midfielder or winger, or even a centre-back moving across.

In our scenario, however, a centre-back moving across is dangerous as this then allows the opposition forward to run in behind and exploit the space that they have left behind, giving them more room in the penalty area. Eventually, it could probably lead to a situation as follows in the next figure (opposite).

In this case, we consider that the opposition right-back has made an overlapping run, with the winger occupying the Atlético full-back and centre-back with a run in between them. The opposition central midfielder (in the middle) is in possession of the ball and makes a quick pass to his right central midfielder. This midfielder can then play his right-back through into space, with the Atlético left-back needing to track him as well as be wary of the winger on his other side. The winger on the opposite flank can also dart into the box in this scenario, so too the forward, meaning

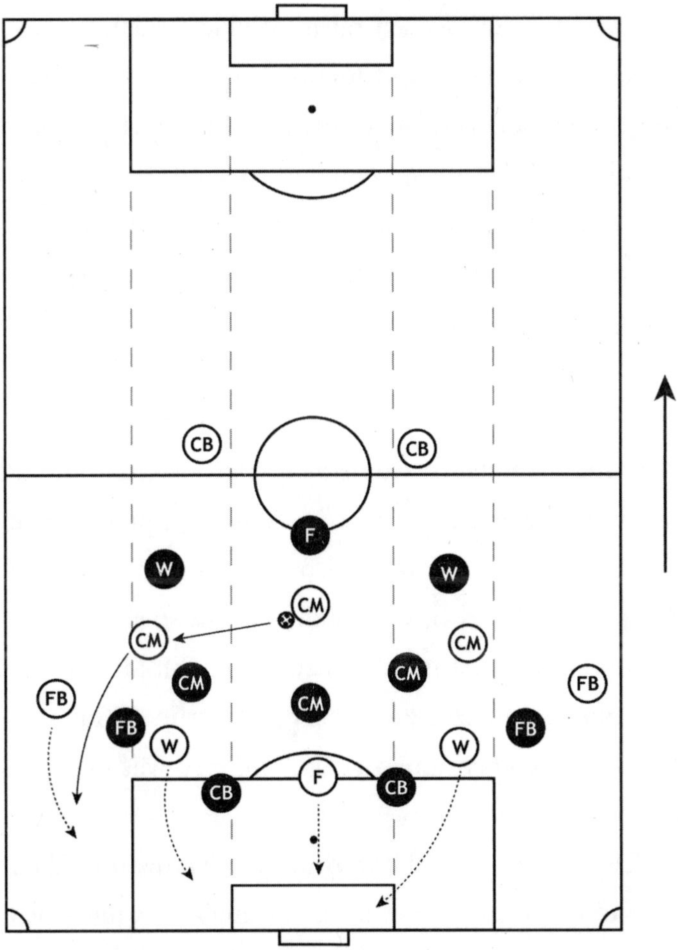

Fig. 3 *Atlético Madrid's vulnerability from crosses / passes from wide areas*

that already there are three options for the right-back in the penalty area.

Of course, we are assuming that most players are static when we visualise this on a diagram, but even if three of Atlético's central midfielders track the two opposition wingers and forward, we can still expect the opposition central midfielders to push forward themselves and find space in and around the box. This basically meant that, once the opposition full-back was in possession of the ball in the wide areas, he had good enough passing options to create a chance of quality for his side.

This was understandably one of the more frequent ways that Manzano's side would concede chances, and while we have viewed it as an entire sequence from start to finish, these were also independent flaws that could be exposed in different phases considering the multiple ways a game sequence could unfold. The fact that most sequences eventually led to the exploitation of the above-mentioned flaws, though, was certainly cause for worry.

Of course, this did not mean that Manzano did not try, but unfortunately even then some issues remained. The switch to a 4-2-3-1, or even a 4-4-2 at times, was one that had been brought about owing to the fact that not only did Manzano want another outright attacking player, but it also meant that his wingers no longer had to play as high as they did and could offer some support to the full-back owing to their naturally deeper positioning. The attacking midfielder or second forward could pair up with the forward up front to form a first line of pressure as the wingers settled into midfield, meaning that they could then ensure that they were not as vulnerable down the flanks.

There was also an attempt to play a higher line to mitigate the space that was afforded to the opposition midfielders in the centre of the pitch, ensuring that all three lines were much closer to each other than they had been earlier. This was also something that Manzano would implement in the 4-3-3 to minimise the space in midfield, but unfortunately it failed to consistently address the aforementioned issues to prevent them from occurring. In the 4-2-3-1/4-4-2, this higher line did serve to make the centre of the pitch more compact than it had been, but a key error was the positioning of the forwards who ended up too close to each other to press effectively.

This would then lead to a situation as given on the next page in Figure 4.

The narrow front two were ineffective in preventing a pass from the opposition back line into midfield, resulting in a similar process as seen earlier, despite the deeper positions of the wingers. A point can be made to then push one striker, or the attacking midfielder, back into midfield, and this indeed was tried by Manzano, but the fact remained that the Atlético structure off

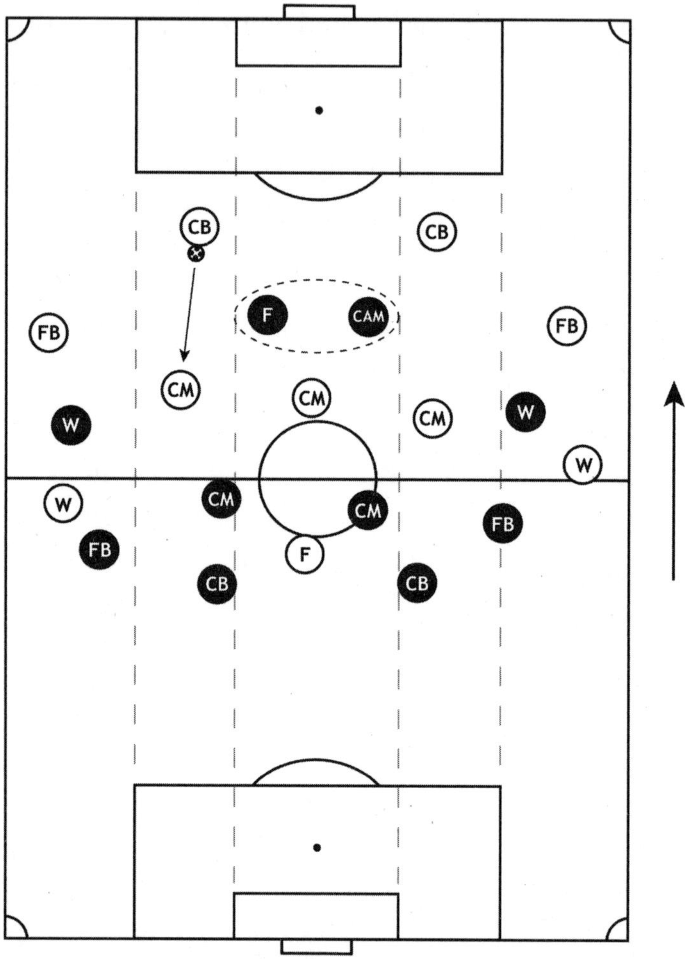

***Fig. 4** Atlético Madrid's narrowly positioned forwards allow opponents to bypass them with ease*

the ball was not properly coordinated and assembled, leading to cracks that opponents opened up. Moreover, it seemed that with every correction that Manzano attempted, new errors would spring up, with their vulnerability in defensive transitions being one that would show across all setups. Let us take the situation shown below as an example:

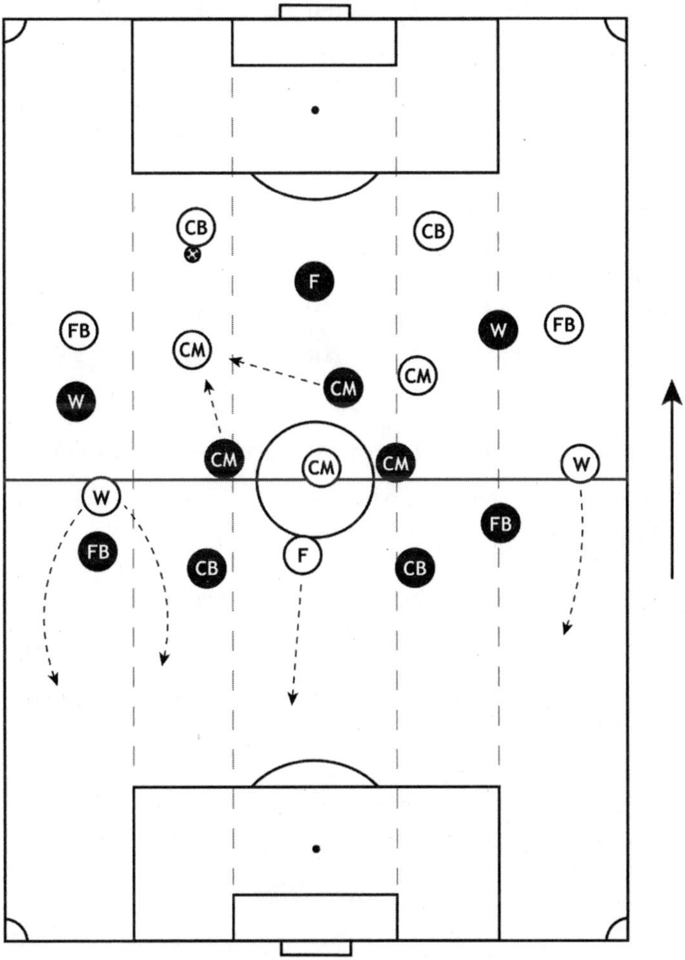

Fig. 5 *Atlético Madrid's vulnerability in defensive transitions*

With Manzano attempting to play a higher line and considering the space that his side were offering in midfield when they dropped back, Atlético found themselves hit on the counter, with opponents looking to get in behind. As we saw earlier, an inefficient first line of pressure still meant that sides could exploit space in midfield, which meant that the Atlético midfielders had to overcompensate in order to close them down. While Manzano had wanted his midfield line to be close to the defence, it could not be done consistently owing to the space afforded to the opposition, leading to the Atlético midfielders having to move out instinctively.

In the situation above, the opposition centre-back has a relatively free pass out to the central midfielder ahead of him. Note that in this structure, we cover the 4-3-3 and a variation of the 4-2-3-1. The latter is clearly visible in the image, but this could also be interpreted as the 4-3-3, where, say, the right central midfielder has stepped up to apply pressure on an opponent while the other two midfielders have held their positions. Getting back to the situation, upon allowing the free pass to the opposition midfielder, Atlético need to close him down, which they can do with either of the two central midfielders moving as shown. The worst-case scenario would be that both the Atlético midfielders move in, but in essence, with just this one pass, the opposition have drawn the Atlético midfield out of position and can now look to bypass them with minimal passes.

We can also see that the opposition front line has occupied positions higher up and, in a way, pin their respective Atlético counterparts to their positions, preventing them from covering efficiently for their midfielders who have stepped up. The wingers are able to make darting runs around the outside or between the full-back and centre-back, while the forward is allowed a run between the centre-backs, and having opened up space in midfield to play into, the opposition is able to play their attack through into space, quickly transitioning from deep in their own half to the Atlético box with ease.

Of course, it has to be added [otherwise why say it?] that when Manzano switched to the other variation of the 4-2-3-1 and set up in a 4-4-2 out of possession, the midfield would find themselves short of a man to cover for the inefficient front line of pressure and be drawn out even more easily, allowing opponents to slice through them like a hot knife through butter.

* * *

Ineffective chance creation

It was hard enough to prevent the frequent concession of chances, but it was then even harder to consistently create more than they allowed, with Atlético finding themselves unable to outscore opponents to the degree that they needed to in order to win games. The stats show that the side managed to score 23 goals up until Manzano's departure, which roughly amounts to 1.4 goals a game, a decent return and the sixth-highest in the league at that point. However, eight of these goals came against the bottom two sides in the division, meaning that in the remaining 14 games Atlético had scored just 15 times. They failed to score in half of those matches as well, dropping valuable points that would have seen them positioned much closer to the European spots and, more importantly, further away from the relegation spots that they were hovering over. A key reason for this can be seen in the next figure.

Now, Manzano had not set up to be a high-possession side, despite having the quality to do so and having the bulk of possession in the odd game. Under his leadership Atlético were not to be known as a side that would keep control of the ball and force opponents back consistently. Instead, they would more often than not lie deeper in their own half in order to ensure defensive solidity, before then relying on quick passing to get up the pitch upon winning possession. This, however, was not just a case of 'parking the bus' before attacking on the counter, but rather a system where Manzano hoped that he could focus on getting the ball forward and directly progressing to the final

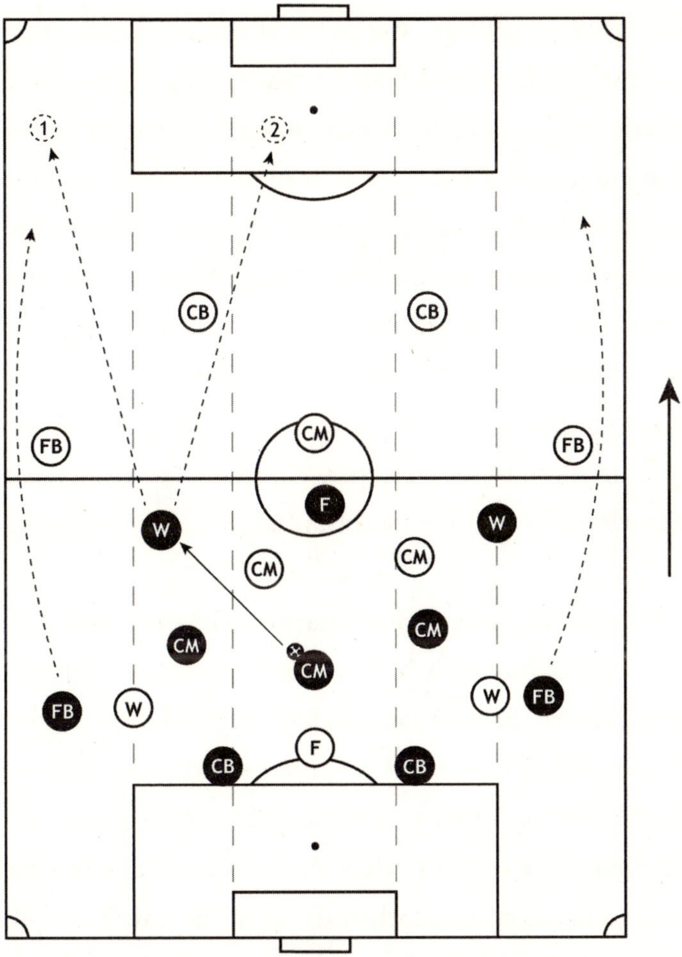

Fig. 6 *Atlético Madrid's difficulties with ball progression*

stage of the build-up, where his team could then look to plan and orchestrate attacks, as opposed to patiently building up right from their deeper positions.

The problem with this, however, links back to some of the issues that we saw earlier. The attacking line was evidently cut off from the rest of the side, meaning that even when the midfield or defence won back possession of the ball, it would not always be easy to find the outlet consistently, having to rely on more medium to long-range passes with a greater margin for error. In the figure on previous page, we have also taken a situation which is not immediately after Atlético have won back possession, but instead a scenario where upon winning the ball back and playing out to the winger, the opposition have had the time to drop deeper, especially the full-backs, ensuring that they are back in place and close to getting in line with the ball, if not already behind it.

Immediately, we notice that the winger is a fair way from goal, and with his passing options all relatively close to him, his main method of progression is to drive forward with the ball on his own. Of course, Atlético were not short of technically sound wingers capable of beating opponents, but they were not blessed with pace and to do so consistently and carry the ball 30 to 40 yards towards goal on a regular basis is not something that players can consistently be asked to do. In waiting for team-mates to support with forward runs and then progress the ball, the winger loses out on time and space, allowing opponents the chance to fully settle in a defensive structure and forcing Atlético to build up from the middle third. Doing this would go against what Manzano wanted his side to do, hence forcing the winger to either carry the ball towards the wings (1), or go directly down the centre (2).

The lack of a consistent way to progress up the pitch and commit numbers in the right areas with the right positions hampered Atlético's ability to get at the opposition, and the ones that suffered consistently were the full-backs. As we can see in the figure, the full-backs are expected to make supporting runs forward, but having occupied deeper positions earlier on, they are now tasked with running virtually the length of the pitch to provide support for an already disjointed attack. There again, any loss in possession would result in them having to drop deeper, meaning that they were being asked to fulfil two separate roles at the same time. Such tactics made for weary legs and poor positioning and decision-making, with the full-backs finding it difficult to occupy positions at two extremes, while completely bypassing the middle third of the pitch, as it was not an area that Atlético looked to build up in.

This is not to say that it was impossible though, and Atlético did find some success at times in terms of ball progression to get higher up the pitch and have the territorial advantage that they wanted. They could then combine down the wide areas that Manzano wanted to play through, but unfortunately even these situations exposed some flaws in the build-up, as we see in the figure below:

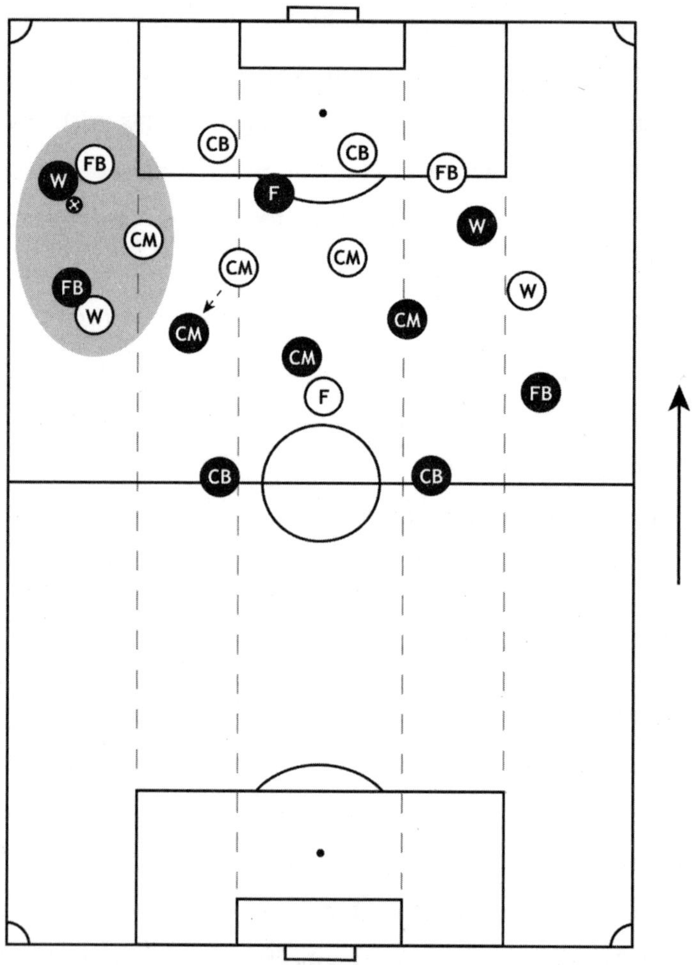

***Fig. 7** Atlético Madrid's ineffective build-up and combinations in the wide areas*

In this situation, we take it that Atlético have indeed managed to get up to the other end of the pitch with their method of ball progression having worked, meaning that their winger and full-back have managed to get forward with some supporting runs from their team-mates. The opposition has also managed to fall back, looking to get into a solid defensive structure to stall Atlético's attack. However, we mentioned earlier that the supporting runs for Atlético were often slower and hence failed to produce good enough passing options and this situation highlights the negative effect that this had on the attack.

We see that the winger and full-back are occupying the wide areas, looking to go deeper down the flanks and exploit the high and wide areas of the pitch. Now, an effective way to do this is by forming passing triangles, which we saw earlier, and by which means it becomes easy for Atlético to pass the ball around and make good movements to attack space in behind defenders. Unfortunately, though, the slower support from the central midfielders meant that these triangles were not consistently formed in time, instead allowing the defence to overload the wide areas with their full-back, central midfielder and winger moving in to crowd out Atlético's players down the flank. Should the Atlético central midfielder then opt to move in to make it a three-v-three, the opposition still have the luxury of moving across and adding a fourth player since they would still have decent cover down the other side.

This meant that Atlético's passing combinations and wide attacks often looked haphazard and poorly coached since they were unable to regularly play clearly defined passes and habitually repeat the same set of passes to get players consistently in the right positions. They ended up having to get to these areas before looking up to find the best possible solution, and in a day and age where the likes of Guardiola, Mourinho, Bielsa and Emery were sat across in the opposite dugout, they hardly stood a chance.

* * *

'We start with a year and I hope we reach ten,' Manzano said in response to a question on whether he would be done at the end of his one-year contract. A leaky defence and an inefficient attack, however, meant that he departed even before the new year, having been in charge for almost exactly half the season. Of course, the fact still remains that the good work to remodel the squad with some astute recruitment laid the foundations for Simeone to take over, much of it down to José Luis Caminero, with some credit to Manzano. Unfortunately, it did not translate into results on the pitch and with a public falling out leading to rumours of a lost dressing room, it was time for Atlético to pull the plug on yet another manager.

'Atlético is going to be strong and powerful.' Somehow, Manzano was not wrong.

3

Recruitment

'The heart equals the budget'

ROME WASN'T built in a day. But when Diego Simeone walked into Atlético Madrid as manager, forget about Rome, he was met with its ruins. Since 1996, Atlético had averaged 14 new players a season, a startling statistic that highlighted the fact that the club had lacked stability and direction for a good 15 years. If Simeone had wanted a clean slate, he didn't have it.

There were issues at the club stemming from the time he was there kicking the ball around on the pitch and, truth be told, there was no telling how long he would last on the sidelines then either. Of course, Simeone's appointment was one to unite and rally the troops, to perhaps paper over the cracks of years gone by, but at the first sign of trouble it could have all gone back to square one.

There were glaring issues in the squad as well, on and off the pitch. Off it, the unrest that surrounded José Antonio Reyes ahead of the transfer window was a situation that needed dealing with and, on it, despite a good run in the Europa League Atlético were statistically one of the worst defences in La Liga. In 16 matches, they had conceded 27 goals, seeing them rank joint third-highest for goals conceded in that period, equal with Sporting de Gijón and only behind CA Osasuna (28) and Real Zaragoza (31). They did rank seventh in terms of goals scored in that time with 23, but the fact was that they did not create enough to consistently outscore opponents either.

For Simeone, following the status quo, tearing down the 'foundations' of the previous manager's side and recruiting wholesale, giving the squad an entirely new look yet again, was not much of an option either considering the finances of the club at the time. And he knew better. He knew what it meant to have faith. Faith in the players, faith in the process, and faith in Atlético. To the world, Atlético Madrid in the 21st century hovered between poor and mediocre, but to Simeone this was a team waiting to be unleashed.

And much like Rome all those centuries ago, it had to be done with consistent planning and execution. When we take a look at the squad that Simeone

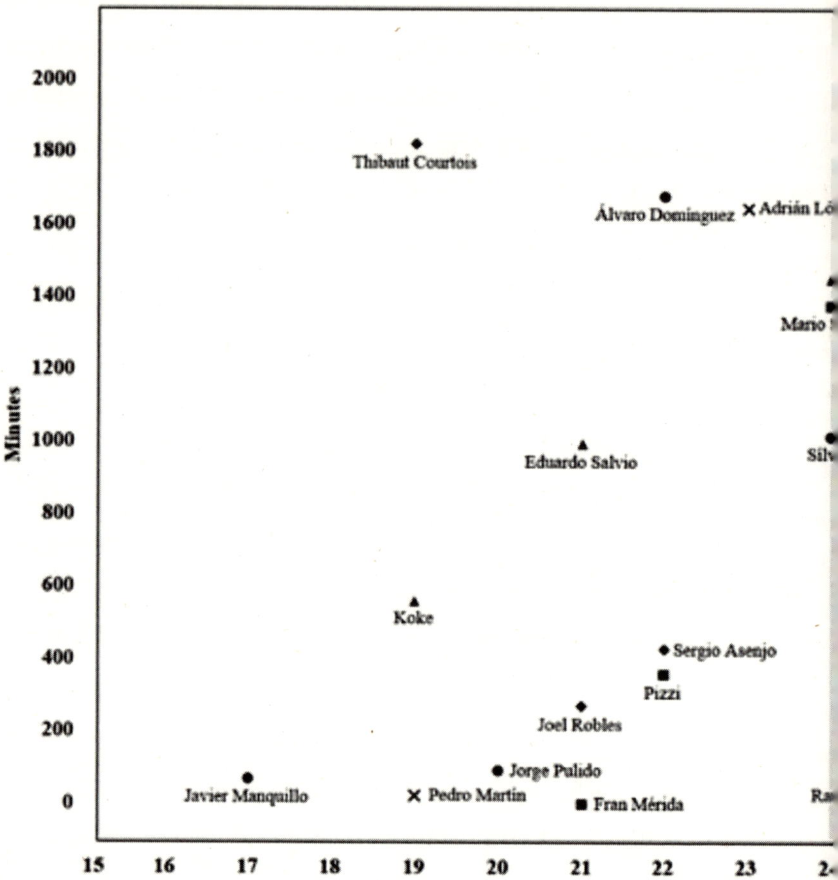

inherited, it did not appear to be too bad in terms of its age profile and minutes. The core group of players, which included the likes of Filipe Luís, Gabi, Miranda and Radamel Falcao, were all in their 'peak' age group, which is generally the bracket between 24 to 30 years of age (some may peak early, while others

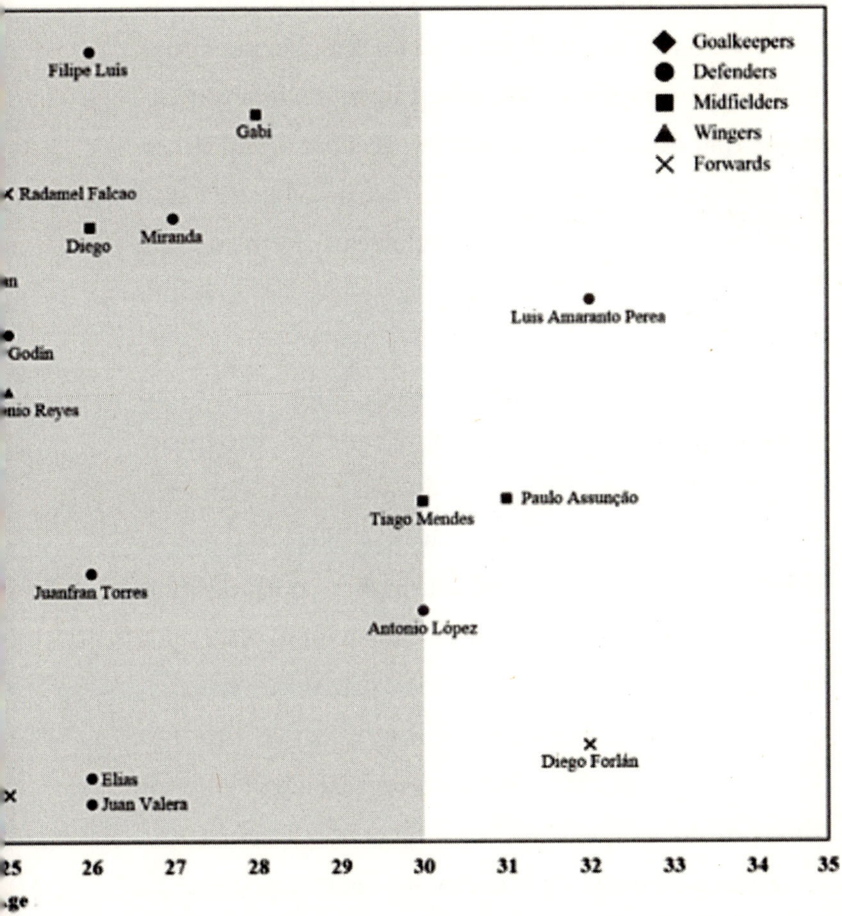

Fig. 8 Atlético Madrid squad profile at the time of Diego Simeone's appointment

peak late, but this is the general range between which this occurs).

There weren't too many players in the age bracket over that, the 'experienced' ages, and there seemed to be a good mix of youth as well, with Thibaut Courtois, Álvaro Domínguez and Adrián López all having a good number of minutes in the side. However, this was not to say that Simeone inherited an excellent squad either. Out of the five forwards that Gregorio Manzano had used, Diego Forlán had left the club early in the season, leaving Falcao and Adrián López as the only regular frontmen available.

Issues with Reyes meant that Arda Turan and Eduardo Salvio were the only other two recognised wingers and barring Koke, who was still a winger at the time, the midfield options were still lacking proper depth, especially in the area of quality youth options. In hindsight, had there been a steady plan in place, this was a squad that could have been primed to succeed, probably not in terms of winning a league title but at least in terms of mounting a regular challenge for European places.

Atlético were at a risk of having their supposed peak phase pass them by and the responsibility for avoiding this fell to Simeone, meaning he not only had to find results on the pitch soon but also discover a way to prolong this period while preparing for the next one, where they could possibly get it right from the start. With the setup that he encountered, though, this task was easier said than done.

Any new manager would love to have a blank cheque and a free run at players to fit their ideologies, but a lack of financial power at the club along with a structure that gave the sporting director, or any equivalent role, the authority to manage transfers meant that Simeone would not always have the final say in the market. While this would steadily improve over the years, he still had to work within his means and the timing of his appointment would leave him with an interesting first window. Having arrived in the latter part of December and not having played a single game before the window opened, it was not going to be easy for *Cholo* to tear the squad apart and build another one in the middle of the season.

The only incoming that did happen was that Pizzi's loan translated into a permanent transfer, with Simeone essentially not adding anyone to the squad that he had. Reyes was given his transfer and moved to Sevilla and that was all the activity that Atlético saw in the transfer market of January 2012. The defence had not been great and the forwards had to score more consistently, but for the next six months, *Cholo* seemed to prefer to deal with any deficiencies using his tactics rather than scouring the market.

From the summer of 2012 though, his recruitment plan was in place.

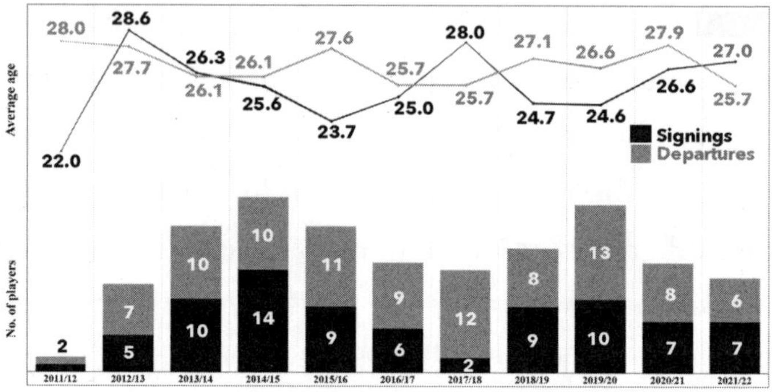

***Fig.* 9** *Average age of signings and departures since January 2012*

Only four times in the next ten years did the average age of signings exceed that of the departures and it was only in the 2017/18 season where the difference was above a year. The focus was on signing younger players and moving the older ones on to, in theory, keep the cycle going and have the squad in and around their peak for a sustainable period of time. Interestingly, Simeone rarely signed more players than he sold as well, with this happening just three times in ten years. It should also be noted that players called up to the senior team from the youth academy are not considered as signings and only players loaned with a fee are considered departures.

The beginning of the 2012/13 season gave Simeone his first chance to overhaul his squad, with seven players leaving the club. Barring Emre Belözoğlu and Fran Mérida, both midfielders who made 17 and 30 appearances for the senior side respectively, the remaining five players featured a considerable number of times for Atlético. Winger Eduardo Salvio had 69 appearances to his name, while defenders Álvaro Domínguez and Luis Amaranto Perea had made 120 and 304 appearances for the first team. The latter left having held the record number of matches as a non-Spanish player for the club. Left-back Antonio López also departed, having made 260 appearances, as did midfielder Paulo Assunção after 147 matches. Of the seven, Salvio, Domínguez and Mérida were the only ones under 30, with the three of them around 22 years old.

As for the arrivals during that season, only one of them, Cristian Rodríguez, went on to make substantial number of appearances for the senior side (98) while the others made around 20 and below each. Only two of the five, however, were under 30 years of age, with Simeone looking to reinforce his side with experience as he attempted to push on from a successful Europa League campaign the previous season.

Despite a comfortable, third-placed finish in the league in 2012/13, the 2013/14 window was not expected to be big for Atlético, even though they had received in excess of €40m for star forward Falcao. There was also the interesting transfer of Martín Demichelis, who signed from Málaga before leaving for Manchester City within six weeks and without a single appearance.

None of the other sales were particularly noteworthy, but in terms of signings one stood out.

The incredibly opportunistic capture of David Villa from Barcelona was the headline arrival and, in addition, Toby Alderweireld and José María Giménez were brought in as well to strengthen the back line. Diego had his permanent move completed after having been loaned in and he had played under Simeone before as well, and excluding Demichelis and Villa, Daniel Aranzubia, a 33-year-old goalkeeper was the only signing above the age of 30 through the season. The average signing age still came above that of the departure age thoughout, mainly due to the fact that Simeone sold a couple of youth prospects, 23-year-old Pizzi, who technically was his first signing, and 21-year-old forward Léo Baptistão, who was sent out on loan to Real Betis.

Winning the league, however, did not mean that the following 2014/15 season would be in any way easier. As is usually the case with underdog sides that win major competitions, the eye-catching prospects get snatched away by the wealthier and 'bigger' clubs and, in this vein, core players such as Diego Costa, Filipe Luís, David Villa and even Adrián López and Diego were prised away from the club. Barring Villa, these were players that were still in and around their prime and their replacements needed to be good. Atlético did not have the same budget as their rivals in Barcelona and Real Madrid, but winning the league allowed them to fund transfers for Antoine Griezmann, Mario Mandžukić, Jan Oblak and Ángel Correa, three of whom are still key Atlético players at the time of writing. Fernando Torres was also brought back on loan and in hindsight it turned out to be a fruitful couple of windows for the club, who managed to replace their stars after being picked apart. They were not expected to defend their title, but by this time it was clear that they were the third-best team, at least, in the country.

The 2015/16 season saw a few more veterans leave, with there being an evident emphasis on a younger core that Simeone was looking to develop. Turan, Mario Suárez and Miranda (on loan) all departed having made close to 200 appearances each, with Raúl García leaving as well after 329 matches. Cristian Rodríguez departed that season and Mandžukić and Alderweireld left after mixed seasons as well, along with Jackson Martínez who left in the winter for about €42m, having just joined in the summer. Yannick Carrasco and Stefan Savić were brought in, with Simeone also bringing Filipe Luís back to the club. Promising centre-forward Luciano Vietto signed from Villarreal to wrap up the higher-profile incomings for the season.

The next season saw Simeone bring in six players, one of whom was Torres, whose loan deal was made permanent. Of the other five, the standout name looking back was that of 19-year-old Diogo Jota, signed from Paços Ferreira in Portugal. Jota arrived for a fee of €7m, but made just three appearances in his time at Atlético. This was also the season where Šime Vrsaljko was brought in and, despite not being Simeone's first choice for most of his time, only left the club at the end of the 2021/22 season. Kevin Gameiro and Nicolás Gaitán were the higher-profile signings in this 2016/17 season, arriving for a combined total of about €60m from Sevilla and Benfica respectively. The standout departure was that of 31-year-old Miranda, who left permanently for Inter in Italy after 178 appearances. Of the other eight, only Vietto and Jesús Gámez made over 30 appearances for Simeone's side.

Only two players signed for Atlético in the 2017/18 season, with Atlético winning the Europa League for the second time under Simeone. Diego Costa returned from Chelsea for €60m and Vitolo was signed for about €35m from Sevilla. There were a fair number of departures, though, with 12 players leaving, and this was the only season where the age of signings was considerably higher than that of the departures. Yannick Carrasco, Theo Hernandez and Óliver Torres were all sold, all three of whom were viewed as very promising talents (and would go on to have good careers), though Torres had not delivered consistently as of yet. Javier Manquillo and Matías Kranevitter were the other more prominent names aged 24 or under to be sold this season. Goalkeeper Miguel Ángel Moyá was also moved on along with Nicolás Gaitán. By this time, there was an evident shift in the way the recruitment was moving and it was clear that the side were gearing up for another cycle of younger players replacing older ones.

In 2018/19, Atlético lost two of their biggest legends in the same season, with Fernando Torres and Gabi departing. The latter left after 413 appearances, having captained the side throughout Simeone's time in charge, and the former exited after almost 360 matches. The loss of two prominent figures and stalwarts would usually result in a period of instability and regrouping, but by this time Simeone's new side had begun taking shape. After moving on Jota and Jonny, the latter after several loan spells, both joining Wolves, Vrsaljko was also loaned out to Inter, making way for eight signings. Thomas Lemar was the pick of the group, arriving for big money (€72m), with Rodri returning after leaving the academy for Villarreal. Álvaro Morata also signed again after a poor stint at Chelsea and it was clear that these three were to form a core for the seasons going forward. Along with them, Gelson Martins, Nikola Kalinić and Santiago Arias were brought in, and so was 18-year-old Nehuén Pérez, whose development so far has been interesting to watch though he is yet to feature for the senior side.

The 2019/20 season ushered in the biggest transition of Simeone's tenure, with the departure of multiple key players and the arrival of future stars. Atlético basically lost their entire legendary defensive unit, with Filipe Luís, Diego Godín and Juanfran all leaving after having made in excess of 300 appearances each and playing key roles in the club's successful sides until then. This resulted in key defensive signings, with Mario Hermoso (centre-back), Kieran Trippier (right-back), Renan Lodi (left-back), Felipe (centre-back) and Héctor Herrera (defensive midfield) being brought in.

Other big names left as well and Atlético were involved in some big-money moves, both in terms of sales and incomings. Barcelona snapped up Antoine Griezmann for €120m and Bayern Munich paid €80m for Lucas Hernandez, with Manchester City swooping in for Rodri after just one season at the club, paying in excess of €60m. In came João Félix from Benfica, arriving for close to €130m, more than four times that of the next most expensive player in Marcos Llorente, from rivals Real Madrid. Carrasco re-joined as well, with *Cholo* bringing him back from China on loan. It was another year of evident squad building, Simeone refreshing the side with a bit of youth to not only replace older members, but also promising younger players who left for big money themselves.

Finally, Gelson Martins departed for a reasonable fee along with Luciano Vietto, with neither really tearing it apart at the club, to wrap up the transfer activity for the season.

Another opportunistic window in the summer of 2020/21 saw another Barcelona forward, Luis Suárez, join *Los Rojiblancos* at the expense of Morata, who joined from Chelsea only to be loaned out to Juventus immediately. Carrasco's loan was made permanent and Geoffrey Kondogbia joined from Valencia, with Moussa Dembélé and Lucas Torreira coming in on loan from Lyon and Arsenal respectively. The departures were mainly of those who had not impressed, with left-back Caio Henrique and forward Nikola Kalinić leaving. There were some important names to depart though, with Thomas Partey being snapped up by Arsenal for €50m and Diego Costa having his contract terminated by mutual consent after falling out of favour. By this stage, the squad was well set and the transition to a more possession-dominant and offensive side was well under way, with the recruitment of younger and more versatile players highlighting the way that Simeone planned to move forward.

The re-signing of Antoine Griezmann on loan from Barcelona along with a big-name signing in Rodrigo de Paul would make Atlético's intentions clear at the start of the 2021/22 season, with the promising 22-year-old Brazilian forward Matheus Cunha also arriving from Hertha Berlin in Germany, fresh off the back of a successful Olympics tournament in which he would score in the final as his country went on to win gold. Twenty-year-old winger Marcos Paulo would arrive from Fluminense in Brazil only to be loaned out to Famalicão in Portugal, and Benjamin Lecomte would sign on loan to provide backup in the goalkeeping department.

The biggest piece of news of the summer window, however, would be the departure of Saúl Ñíguez, arguably one of the club's best-ever homegrown talents and a true fan favourite, on loan to Chelsea in the Premier League for a breath of fresh air as his performances had started to waver. The season would not go to plan though, and Atlético's defence was uncharacteristically vulnerable, all the more so when Newcastle United snapped up Trippier in the January window. Replacements were surely needed and in came Daniel Wass from Valencia along with Reinildo

Mandava from Lille, with the latter immediately securing his place in the side and already becoming something of a fan favourite.

Atlético still have some work to do in the coming window to tighten up their squad and get back to their best, especially needing some solidity in midfield considering that Herrera has already, at the time of writing, secured a move to Houston Dynamo in the MLS at the end of the season. The extent to which the club will invest is still unknown, though Simeone is now backed far more than he initially was, and with some of the other major European clubs already eyeing a few Atlético prospects, there will be an interesting window ahead.

A recruitment plan is all well and good though, but perhaps the most obvious and yet understated part of transfers nowadays is the actual fees involved. Player fees and transfer windows are looked at in isolation, but in reality, a manager has to work within set margins over a long period of time, especially at a club like Atlético Madrid. It is, therefore, remarkable to see how the buying and selling of players below translates into numbers in the form of transfer fees.

Not only have Atlético recorded positive net spends (meaning they received more than they gave) in nearly half the seasons, their overall net spend of €112.2m

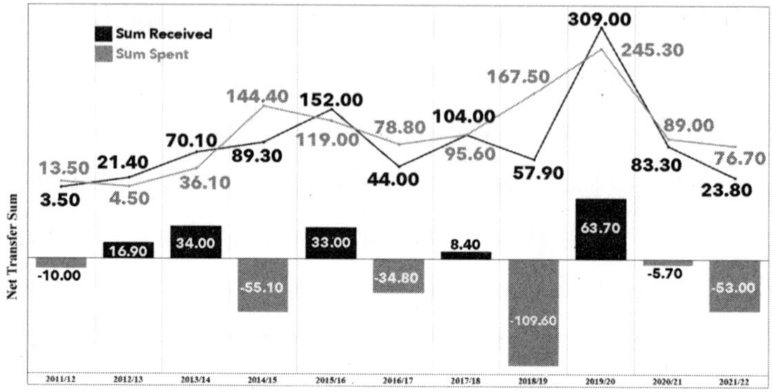

Fig. 10 *Amount spent and received in transfers since January 2012 (million euros)*

is nearly five times smaller than that of Barcelona (€551.92m) and comparable with that of Real Madrid (€146.5m) despite having bought nearly twice as many players and selling only about ten players more in the same span. It is the state of modern football where budgetary restraints heavily impact the ability of a club to consistently fight for the top spots and, while sides like Leicester City and Lille have managed to break this barrier on occasions, Atlético's decade-long battle right across Europe is even more astounding simply owing to their longevity at the top.

Of course, with more success and an improved reputation there does come more money, as can be seen from the generally increasing trend of expenditure, but it is equally interesting to note how the sum received increases with this as well. According to a

Transfermarkt report in late 2021, it was found that Simeone had generated the most money with sales and transfers of players in the 21st century, totalling €1bn at the time. While spending power has increased owing to their on-field exploits, the club cannot afford to match their rivals with that alone and thus have cultivated a healthy transfer environment, where they are able to offload players for good money while increasing their investments in the squad. In 2012/13 and 2019/20, the seasons before their league titles, Atlético had registered net incomes by means of transfer fees, something which is truly remarkable in an age where teams have to invest heavily in incomings over a couple of seasons at least in order to win major trophies. This shows that, despite losing important members of the squad, Atlético are able to put the big money received to good use with smart signings, meaning their on-field performances are not always affected by the loss of a player or two, and therein lies the beauty of *Cholo*'s recruitment plan.

This is not to say that every player has been a resounding success, with players such as Toby Alderweireld, Mario Mandžukić and Diogo Jota having done exceedingly well elsewhere but failing to consistently perform at Atlético, and other big signings including Cerci, Vietto, Martins and Vitolo having not lived up to their billing either. In such cases, Simeone's ruthlessness prevails, with the manager simply not giving players much of a look in if they are not convincing. There are, of course, exceptions to this as well, with prominent stars such as Marcos Llorente and Yannick Carrasco going on to turn their careers around from such situations. The former originally signed as a defensive midfielder and the latter seemed unsettled as a winger in Simeone's system, but they have since been assigned new roles and moulded into versatile players. This has seen them flourish.

Finding undervalued assets is one part, but finding assets capable of fitting into Simeone's systems has undoubtedly been the key to Atlético's success, and the backbone of the recruitment strategy. The integration of talent into a squad, a key stage of the scouting and recruitment process is certainly something that *Cholo* and his team have been able to excel at consistently and has also then allowed for flexibility in formation and tactics, be it before the game or for in-game tactical tweaks. Not only does this show good recruitment in identifying talent, but it goes to show the ability of Simeone and his technical staff to further develop the talent that they bring in, which is yet another part of recruitment that often goes unnoticed.

As the years have gone by, this recruitment plan has made Atlético a wanted destination for talent as well, and not a club where players would think that their careers would stall. For future stars, it can be seen as a stepping stone to big-budget clubs, with Atlético providing the option to showcase their skills away from the limelight of La Liga's two biggest names. For others, Atlético can be viewed as an option to prove themselves to the world, fighting season on season against Europe's elite and showing that, on their day, they can take anyone down. That is not to say that the club is not already viewed as one of the best in Europe already, but this is perhaps Simeone's greatest achievement on the recruitment front, the fact that he has been able to make Atlético an option for entirely different types of players at various stages of their career. He cannot, and will not, turn the side into the *Galácticos,* but neither is his side made up of 'best of the rests' with nothing to prove.

Cholo's ability to come up with a concoction that neatly blends the assortment of players picked from the market season on season is an attribute that not all managers possess, and then uniting them to give their all for the badge of *Los Colchoneros* every single minute is something even rarer to find.

4

Chaos Calling: Midfielders

'We aspire to be an annoying team'

ANNOYING. FOR anyone who played against Diego Simeone, he was annoying. Whether he was sitting ahead of the defence or pacing down the touchline, if you came up against Simeone that day, you were bound to leave the game frustrated. A cheap foul before walking off nonchalantly or his pitchside antics after a goal, the result was secondary. And as much as you tried to avoid it, the annoyance would creep in, slowly breaking through your shell before completely consuming you, almost like a virus. Just ask David Beckham, because before you know it you could be seeing red.

This is just what Simeone the player wanted. He wanted to get under your skin, unsettle you, unnerve you, and operating in the heart of midfield, he had the best position to do so. Where others saw the midfield as a vantage point from which they could gauge and assess the entire game, Simeone saw it as the best place to cause destruction. His eyes searched for any possible weakness, any potential advantage, and his mind and body were ready to commit wholeheartedly. Where other star midfielders command and dictate the game with the ball, looking for an opportunity to thread that perfect pass, Simeone saw things differently. He was not just a destroyer either, like many defensive midfielders who graced the pitch with him, he was a monster. His was a position from which he could orchestrate the play, controlling the flow of the game without the ball and pull the strings for his side, and he knew just which strings to tug on.

Is this what makes midfielders good managers? Simeone isn't the first, or greatest, central midfielder to become a successful manager and you only have to look across to the white side of Madrid to see the success that Zinedine Zidane has had. The Frenchman won three Champions League titles in succession as their coach and was so good that Real had to plead with him to return when Julen Lopetegui and Santiago Solari both failed. Even English legends Frank Lampard and Steven Gerrard made waves with their sides. Lampard, after a good stint with Derby County, qualified for the

Champions League with a young Chelsea side after a transfer ban in his opening season. His fairytale was rather unceremoniously cut short, but he did bring in several of the players who eventually went on to win the Champions League without him. Gerrard, on the other hand, worked in the youth setup at Liverpool before moving to take the job at Rangers and his work in the 2020/21 season was simply astounding. Unbeaten throughout the Scottish Premiership campaign, having dropped points in just six games, Gerrard's side finished a whopping 25 points ahead of their closest challengers, eventually landing him a job in the Premier League with Aston Villa.

Then there are the Spaniards, Xavi and Mikel Arteta, who are slowly working their magic and rightfully staking their claim to be a part of football's next wave of top tacticians, and we need not even mention Pep Guardiola. The fiery Italian Antonio Conte needs no introduction either, having won three Scudettos with his old club Juventus before winning the Premier League comfortably in his debut season with Chelsea. He then took Inter Milan to the Europa League Final and comfortably won the Scudetto the following season, ending Juventus's extended era of dominance, all the while jumping and celebrating like a child, something that rather comically irked José

Mourinho whenever they faced off. His equally – if not more – aggressive counterpart Gennaro Gattuso had mixed spells at both AC Milan and Napoli, but he did manage to win the Coppa Italia with the latter as well.

Perhaps having been in the heart of midfield, these players have developed an extensive understanding of the game, making them natural tacticians over the course of their career. Or perhaps their constant contribution to everything that their side does has left them with an unbreakable attachment to the game, an addiction bordering on madness fuelling the need to be involved in the chaos.

Where there is madness and chaos, there is Simeone. And he takes it to the next level.

'I don't like this, I don't feel it,' said Simeone after paying Guardiola a visit to study his Barcelona side a few years before taking the Atlético job, and this is what differentiates the Argentinian from the host of managers listed above and beyond. Where the others bury their chaos and addiction deep in their intricate tactics and hide their aggression, reserving it only for the hottest of situations, Simeone bares it all out in the open. His madness is openly visible all across the pitch, and his passion and aggression are loud from the touchline.

Unfortunately for Simeone though, as a manager he is now restricted to the confines of his technical area, and try as he may to cross them on occasions, for 90 minutes and beyond he is nothing but a voice among the crowd, albeit the most important one. A chief instigator right in the thick of the action in his playing days, now he is restricted to the borders of the pitch. The most important weapon still lies within him though, that of his penchant for chaos, and as much as he would love to unleash this from the sidelines, he knows it is better used on the field. And what better place to hide it than the position that he knows best?

It would be a shame if Simeone's midfield was completely unlike him, depriving us of the chance to see hints of *Cholo* strutting about in the middle once again. It is not entirely evident at first though, since there is no player exactly like Simeone, but with every cheeky tackle or mischievous look, the ghost of Simeone the player springs to life in each of his midfielders, almost as if the man himself had it bottled up to hand out to them before every game. While it may seem that Simeone's Atlético are centred around their defence, the midfield is the rock upon which the side is built, and it is only right that this cornerstone is sculpted in the image of its master.

Despite the many positional and tactical tweaks that the midfield has undergone since the day *Cholo* took over at Atlético, this department has largely remained the side's engine, driving it forward consistently over the years. It is, therefore, key to first analyse the duties of the midfield when attempting to break down Simeone's *Rojiblancos*.

Now, in general, midfielders have a more dynamic role in any football side, providing the link between defence and attack and possessing the ability to move into either, or both, lines depending on the situation. Of course, with the evolution of the game over the years, and especially over the last decade, it has been all the more crucial for each player to be dynamic in their own way, highlighting how much sharper the modern-day midfielder has to be to excel at the top level. And when crafting the ideal Simeone midfielder, sharpness and dynamism are two of the main ingredients.

When we look at *Cholo*'s initial 4-4-2 setup, it has just the two central midfielders lined up alongside each other and with defensive duties prioritised, there was not really anything expansive expected from either of the two. However, these were not just additional centre-backs that would drop in and add numbers to the back line either, and the real key to their success would lie in their excellent positional awareness.

Even though we said that the two midfielders lined up alongside each other, this was not entirely the case in games, with Simeone staggering his midfield when

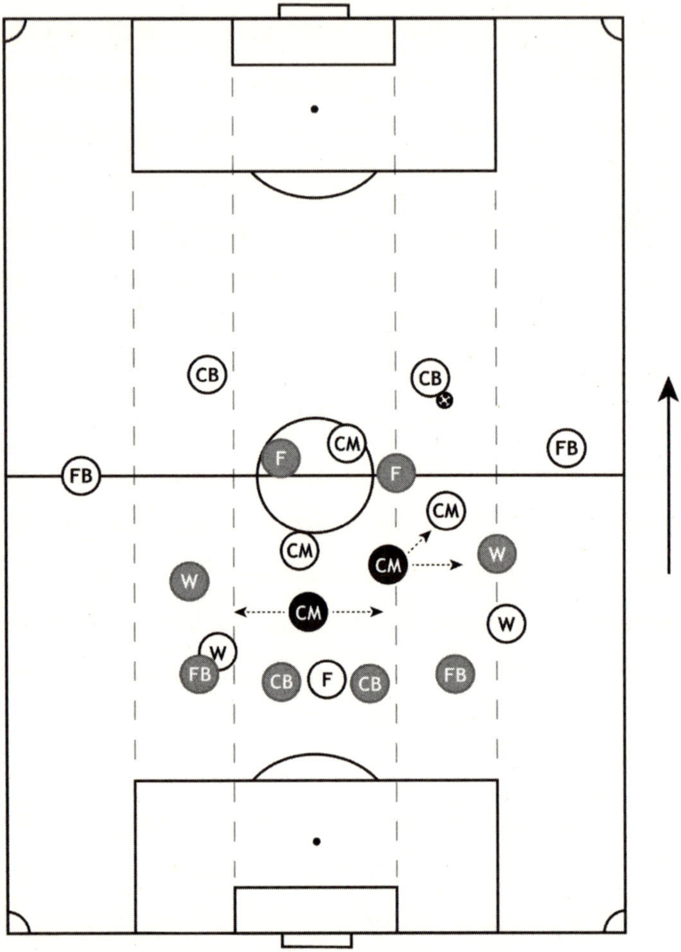

Fig. 11 The staggering of Atlético Madrid's central midfielders to protect central spaces

out of possession. This meant that the ball-side central midfielder would step up ahead of his counterpart and would be ready to press forward if needed.

With just the two players in the middle to stunt any central progression, staggering them is perhaps the best way of blocking out any passes through the middle. Having them in a flat line would allow some space behind the midfielders and would just make it easy to play around them with quick passing combinations, but the staggering allows the midfielders to cut off passing angles better and also to cover for each other should either one of them be beaten.

But are they always staggered? The simple answer is, no. One of the main drawbacks of the 4-4-2 formation in the modern game is that the two central midfielders can be outnumbered in midfield consistently, with opposition sides more often than not opting for a three-man midfield. While Simeone's setup does call on the forwards and particularly the wingers to compensate for this (we will see how this works later), it is also equally important that the two central midfielders themselves are not venturing out of position too early and conceding space to the opposition. As a result, they start out alongside each other along a flat line as the opposition start to build up, staying closer to the centre-backs and minimising space centrally, before they slowly shift across to their staggered position once the opposition naturally move the ball sideways.

Figure 11 also shows the individual roles of the two central midfielders in this process, with the side having forced the opposition to play towards their left flank and Atlético's right. While one opposition central midfielder has already dropped deep to facilitate the build-up (between the two Atlético forwards), the pass to him is not on and hence his counterpart has had to drop to receive between the Atlético forward and winger. This pass would effectively bypass Atlético's first line of pressure and, if allowed, could lead to the side being outnumbered in the middle of the pitch very quickly, with the deep central midfielder and full-backs of the opposition pushing forward immediately. Hence, the ball-side midfielder for Atlético would push up and follow him, making him a more difficult passing option and leaving the opponents' centre-back with no other choice but to play it to his left-back.

This is still not enough though and with this movement, the Atlético midfielder has put some distance between himself and his team-mate in midfield, allowing a potential gap for an opponent to drop into. There is also the chance that the opposition central midfielder receives the pass anyway and should he have the technique to evade this pressure and turn his man, he would find himself with space centrally to drive into. To mitigate this, the deeper Atlético central midfielder shifts across to his right, ensuring that he covers the depth behind his team-mate and can also step out quickly to snuff out danger if his team-mate looks like he could be beaten.

Ultimately, this eventually fulfils Atlético's aim of forcing the opposition out wide, having cut out all possible central passes with the positioning and movement of the two midfielders. Once this is done, the midfielders have their next task, which is to suffocate the opposition out wide.

Having forced the opposition out wide, Atlético naturally would look to use their wingers and full-backs to occupy these spaces and contain the opposition. A forward would also drop in to add numbers, and from Figure 12 we see that without the central midfielder of Atlético there is a three-v-three situation out wide. The centre-back has played the ball out wide to his full-back, with Atlético promptly shifting across and stepping up slightly higher considering the full-back has received the pass in his own half.

When a full-back receives the ball out wide, he is effectively limited to passing in three basic directions – forwards, backwards and towards the centre of the pitch. Anything towards the touchline is naturally cut off, hence making it an extra defender for the opposition. Simeone looks to use this to good effect by not only creating an overload out wide, but by using the midfielder to do so.

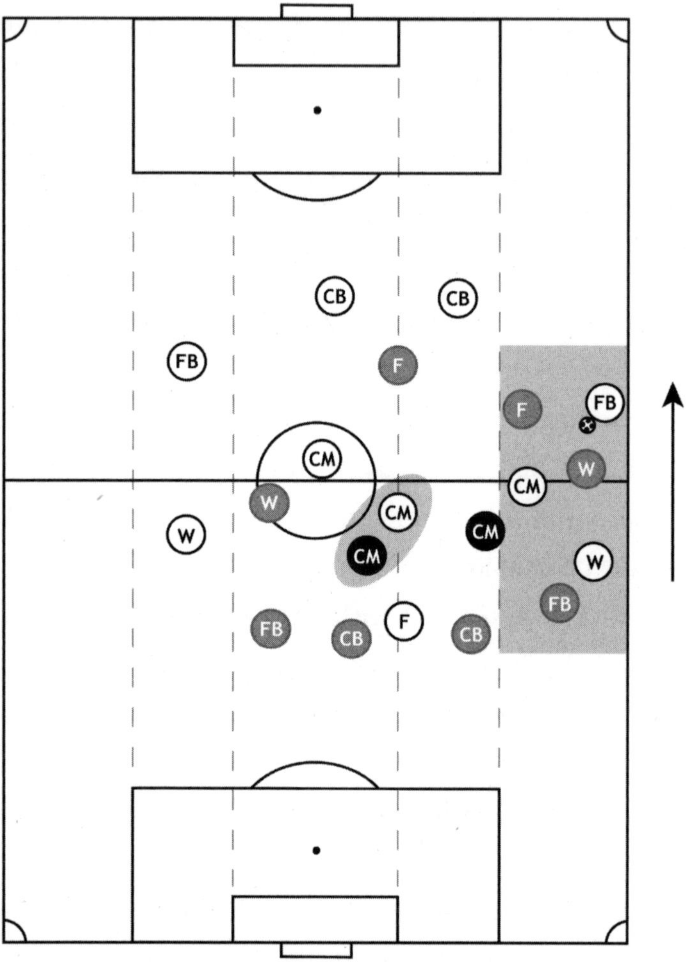

***Fig. 12** Atlético Madrid's central midfielders stepping in to cause wide overloads*

We saw earlier how an Atlético midfielder stepped up and followed an opposition midfielder and now this opponent has moved out wide to offer support for his full-back. However, he does not shake off his marker though, and the Atlético midfielder follows him into this wide area, creating a four-v-three in favour of *Los Rojiblancos*. While it is still possible to move out of the flanks with some smart passing and movement when faced with a three-v-three situation, the opposition full-back now struggles to find a proper pass, having been outnumbered out wide. Furthermore, he does not have the luxury of time and space, highlighting the use of the touchline as an extra man with the Atlético players closing in on him.

Committing to a four-v-three out wide, however, needs two things to happen in order to be successful. The first is that the team with the numerical superiority, in this case Atlético, swarms the opponents and closes them down quickly rather than employing a more passive press that allows the opponent with the ball time to work out his next move. The importance of this is to prevent the second situation from occurring, which is when opponents are able to move out to other zones quickly where they are now afforded more space.

In the case shown in Figure 12, this vacant space is available centrally and we can see how the other two opposition central midfielders are able to drift between the forward and midfield lines of Atlético. Considering that Simeone's side have swarmed their opponents in the wide areas, there is still the chance that they look to take advantage of this central space by playing a quick pass out in the general direction, allowing their team-mates to receive in space and quickly change the direction of attack. This then leaves Atlético vulnerable through the middle, which is something that they simply do not want to allow.

As a result, the second thing that needs to happen to deal with such a situation is the movement of the other Atlético central midfielder to cover the pass out. Of course, in the above example, it is not possible for him to cut out the passes to both opposition midfielders, but considering the pressure applied on the opposition full-back by his team-mates, it is the closer pass that has the higher chance of succeeding, and hence the Atlético midfielder would move up and mark his opposition counterpart, much like his team-mate did in the wider areas. The opposition are now forced to come up with something special if they want to directly escape this pressure, but more often than not they would find this difficult to do.

Teams like Real Madrid did try to do this at times, pushing players to neutralise the overload down the flank, while also keeping players on the far side to allow them to receive any switches in space. This, however, left space centrally for Atlético to attack should they regain possession, and the sheer difficulty of playing a crossfield pass under pressure from multiple opponents made this a tactic that was incredibly difficult to pull off. Even the few times that it did work, the passes would often be floated across without any real incisiveness, allowing Atlético the time to shift across quickly before the ball reached its target.

While this did provide a good amount of success in stunting opposition attacks early, it was not the only thing that the central midfielders offered in defence though. With opponents playing right into Atlético's hands by playing out wide, they then wanted to find any possible way of breaking through the middle, meaning the pair had to be on high alert all the time and even find intelligent ways of dealing with their opponents. We know that they were often outnumbered, or at least matched, in midfield and this meant that they could not look to directly mark their opponents either, instead having to coordinate with their team-mates and use good movement coupled with excellent awareness to track opponents.

To exploit the central spaces, the opposition would not directly play through the middle right from the back, rather they would move the ball wide before looking for quick passing combinations through the middle. This served as a means of drawing the Atlético players wide and, before they could get into position and cause the overload, catching them out of position with the central passes. To make the most of it, they could also push their third midfielder up the pitch, rather than having players drop deep to start the build-up, in order to outnumber the Atlético midfield as we mentioned earlier.

On paper, it does sound very effective and it probably does not require the same amount of technique and skill to bypass the Atlético players, considering that the opposition has the overload in this case. The only thing that is required is a high tempo of passing, and with a few passes, the opposition can quickly move into midfield and slice right through. So how does the Atlético midfield deal with this then? This is something that we would refer to as 'baiting'.

Figure 13 (overleaf) shows a situation where the opponents have looked to push their side forward, with only the full-backs staying further behind in the build-up phase. The three opposition central midfielders have been pushed between the lines and, with the full-back having just received the ball, Atlético are looking to shift over and overload the flank.

Immediately, we see that the full-back in possession has three passes on for him, with two central midfielders open and his winger available further ahead. The pass to the winger is perhaps the more direct option, but this would once again force

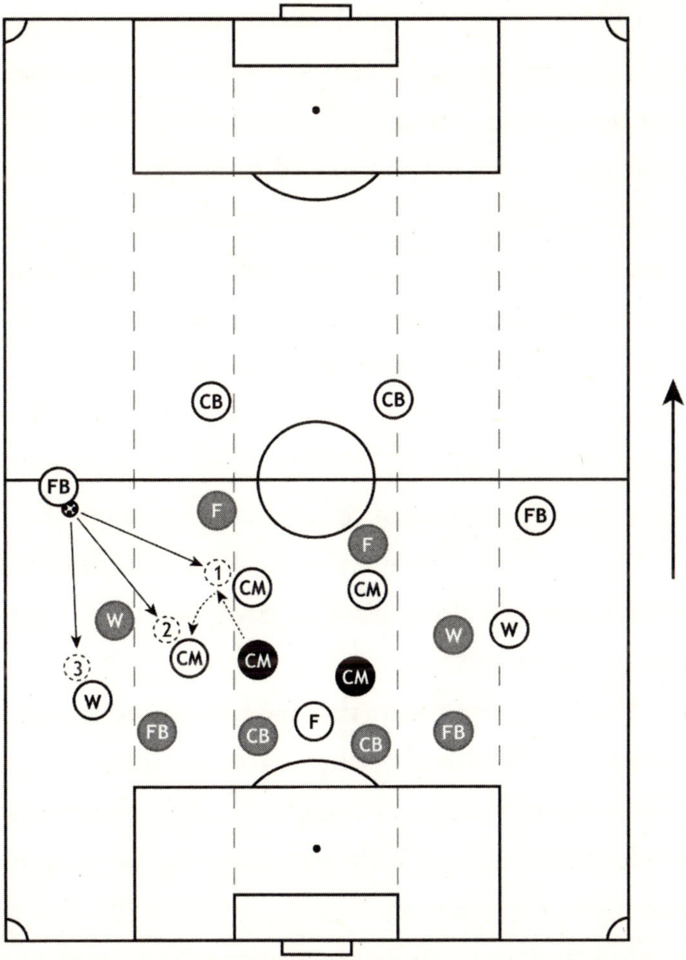

Fig. 13 *Atlético Madrid's central midfielders 'baiting' opponents with passes of higher difficulty*

his team to the wide areas where Atlético will then look to crowd them out. As a result, the passes to the two central midfielders are the ones that would pose the greatest threat to Atlético.

Of the two passes available, we see that pass 1 is the easier one, with the central midfielder in question having a good amount of space in midfield. The Atlético forward has not moved across yet to cut this pass out, leaving his man free in between the lines. Pass 2 is the more incisive and threatening one, as it could effectively bypass two lines of Atlético pressure, slicing through not only the forward line but also the midfield as well. However, this is more difficult, as the Atlético winger can cut this off with quick steps to his right once he senses that the pass is going to be made. Moreover, the ball-side Atlético central midfielder is close enough to close this man down should the pass still go through as well.

This does not mean that pass 1 will be allowed though, and this is where the awareness and movement of the Atlético midfielder comes into play. Understanding that 1 is the ball that is on, he commits himself to stepping up and cutting the pass off, causing the full-back to reconsider his options. Now, what was the easier pass has been blocked off, with pass 2 being the only other way to cut through the midfield. This, however, has become an even more appealing option for the full-back, who senses that all he has to do is beat the winger in order to slice through and find his team-mates with loads of space ahead of the defence.

What the full-back, on most occasions, fails to realise though is that he has now effectively been forced, or 'baited', into playing this pass which is not as excellent an option as it may seem. With most right-backs being right-footed (and left-backs being left-footed for the inverse case), the natural angle to play this pass is tight, and now that the Atlético midfielder has moved, the winger is on higher alert to cut out this pass. The distance between his two passing options is minimised as well, since the midfielder for pass 2 has to drop slightly to get out of the line of Atlético's winger. The most important thing though, is that the Atlético midfielder knows this, and hence is already waiting to make his next move.

Having moved to cut off pass 1, the Atlético midfielder's job is only half done, and his next duty is to cut off pass 2 as well. With that being the only option that he has allowed through the middle, his job becomes easier thanks to his winger who has worked to make it even more tricky for the opposition. All he has to do now is wait for the opponent to engage in making this pass, and he can then quickly move back and intercept the ball. The timing of this movement is key, and this is what completes this manoeuvre, with the midfielder waiting for the moment just as the pass is played before quickly darting across and receiving it, his opponent falling for it hook, line and sinker.

This clever bit of play allows the Atlético midfielders to deal with any numerical deficiencies in midfield, using their movement to effectively cut off multiple passes. It also then goes to show the quality of the midfielders needed, and how important the execution of such sequences is to the overall defensive tactics of the side. Hingeing it all on good execution may seem risky, but the fact that these duties are carried out consistently over a period of time also shows us the level of coaching and training involved to drill these responsibilities into the players, making such situations comfortable for them.

While these tactics were a primary feature of the early 4-4-2, we have only considered opposition sides building up from near the halfway line until this point. In the earlier seasons, Simeone was comfortable sitting well behind in a low block, only using a mid-level block at most. However, with football developing rapidly season after season, more and more sides looked to build up from further behind, meaning that Atlético could not just sit back and allow the opposition nearly half the pitch to run into. Countering this would not be as simple as just pushing the side further ahead with the same roles either, as the side would then be vulnerable to being stretched easily and risked allowing too much space for the opposition to play into.

Moreover, Simeone also realised that the side itself required a different midfield setup for the modern era, with a pair of gritty central midfielders not just hard to find but also difficult to use effectively in and out of possession. While the two central midfielders still had to share defensive duties, they could no longer be split equally either, and the earlier method of having the ball-side midfielder step out while his team-mate covers would not work consistently simply because there was far more space that needed covering when looking to press higher.

'Destroyers', or players who could sit at the base of midfield and deal with most defensive situations, were slowly becoming the mainstream, especially for the bigger sides looking to employ a more possession-based system and push their other players well forward, leaving large spaces that needed covering. While Atlético were not necessarily a possession-based side yet, Simeone understood that having players in this mould would still allow him greater flexibility to press higher, being able to cover more space in midfield with the protection that a 'destroyer' offers.

This then led to a slight tweak in the system, where instead of having two central midfielders alongside each other, they would play one ahead of the other, with the forward player having the freedom to venture forward and press, while the 'destroyer' could stay behind and offer solidity to the back line if the first two lines were bypassed. Again, this would require the support of the wingers especially, but with our focus currently on the midfielders we now see that both of them would take on fairly different roles and offer something different out of possession, seeing Simeone move away from the tactics that he had employed earlier.

Figure 14 shows this shift in greater detail, with Atlético Madrid now looking to press opponents much higher than before. They are still in the 4-4-2 formation, although the shape above can also be interpreted as a 4-4-2 with a midfield diamond or a 4-1-3-2 as well.

As we can see from the figure, the goalkeeper is looking to start the build-up, with his two centre-backs having dropped to support him. Being in the box, the Atlético forwards cannot close them down just yet, but they are poised to move in once the initial pass has been made. Crucially, though, an opposition central midfielder has also dropped in between the centre-backs, and the Atlético forwards, to provide another passing option for the goalkeeper.

This player is key to the build-up, as his pass is fairly easy if not pressured, and the goalkeeper is able to take both Atlético forwards out of the equation very early on. If the forwards remain narrow to cut this out, that then allows the goalkeeper to play to his centre-backs who may then find a passing option in the channels to bypass the forward line. As a result, an Atlético midfielder needs to step up to follow this man and cut out the passing option, leading to the shape seen above. If the side had maintained their previous 4-4-2 setup with the midfielders alongside each other, the flatter shape would have struggled to effectively cut out this pass as they would have also left space in behind for the other opposition midfielders to exploit.

This structure also sees the midfield initially overloaded by the opponents centrally, and we can see how the 'destroyer' has to account for two opposition players. This, however, is in fact another way of 'baiting' the opposition into playing a longer pass into either of the two players, forcing them to abandon their short build-up and go longer into midfield. Notice how the wingers are crucial to this as well, with their narrower structure allowing them to close down the opponent closest to them and hence support the 'destroyer' as they look to engage whichever player that the long pass has been played into. It also means that it is not a direct aerial duel between one Atlético midfielder and his opposition counterpart, but that there are men on hand to sweep up the second ball in case the header is lost.

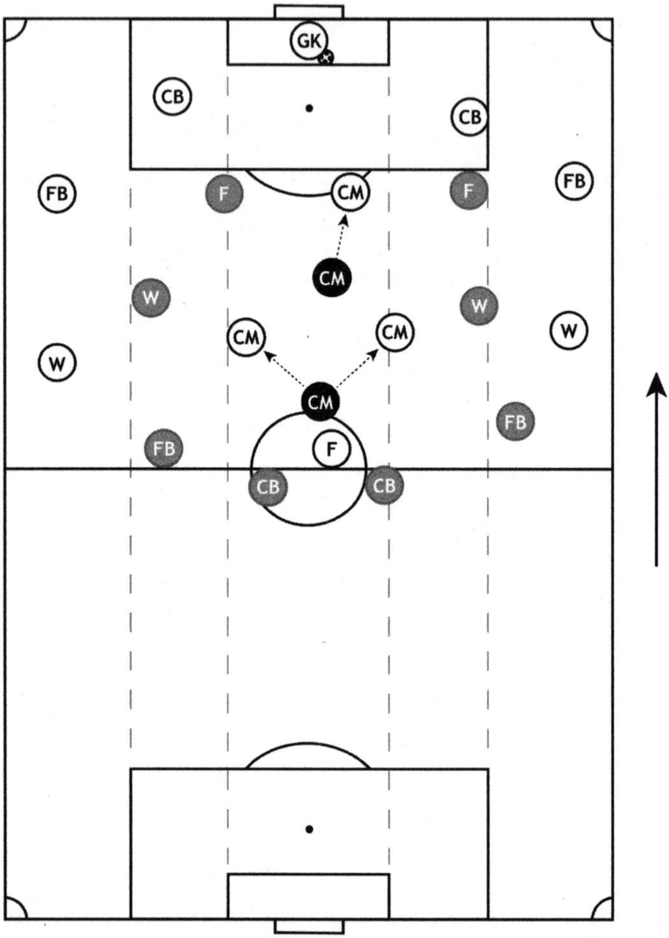

Fig. 14 *Use of a 'destroyer' and a midfielder with more freedom to press*

This effectively means that the goalkeeper's options are now fairly limited to simpler passes, unless he is willing to take the chance with the longer ball out being contested. With the shorter route offering more safety, he can play the ball to either centre-back or full-

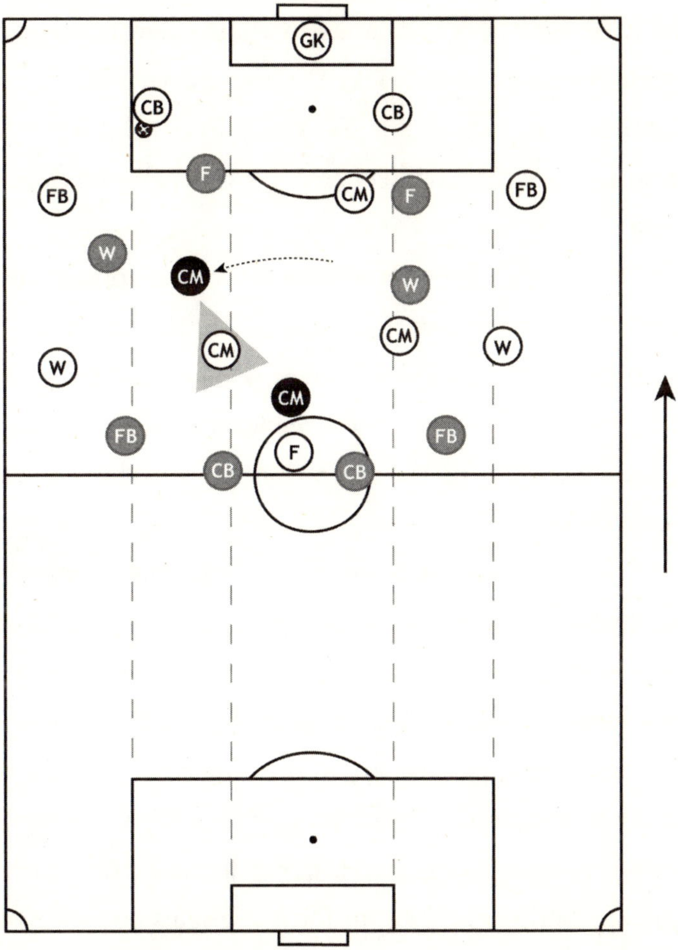

***Fig. 15** Midfielder shifts to account for the pass to the centre-back*

back, with the pass to the nearer central midfielder too risky an option considering the pressure on him from the Atlético midfielder. Again, out of these options, the pass to the full-backs is somewhat more difficult owing to the longer distance and the need for it to be extremely accurate, so as to allow them to receive with time and space near the touchline. Hence, to further analyse how this Atlético press works, we will assume that the goalkeeper plays the ball out to his centre-back.

We see that the ball has gone out to the opposition's right-centre-back, with Atlético now shifting across accordingly. The forward can now move in to engage him and the winger can move closer to the full-back to apply pressure should the next pass be played out to him.

In such a scenario though, one of the opposing central midfielders, who was initially further ahead and under the watch of the 'destroyer', is now an available passing option in between the lines owing to the natural passing angle opening up. While it is still possible for the 'destroyer' to follow him and apply pressure, this pass is still a fairly decent option since the opposition can look to form triangles out wide or overload the middle, and the midfielder has the time and space to turn his man as well. It would also call for the rest of the Atlético players to shift inwards, for example the right-winger would have to move centrally to cover the player closest to him, and this opens up large spaces down the opposite flank for the opposition to play the ball into.

As a result, to prevent the press from being rendered ineffective with this relatively straightforward pass, it is the higher Atlético midfielder who shifts across to his left to cut out the angle. What he is doing is basically placing his opponent in his cover shadow, which means that his positioning effectively keeps his opponent behind him, covering off any potential passing angles that the ball carrier has to this player. With the ball being shifted out to the centre-back, this midfielder has the freedom to leave the man he had been marking earlier, since the forwards can now cut off the pass instead with their positioning and movement.

This also means that the 'destroyer' can stay behind to cover depth and is still capable of shifting across to either side if needed later on. His positioning, just ahead of the defensive line, also adds the extra support in numbers in case the opponents are still able to beat the pressure and run at the back line. Much like we saw in the deeper block earlier on, one Atlético midfielder has been given the responsibility of marking two opposition midfielders, with the other having to cover for him if necessary. This simple yet effective tweak has maintained the earlier principles, but switches up the execution to suit the newer style of play.

That is not all though, and while this change does allow Atlético to press higher effectively, what it also does is offer a whole new dynamic in possession. It has never really been a necessity for Atlético midfielders to get involved in the build-up, though their slick and incisive passing has created numerous chances for the side, with most of the attacks being direct and into the channels for the forwards. However, in keeping up with the changing times, Simeone understood that the earlier brand of football would not be entirely sustainable in the modern era, and certainly not for a side looking to act as a European heavyweight.

Atlético didn't often have the ball for long, but they now had to be more patient when they did, and once again the midfielders would prove to be key to this new development.

One of the most common ways of using midfielders in the build-up phase is by allowing them to drop between the centre-backs to facilitate ball progression. What this effectively entails is that one central midfielder could get back and receive the ball in space, allowing him to find better passes forwards ideally to break the opposition lines and find team-mates in space.

This is what Atlético set out to do as well, with the 'destroyer' splitting the centre-backs and forming a makeshift back three in possession. Moving into this shape allows the full-backs to get forward and stretch

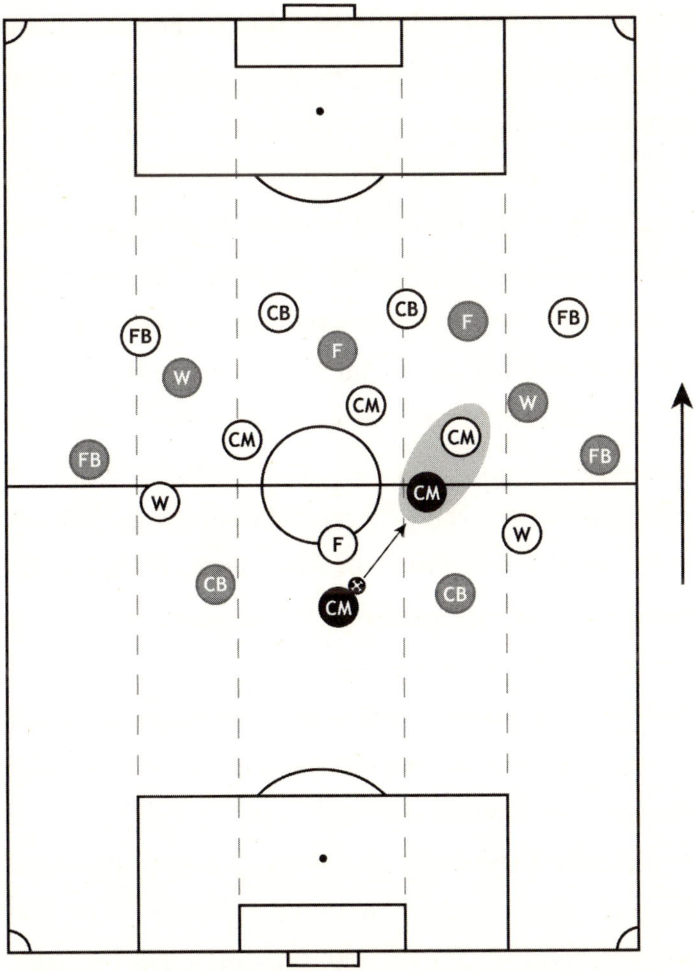

Fig. 16 *Atlético Madrid using a midfielder to form a makeshift back three in the build-up*

the field of play as well, which could then open up central spaces to play passes into. It also goes without saying that the 'destroyer' in question should have a good passing range, with players such as Thomas Partey and Rodri proving to be ideal for this role and essentially being evolved versions of Gabi, their predecessor, owing to the improvement in passing range.

Once this shape is created, the other central midfielder then has the freedom to drop into the pockets of space ahead, with the aim of receiving the ball behind the opposition's first line of pressure. His role is to drift across the pitch as the ball moves across the now back three, providing them with a central short passing option. He can then, ideally, receive and turn into space, from where he can pick out forward passes to his team-mates, breaking lines again and allowing them to quickly attack the back line. However, while it seems sound in theory, it relies heavily on the technical ability of the player, who, as can be seen from Figure 16, has to receive the ball with an opposition midfielder closing him down.

Also, this shift to play a bit more possession-based football did not click immediately either, and the other supporting players could not effectively provide their midfielders with the necessary options that they required. This meant that, while Atlético did have technically sound midfielders capable of playing under pressure, they were still often left with much to do upon receiving. Figure 16 highlights this as well, and we can see that apart from the one Atlético midfielder between the lines, there is no other passing option for the ball carrier, which not only forces him to play just the one pass out, but also allows the opposition to quickly close his team-mate down once he receives since he has no other supporting player to lay the ball off to.

This is not to say that the build-up was always ineffective, and it did have its moments where it clicked with some good movement and rotations, but overall Simeone did not see the same level of success with this midfield arrangement in possession as much as he had defensively. Atlético Madrid were still a good team, but one that continued to thrive on a more direct style of play, albeit with a bit more individual technicality to sustain attacks and possession for a bit longer, and often focusing more on final-third creativity as opposed to a consistent build-up from the back. *Cholo* would not entirely scrap the idea of a more possession-based setup though and, with the introduction of the 5-3-2 formation, it would return.

With the shift to a back three, the build-up phase no longer requires the central midfielders to drop into the back line and specifically in the 5-3-2 formation, three central midfielders are now available to receive passes in between the lines. The wing-backs in this formation can provide the width naturally while the two forwards stay ahead and continue on in their role.

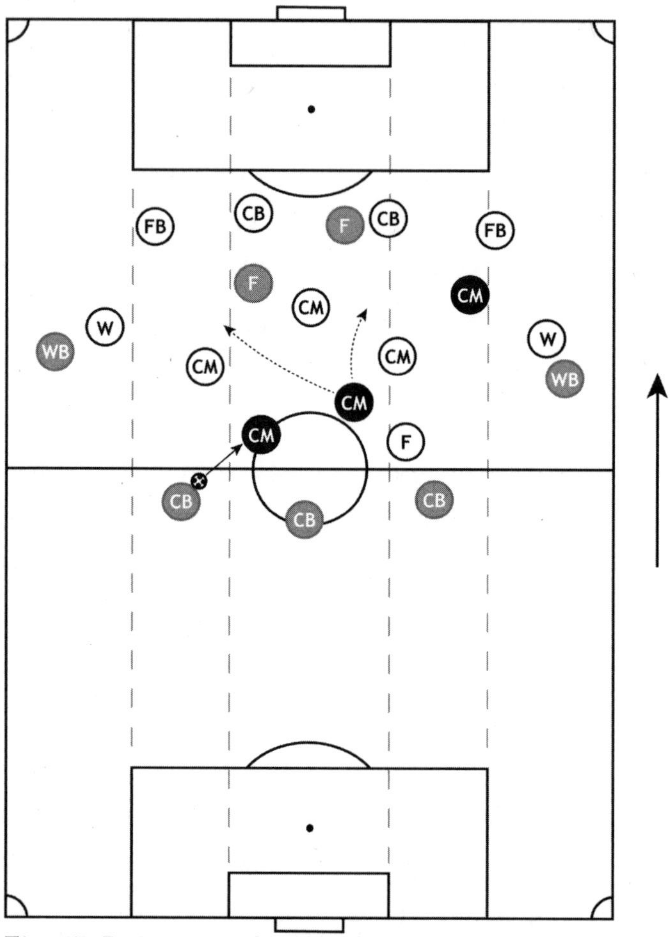

Fig. 17 *Positioning of midfielders when building up in the 5-3-2 formation*

This formation change now provides a variety of options when playing out from the back, the crucial thing being that the players are able to receive in more natural positions. For example, we saw earlier how only the central midfielder was available between the lines in the build-up using the 4-4-2 shape, and should any other player look to drop deeper to support him they would be vacating their natural position to do so. In this case, though, the forwards can continue to trouble the last line while the wing-backs stay wider, with the central midfielders able to receive in numbers in the middle.

Having laid the foundations to build up from the back, Atlético now have multiple ways of doing so, the simplest one being the case shown above in Figure 17. Here, after some shifting of the ball among the back line, two central midfielders have dropped deeper to receive the ball beyond the first line of pressure, forming a 3-2 shape at the back. It is not possible for the opposition forward to cut out all the available passes to these two players either, meaning that the ball is easily played into midfield. We saw earlier on how, with just a single Atlético midfielder in midfield, the opposition could easily mark him out of the game to prevent central progression. In this case, however, despite it being a three-v-two in favour of the opposition in midfield, Atlético also have their forwards and one more advanced central midfielder looking to drift in behind the second line of opposition pressure, meaning that not all of the other team's midfielders are available to engage the two deeper Atlético players.

For example, the deepest opposition central midfielder cannot vacate his zone as he would be leaving his two centre-backs to deal with two Atlético forwards and the opposition's left central midfielder has to worry about Atlético's advanced midfielder, considering that he is in a position to cause a two-v-two situation out wide along with the wing-back. As a result, despite having numerical superiority, Atlético still have the upper hand with more passing options available, and the fact that they have the two deeper players also allows them to have more control and shift the ball around in case of opposition pressure as well.

This could, however, easily change if another central midfielder was posted forward, and this is something often seen against sides that look to defend deeper. In such cases, Atlético have just the one central midfielder dropping to receive, while the other two look to get in between the lines or stay slightly further ahead to provide more incisive forward options to slice through the defence more easier. This allows for tactical flexibility within games as well, since the side can alternate between the different build-up options available to them and look to have more control over possession in midfield. Moreover, with the three central midfielders, Atlético can now look to push at least one of them higher, having more defensive security at the back and with two, not just one, midfielders covering. This in particular forms a crucial part of Simeone's shift to play more sustainable attacking football.

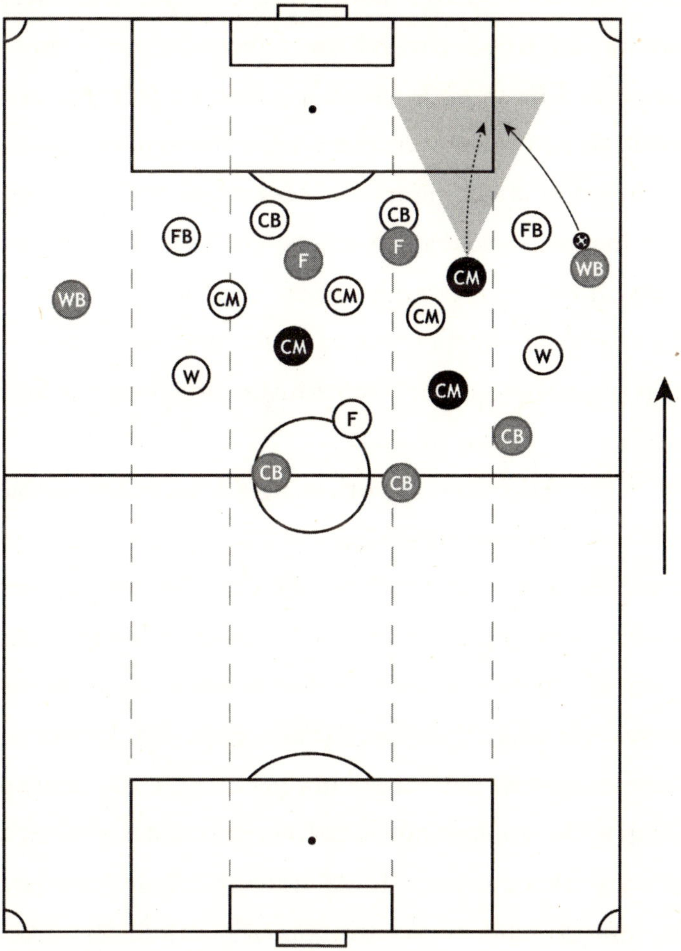

Fig. 18 *Atlético Madrid's central midfielder is given the freedom to attack the channels*

Figure 18 visualises an example of such an attack, and this is perhaps one of the most commonly seen attacking sequences with the current Atlético side. In Figure 17, we saw how one central midfielder had remained forward in a more advanced position and was allowed to drift between lines to receive the ball closer to goal. The most interesting point to note was the positioning of this midfielder, who does not exactly act as a central attacking midfielder or split the forwards, but instead looks to stay in the channels and station himself between the opposition full-back and centre-back. Figure 18 follows on from this and shows us why this positioning is key to creating an attack that proves difficult to defend against.

Since Atlético play with wing-backs, they are able to stretch opponents wider when in possession and use the entire width of the pitch, forcing opponents to do the same and follow their wide players. This means that the opposition full-backs have to allow space between them and their centre-back and, at best, they can get some support from their central midfielders or wingers. However, with Atlético playing three central midfielders of their own and having a further two central players in their forwards, it becomes difficult to cut off all the space afforded centrally, meaning that the Atlético midfielders can generally roam around in midfield and find pockets of space to drop into.

The most dangerous space to attack is, of course, the channel between the centre-back and the full-back, and this is exactly what Atlético want to do. Having moved the ball out wide as shown in Figure 18, the Atlético wing-back has drawn the opposition full-back out, while his forward pins the centre-back to his central position. The opposition are still looking to protect this channel though, having kept one of their central midfielders on the Atlético midfielder as he initially moves wide to provide a passing option for his wing-back. However, this is effectively just a one-v-one situation and, with the Atlético midfielder already ahead of his man, he is afforded the space to dart quickly into the channel and receive a through ball in behind the defence. Should the opposition look to position their man ahead of the Atlético man, then he can still make the run in behind him, showing how the one-v-one situation is not exactly the most effective means of stopping this, unless the defending side is fully prepared to track such a run or they commit an extra player to block out the zone.

For an already stretched side, neither of these is entirely possible and each would prove to be extremely difficult, highlighting the effectiveness of such a sequence to consistently create chances for the side. Marcos Llorente is one of the main players tasked with this role, and with his darting diagonal runs he can consistently threaten opposition defences and set his team-mates up with clever crosses and cut-backs into the penalty area. Having been largely passive in attack in the initial 4-4-2 formation, the Atlético central midfielders now play a crucial role in generating sustainable means of chance creation, making use of the incisiveness and directness of the older generation to complement the movement and technicality of the new.

The new responsibility adds a different dynamic to the midfield, allowing the individual players to showcase their quality on the ball and play a more expansive brand of football for extended periods of the game. However, this is still Simeone's Atlético Madrid, and, for all the buzz about the attack, the defensive aspect remains equally, if not more, important.

Although there are now three central midfielders, one more than in the 4-4-2, they are the only players blocking off the central lanes and hence find themselves effectively one man short in the middle line. While they may not necessarily be overloaded in the middle, it does become important for them to use their positioning to good effect to ensure that they not only cut out the spaces between them, but also work to ensure that they do not allow too much space on either side as well. If allowed, opponents can look to cause overloads and

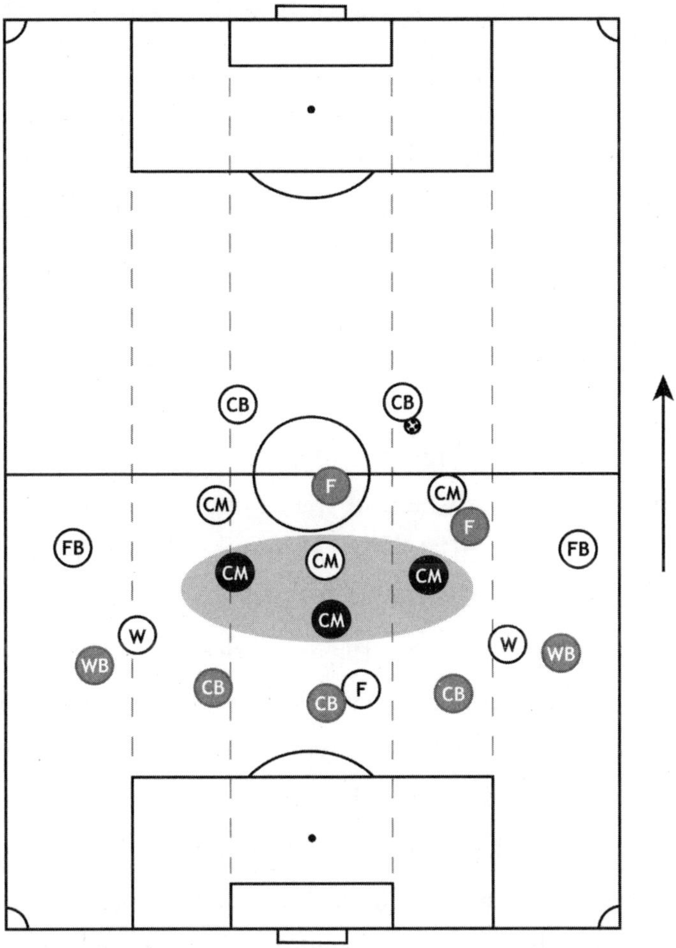

Fig. 19 *Atlético Madrid's staggered and compact midfield shape in a 5-3-2 formation*

get players into the channels, considering how narrow the midfield shape has become, making it difficult to force opponents completely to the flanks. This means that Atlético's midfielders have to tread a fine line and, most importantly, they need to work in tandem with their team-mates.

The key principles, however, remain largely similar to those we saw earlier. Simeone still uses the staggered midfield, now with two central midfielders ahead and on either side of a deeper-lying midfielder, forming a V shape in the middle of the pitch, with the positioning of these midfielders seeing a slight tweak. In the 4-4-2, one central midfielder would be allowed to push forward and press an opponent, while the other covered the depth behind them, but in the 5-3-2 all three central midfielders work to effectively cut out a pass to a centrally positioned opponent.

Looking at Figure 19, we notice that the three Atlético midfielders have effectively surrounded an opposition midfielder, and while the pass does largely remain available for the ball carrier, in this case the centre-back, it proves to be a risky option as the receiver can easily be closed down by all three players. Along with the right movement from the forward, Atlético are able to form a tetrahedral or pyramidal shape in midfield, effectively blocking out a pass to the opposition's central player.

This would then result in the opponent pushing their other midfielders deeper to receive from the back line, where they fall under the responsibility of the forwards, or they would play the ball out wide, allowing Atlético to once again shift across and crowd the flanks. Rather than actively pushing for the man-to-man press, Simeone has now been able to shift to a more zonal pressing system in midfield, cutting off the central passes with a good shape made by excellent positioning. Should the opposition then look to push their other midfielders deeper into the channels and either side of this V-shaped midfield, the Atlético players can simply rotate or shift across, with the closest midfielder moving in to cover the opponent while the furthest can move slightly ahead and across to step closer to the centrally positioned opponent, leaving the deeper-lying midfielder to continue in his role of providing the necessary cover for them.

The evolution is remarkable and yet Simeone's midfield hinges on the same principles that it always has: defensive organisation, movement and incisiveness, with each player given a distinct role that brings out their strengths, but even when the personnel changes, the system continues to work as a well-oiled machine. The bulk of the credit does go to the manager himself, but what would the system be without his players? In this regard, it must be said that the midfield of Atlético Madrid has been graced by some truly talented and legendary figures, to whom a homage is necessary.

Gabriel Fernández Arenas (Gabi)

Best known for his role as captain for the majority of the Simeone era, Gabi had been part of the Atlético Madrid first team as early as the 2003/04 season, sharing the dressing room with *Cholo* himself. Born and raised in Madrid, he was a youth team prospect, and managed to make the Spain squad for the Under-20 World Cup in 2003, playing every game en route to a runners-up medal, losing 1-0 to Brazil in the final. However, his path to the top only became longer from then on.

Not finding regular game time in the senior side, Gabi was sent on loan to newly promoted local rivals Getafe for the 2004/05 season. There, with regular game time, he found his feet at the top level, ending the season with 32 La Liga appearances, two goals and an assist to his name, having helped Getafe to a 13th-placed finish, just three points behind parent club Atlético themselves.

His performances did not go unnoticed back home and, in the following season, he was integrated into the first team, featuring another 32 times in the league under several managers in what proved to be a period of instability for Atlético. He had by no means taken the league by storm and, truth be told, had not even nailed down his starting position that year, with his playing time only decreasing the next. He was inching towards his 24th birthday by the time the 2006/07 season was reaching its conclusion and, taking the step of leaving his boyhood club in search of regular starts, he signed a pre-contract agreement with Real Zaragoza in February 2007, a move that would see him join that summer. Gabi's top-level career was far from over, and in truth, this move would just be the beginning of his rollercoaster ride back up.

Having been relegated with Zaragoza in his first season, Gabi stayed on and earned promotion back to La Liga immediately. He then prevented the side from going back down again and his name was already on the radar of top Spanish clubs who had begun to circle around for his signature. Zaragoza wanted to keep hold of their star man though, and the next season, he was made their captain and also allowed to flourish in a more advanced role, seeing him net a career-best 11 goals that would keep the team in the top flight, with two crucial goals on the final matchday allowing Zaragoza to escape relegation. By now, it was clear that Gabi had the ability to fight for the higher positions, and in the summer of 2011 Atlético Madrid knocked on his door once again, with the Spaniard returning to his first club.

It certainly was not a pleasant return though, and within six months Gregorio Manzano was gone, signalling another tumultuous period for Atlético. What happened next, however, is already a part of folklore. After a Europa League and UEFA Super Cup in half a season under former team-mate Simeone, Gabi was handed the chance to captain the side he grew up supporting, embracing the opportunity to spearhead his team on the pitch. His journey had taken longer than he would have liked, but eventually he was right where he wanted to be.

Gabi went on to become a figurehead in the Atlético dressing room as they went from strength to strength, and he led by example. It was his 49th-minute corner at the Camp Nou in May 2014 that found Diego Godín, bringing home the La Liga trophy for the first time since 1996. He went on to win a Copa del Rey and a Supercopa de España, claiming all the domestic honours before taking home yet another Europa League, totalling six major trophies in his seven-year stint, with the elusive Champions League being the only one he never managed to lift as captain.

It was also a shame that despite making the youth sides of his national team, Gabi never managed to earn a senior cap for Spain despite his consistent performances and even being hailed as one of the best performers across Europe for multiple seasons. He would eventually find himself seventh on Atlético's list of appearances when he left in 2018, and with 417 appearances for *Los Rojiblancos*, Gabi called it quits at the top level and moved to Qatar to join Al-Sadd, playing alongside fellow Spanish international Xavi. He would win the league in his first season and take the armband there too, following Xavi's move to become manager of the side for the 2019/20 season. Finally, at the end of 2020, Gabi announced his retirement from professional football, leaving behind an illustrious career that included playing a crucial part of Atlético's meteoric rise to the top.

He did return to Atlético as well, this time as a coach, working within the youth setup and at time of writing, he is all set to take over as coach of Getafe's B team for the 2022/23 season and, even if it is only on the sidelines, it will be good to see Gabi back in action again. Who knows, maybe he is once again starting his path from the academy to the senior side, this time as a manager.

'I always say that playing with Atlético Madrid was my childhood dream, so I cannot ask for more than what I am living these years,' he admitted.

Gabi did more than just play for his boyhood club. Blood, sweat and tears, he gave it his all, ensuring that his side garnered the attention of the footballing world, much as they had captured his all those years ago.

* * *

Tiago Mendes

Another key midfielder under Simeone, Tiago's playing career took him across four of Europe's top five leagues, with the Bundesliga being the only one that he missed out on. The Portuguese midfielder started his professional career at Braga in his homeland, before moving to Benfica in December 2001. His career-best 13 goals in his first full season with the Portuguese giants helped them to second place in the league and, at the end of the next season, José Mourinho came calling at the start of his first season at Chelsea.

He soon became an invaluable part of that Chelsea side and, paired alongside Frank Lampard and Claude Makélélé, featured in 34 Premier League matches en route to winning the title. He was a classic Mourinho-type player with his work rate, technique and vision and this would eventually stand him in good stead later on at Atlético. However, the following 2005/06 season saw Chelsea sign Michael Essien from Lyon and, understanding that his chances were henceforth going to be limited, Tiago left and went the other way.

With Lyon, Tiago played more of an anchor role and won back-to-back titles in a midfield boasting the likes of Juninho Pernambucano, Florent Malouda and Mahamadou Diarra. When the latter left for Real Madrid after their first title, Tiago ended up playing a more significant role on the road to their second, and was also part of the Portugal side that made it to the World Cup semi-finals in 2006, but did not start in their last-four defeat to France.

In hindsight, his time in the national team was somewhat irregular and despite playing five times in the 2006 World Cup, he was in the squad but had not featured in the Euros two years earlier, and in 2008 he missed the final list for the Euros as well. He did feature in the 2010 World Cup, however, although his game time was limited and despite having officially quit at the end of the tournament, he made a return to the side in their Euro 2016 qualifiers. He would miss the finals though, having not recovered from a broken leg, and he ended his international career with 66 caps for the senior side.

Back at club level though, Tiago moved on from Lyon to Juventus in June 2007, but his time in Italy was by far his toughest at any club. His performances in 2007/08 were heavily criticised and, at the start of the next season, Juventus looked to send the midfielder on loan back to the Premier League with Everton. Tiago would refuse the terms, however, and negotiations came an unexpected end when he locked club president Giovanni Cobolli Gigli in a toilet stall, only for club captain Alessandro Del Piero to find and rescue him an hour later. The story itself would be confirmed on live TV by Cobolli Gigli, and while it would not be out of the ordinary to expect the player to be moved on immediately, Tiago stayed for nearly two more years, with injuries and suspensions hampering his already limited appearances.

Redemption would come in the form of Atlético Madrid in January 2010, with Tiago signing on for a season-long loan deal, eventually moving permanently to the Spanish capital. His first season as a full Atlético player kicked off under Manzano, ending with the Europa League and revitalisation under Simeone. Along with Gabi, he would forge a formidable midfield partnership, playing a key role in the side that won the league in 2014 and, despite trying to force a move back to Chelsea (which eventually fell through) at the end of that season, Tiago remained with *Los Rojiblancos* for three more years. The latter stages of his career were unfortunately riddled with injuries though, meaning that Tiago was not often at his best after that glorious campaign, eventually hanging up his boots in 2017. He would only officially leave the club a year later, after serving as an assistant coach under Simeone for one season.

A player who has pretty much seen it all, Tiago might not go down as one of the greatest midfielders ever, but his valuable contributions have seen him pick up honours nearly everywhere he has been. His knowledge and experience have certainly paved the way for a good coaching career, and having made the swift transition to Atlético's coaching staff before taking up other coaching roles in the Portugal youth national teams, he was also announced as the coach of Vitória de Guimarães in the Portuguese first division in 2020. Supposed disagreements with the board meant that he was only in charge for three matches, but he has since returned to the youth setup of his national side, working on breeding the next set of talent back home.

* * *

Saúl Ñíguez

Saúl is perhaps one of the most loved academy graduates at Atlético, but funnily enough, they weren't even his first club in the capital. Having joined the Real Madrid academy at the age of 11, Saúl had a horrible time before making the switch across the city in 2008. He quickly progressed through the youth ranks and his technical ability was visible for all as he became a regular for the Atlético B team, aged just 17. He made his debut for the senior team at the same age in the Europa League in 2012, playing the last six minutes of a tie against Beşiktaş.

His La Liga debut would come the following year, as he made two substitute appearances towards the end of the 2012/13 season. The following season should have seen him lift the title with *Los Rojiblancos,* but Saúl was busy making headlines of his own out on loan across the capital at Rayo Vallecano. The Spaniard played 34 games for the relegation-threatened side and even played at centre-back at times for an offensive-looking team, showing immense responsibility at the young age of 20.

Atlético knew that they had a serious player on their hands and swiftly promoted him to their first team the following campaign, where he made 35 appearances across all four competitions they were involved in. Simeone utilised him in midfield and down the wing as well, once again showing Saúl's versatility, and he ended that season with four goals and two assists. The biggest test of his character was yet to come though, and a kick to the kidney in a Champions League last-16 tie saw Saúl initially sidelined for just 39 days before seemingly making a full recovery and getting back to regular first-team action.

However, going into the 2015/16 season, and just approaching his 21st birthday, not all was fine for the Spaniard. 'In every training session and every game, I pissed blood,' Saúl said in an interview later on. He was playing with a catheter and yet, with the departure of Mario Suárez along with an injury to Tiago, he was becoming a mainstay in the side, occupying roles all over the pitch during Atlético's run to the Champions League final and, most notably, scoring a magnificent solo effort in the semi-final first leg at home to Bayern Munich, where after receiving near the halfway line, he dribbled past five players before coolly slotting the ball into the bottom corner. All this while he was racking up the appearances in Spain's youth national teams as well, eventually making his full senior debut in September 2016, though he had been an unused member of the squad as early as 2015.

He would not stop there, and the 2016/17 season saw Saúl make 33 La Liga appearances and start all but two games in Atlético's Champions League campaign that saw them reach the semi-finals, with Saúl himself scoring in the second leg against rivals Real Madrid. At the end of that season, Atlético would reward him with a nine-year contract and slap a whopping €150m release clause on the then 23-year-old, effectively tying him down to the club. Despite rumours of other big clubs vying for his signature, most notably Manchester United, Saúl never looked like leaving and started his 250th match for the club in August 2019 in a win against Getafe.

Oh, and remember the catheter that we mentioned earlier? Saúl played with it for two seasons, starting nearly every game during that time. He was 22, ready to remove a kidney just to play for Atlético until assistant coach Germán Burgos knocked some sense into him. Yet, he still pushed himself to the limit and then some, a fighter in every sense of the word. His battles have brought him five major honours with Atlético, including the Europa League and the UEFA Super Cup, and Saúl remains a warrior, loved by the Atlético faithful and admired by the world.

He has gone on to continually display his profound technical ability, playing in any role across midfield, while also slotting into the defence, playing at left-back or centre-back. It is almost unfathomable that a player, who was now 27 as of the end of the 2021/22 season, can be so good virtually everywhere on the pitch and look as comfortable off the ball as he does on it. Despite a loan move to Chelsea for the 2021/22 campaign not entirely clicking, Saúl is still an excellent player who Atlético will be ready to welcome with open arms upon his return. With a bit of confidence and regular game time, it should only be a matter of time before he finds the form that saw him become one of the most sought-after players in the world, and when this happens we are certainly in for a treat.

* * *

The midfield has perhaps undergone the biggest overhaul under Simeone's tenure, with the entire positional role seeing a massive change. From the nitty-gritty of Gabi and Tiago to the technical ability and expansiveness of Saúl, Thomas Lemar and Rodrigo de Paul, the midfield is now filled with players capable of holding their own defensively, but also taking charge of games in attack. It is certainly not easy to find a system capable of bringing out this attacking flair while prioritising defensive solidity either, but Simeone has laid down the marker with his intricate midfield setup.

Midfielders are at the heart of everything that the side does, covering the lengths of the pitch and waiting for their moments to pounce, swarming their opponents like bees, suffocating them until they win the ball back, before slicing right through with precision and guile to open up opportunities of their own at the other end. The eyes might deceive though, and it may even look ugly at times, uncoordinated and messy, appearing devoid of any clear instruction like a bunch of school kids all wanting the ball at the park. After all, how else can you describe a situation where three players find themselves in the same spot in the modern era?

In a side that takes after Simeone, the midfield bears the most striking resemblance. It is, after all, the position that the man himself knows best, and trust him to ensure that he covers all bases. It is a position that demands intelligence, awareness and skill, in order to dictate the flow of the game just as the manager requires. It is also a position that does well to mask these traits, using aggression, deception and wiliness as a facade to draw attention away from the intricacies of play.

In the centre of the pitch, it is madness, it is chaos, it is annoying. And it is perfect.

5

Hidden in Plain Sight: Wingers

'Games aren't won by those who play well, but by those who play safe'

FOR DECADES, football has reserved a special position for players with a certain spark, who capture our imagination and do things that were previously not thought to be possible. They were deemed to be the primary outlets in attack, bursting down the flanks and showcasing their skill, taking defenders on and putting them on the ground. Attacking could only come one way, and that was when these players picked the ball up and floated it into the box, letting their team-mates finish the job.

As the game evolved though, wingers would go on to be more than just players who could cross the ball, and from Johan Cruyff to Lionel Messi, creative and more direct wingers would become mainstays in most top sides. These were players who were now expected to score as much as they created, and only the brightest and most skilful could reach the top. Vision, technique, agility and intelligence personified, the greatest would make an entire stadium hold its collective breath as they received the ball, before snatching that same breath away with dazzling footwork in the moments after.

What would football be without these beautiful wingers? Some might call it lifeless, devoid of any excitement or thrill, and while they might have a point, a certain Frenchman clearly disagreed. To him, a system without wingers would be one thing only, successful. While names such as Arrigo Sacchi, Rinus Michels and Sir Matt Busby might ring a bell, not much is widely spoken about Albert Batteux, a gentleman from France who would go on to become the most successful manager in the history of the nation's Ligue 1, even to this day.

Born in Reims, Batteux would go on to play for his hometown club, Stade de Reims, and after a fairly successful, albeit war-interrupted, career, he would retire at the age of 31, immediately moving to the sidelines and taking over as coach of the club. This was an era where coaches were much older and senior figures, but this did not matter to Batteux, who would go on to dominate French football. Long story short, he would win the league title in five of the next ten seasons, making it to two of the early European Cup finals, including the very first, only to lose to Real Madrid and the legendary Alfredo Di Stéfano both times.

Batteux would also take charge of the French national side alongside this from 1955 to 1962, steering them to third in the 1958 World Cup with a strong core of Reims players. He would then leave both club and country roles in successive years, moving down to the lower leagues before returning to top-flight football with AS Saint-Étienne in 1967, winning three titles on the bounce to take his total tally to eight. His managerial legacy would end a few years later, but the style of play would carry on even up until Euro '84, with his former player, Michel Hidalgo, coaching the national side to victory. But what made his philosophy so successful, and how could it be so without wingers?

Instead of the common 4-4-2 formation, what Batteux had done was pioneer the 4-2-2-2 setup, effectively forming an extra midfield line by playing the wingers through central areas of the pitch. No longer playing out wide, these wingers now resembled a pair of attacking midfielders, playing ahead of two defensive midfielders and behind two forwards. Hidalgo himself would tweak this formation to create France's famous *Carré Magique*, or 'Magic Square', at Euro '84, which was essentially a midfield diamond consisting of the likes of Luis Fernández, Alain Giresse, Jean Tigana and Michel Platini. Champagne football, they would call it, for it was smooth, silky and simply beautiful to watch.

Enter Diego Simeone.

Champagne would never be used to describe his football style, but when the spray came down over 30 years later in 2014 to celebrate Atlético Madrid's La Liga title win, the argument could be made that *Cholo*'s side had some resemblance to the French ones all those years ago. It was nowhere near as silky or offensive, but it took advantage of one key feature. While the side did sit compactly in a 4-4-2 when out of possession, this certainly was not the case in possession, however short this period was. Atlético did not have wingers who would consistently run down the touchline and float crosses into the box, and neither did they have wingers who would pull off a sublime piece of skill to beat a defender. In fact, Atlético did not have wingers at all.

Simeone himself was all of 14 years old when the *Carré Magique* triumphed, and there is no real evidence to suggest that he took any inspiration from that system or its predecessors, but, in essence, he set out to create yet another extension of the base formation. Atlético would play in a 4-4-2, but one that would largely resemble the 4-2-2-2 in possession, creating a winger role that would be best described as a hybrid between the modern winger and an attacking midfielder.

Though originally seen as a system which can allow for fluid football with passing and movement between the lines, *Cholo* saw its merits for his more defensive approach and set out to make the most of them. Firstly, the setup naturally allowed his wingers to have more central starting positions, often occupying areas in the channels rather than sticking to the touchline. This then led to the next advantage, which meant that due to this central positioning, the players would now be closer to each other, effectively minimising passing distances. This also meant that the side did not require their midfielders to play longer passes to find their wingers, which would subsequently improve their passing success. Finally, the system would ensure that the game was played over a much smaller area of the pitch, making it easier for the players to cover ground and interact with each other.

What this setup also did specifically was that it ensured that long balls from deeper positions, e.g. the centre-backs, could be recovered more consistently as Atlético now had multiple players ready to challenge for the second ball. Rather than looking to play out from the back with options ahead, Simeone had transformed this into an optimal model for winning long balls, making it more than just an outright duel between two opposing players by ensuring that there was ample support to either receive the second ball, or crowd the opposition and recover possession higher up the pitch.

It is clear that Simeone embraced the positional aspect of this role, and his goal was to maximise output when in possession, focusing on the quality of football in those few moments while ensuring his side could quickly move into a compact and solid shape off it. Having deemed 4-4-2 as the best shape in defence, 4-2-2-2 would allow for a very natural shift when possession was regained, rather than requiring the previously compact wingers to have to suddenly move wider and spread out, before repeating the process should Atlético then lose possession.

A fair question can then be asked, though, that if the wingers were to stay central and make the playing area effectively smaller, would the wider zones of the pitch become redundant for Atlético? And following on from this, do the side not risk suffocating themselves in the middle of the pitch? To answer these, we will once again turn to our tactics board to see how Simeone deals with such situations.

Up to this point we have only mentioned how *Cholo*'s narrow wingers served to compress space, but naturally when this happens, larger vacant spaces become available

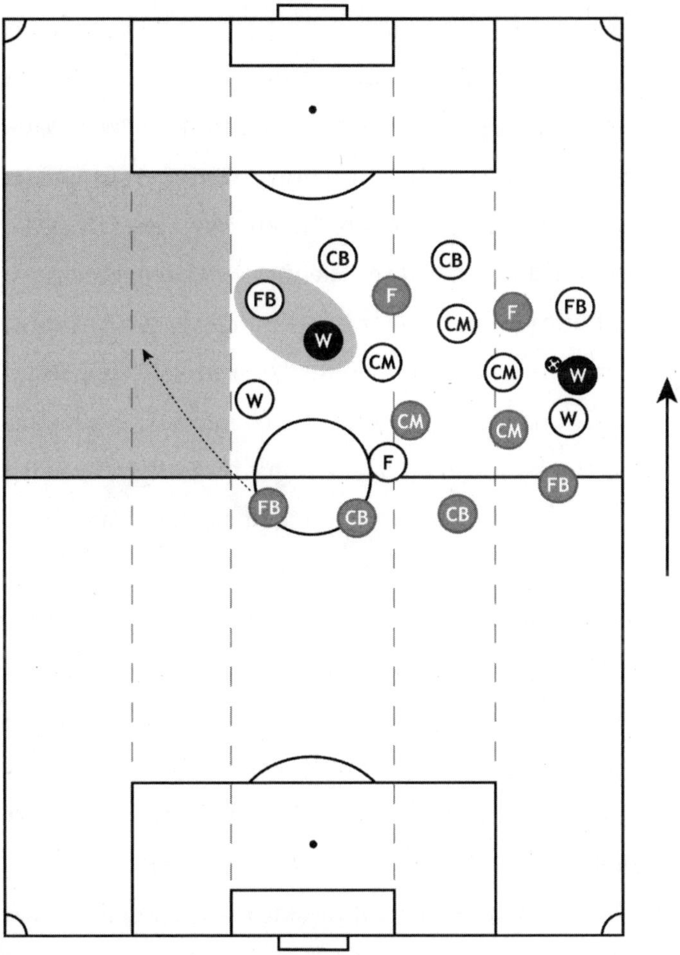

Fig. 20 *Narrow wingers compressing the playing area to create spaces out wide*

in other portions of the pitch. The playing area, after all, has fixed dimensions, and when you strive to fill just one portion of it at a time, the remaining areas will remain empty. Usually making the pitch smaller would suit defending sides, as this allows them to focus their efforts on one concentrated zone, and to commit to crowding opponents out in that zone to win back possession. On the flip side, however, this means that the team in possession can dictate the areas that the game should be played in, leaving the defence with no choice but to follow. It is this advantage, however slight, that Simeone looks to make use of with his wingers.

In Figure 20, we see a situation where Atlético have moved the ball to their right flank in possession, with the right-winger having the ball near the touchline. His team-mates are looking to cause an overload down the flank to provide him with passing options, something which we have often highlighted, and hence the opposition are drawn that way as well. The key to narrowing the playing area lies with the left-winger though, and his positioning is crucial for this next segment.

The width of the defending side is largely determined by the distance between their two full-backs, and to effectively compress the side Atlético need to ensure that the entire back line is shifting across to the ball side. In this case, their right-winger has occupied the opposition's left-back and with the forwards shifting across, the opponents' centre-backs have also moved over. The right-back, however, now has two options depending on the movement and positioning of Atlético's left winger.

Should the winger stay wider (creating Simeone's distinctive asymmetric setup with one narrow and one wide winger), the full-back can allow more room between himself and his centre-back to track him. Alternatively, though, if the winger moves inside, the full-back would need to do the same to defend the space between himself and his centre-back. In our case, since both wingers have been asked to compress the pitch, Atlético's left-winger follows the second situation and, in doing so, he draws his man centrally, effectively pinning him to a narrower position. As is evident from Figure 20, this manoeuvre has meant that the winger has created a vacant space down his flank by virtue of him trying to compress the opposite flank with his inward movement.

One of the slight drawbacks of the 4-2-2-2 shape, however, is that there is no outright attacking player available to exploit these wider areas, and hence managers have to use their full-backs to do this instead. We will dive deeper into the details of the full-back's forays into this space later on, but as revealed in Figure 20, he is then tasked with stepping out of the defensive line to attack the vacant area, providing the side with the option to switch the play to him. The opposition now have to scramble to defend the excess space without losing their own shape, causing them to expand out wide, now creating central avenues for Atlético to slice through.

By simply tucking the wingers inside, Simeone has not only ensured that his players always have short passing options and can concentrate their attacks through one zone, but that they can also create space simultaneously, opening up an alternative avenue of progression should they get crowded out. Funnily enough, this is exactly what Atlético's defensive structure looks to prevent the opposition from doing, and we saw earlier how the side likes to remain centrally compact, forcing opponents out to the wings before closing them down and preventing the crossfield pass.

What makes it difficult for the opposition to simply use Atlético's formula against them is the fact that, even in possession, *Los Rojiblancos* maintain their wide overloads, with the winger forming a crucial part of the four players who move out wide. The key point to note is that even as the winger occupies a position down the touchline, he is still relatively close to his team-mates, meaning that instead of the attacking structure having been expanded to occupy the wider areas it has simply shifted across.

The opposition would then need to commit five players to the flanks to cause an overload, which basically pushes half their outfield players to one zone of the pitch and would leave them completely open should the ball be shifted out of that zone. While sides have looked to beat the overload simply by having their players enter the wide areas first, it does prove to be difficult to deal with, considering that Atlético's direct and quick tempo in possession generally allows them to shift the attack quickly elsewhere if need be.

Moreover, Simeone likes to use his wingers to add a certain unpredictability to his team as well. Compared to 4-4-2, 4-2-2-2 allows for many positional and formational shifts throughout a game, as the two wingers in this setup can very easily switch positions with their team-mates or alter their starting positions to create different shapes.

This results in a high level of fluidity, and the same players can often be found in different parts of the pitch during the game, which once again points to the versatility of the Atlético players. In pursuit of quick, counter-attacking football, such fluidity is also important to allow the side to have multiple options in transitions, as each player could shift to fill in the position of another if they have moved out to receive the direct pass.

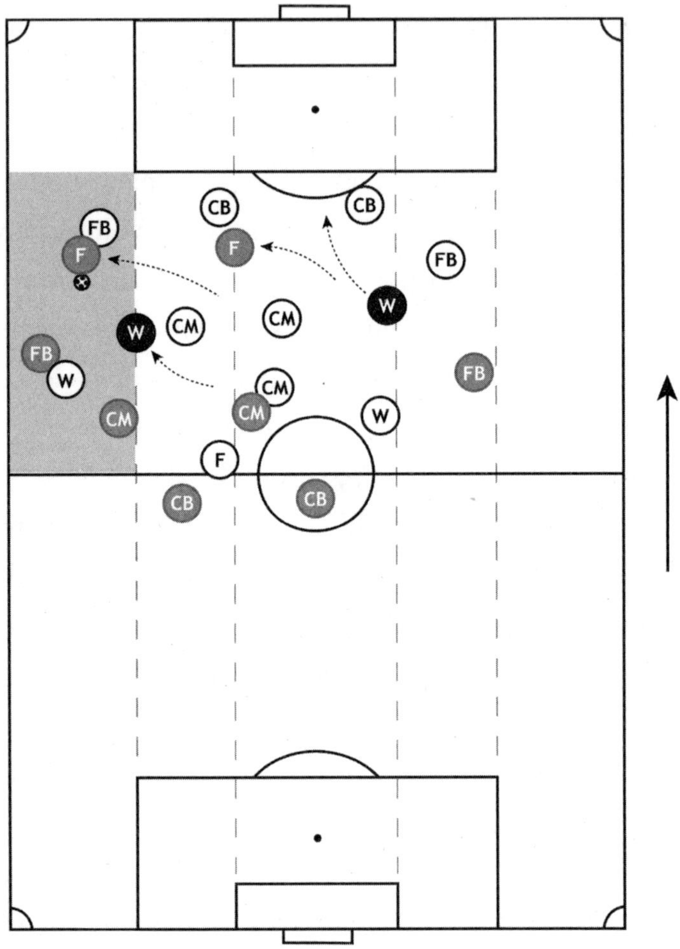

Fig. 21 *Wingers engaging in positional shifts to cover for a forward that has moved wide*

Figure 21 not only shows an example of such positional shifts, but also highlights how the wingers form a key part of them. In this case, Atlético have worked to overload the wings with yet another combination that sees the full-back providing width and the winger taking a more central role. The central midfielder is the deepest player, while the forward is the furthest away in this overload, having moved out wide to receive the longer pass from his deeper players. This combination allows the winger to have more freedom to attack the channels, rather than being trapped out wide near the touchline and minimising his efficiency.

With his positioning, the winger also initiates a positional shift, allowing for a rotation among the front four. By stationing himself close to the channels in this overload, the winger allows the forward that has received the ball to move much wider, engaging the opposition full-back. The winger himself has also drawn an opposition central midfielder towards him, and has slowly begun creating some space in the middle of the pitch. With his counterpart having moved wide, the other forward also shifts across naturally, pulling his centre-back along with him and increasing the gap between the opposition centre-backs. This sequence has now created space for the winger on the opposite side to run into.

With a far narrower positioning than an average winger, Atlético's right-winger can now attack space not just between the centre-back and full-back, but between the centre-backs. The space allowed to him sees him join the front line with this run, effectively changing his role from that of a winger to a forward. While not directly swapping positions, he has exchanged roles with the ball-carrying forward, who has now become a left-winger himself, and Atlético's left-winger, despite still being down the left, is theoretically now a right-winger. The 4-2-2-2 shape largely remains intact, though the 'winger' line is now completely down the left, and it is only the individual players within this shape who have changed.

While such a sequence does leave Atlético's right side vacant, it is not much of a drawback as the side want to use their overload down the left to progress the ball before looking to play their forwards into space in and around the box. This shift ensures that they can do exactly that without technically losing a forward, allowing them still to have the two front line options despite committing one forward to the flanks for the overload. Moreover, neither player is too far away from their initial position either, and a natural shift back is easily achievable should possession be lost or sustained long enough for the side to have to get back into shape.

This would not be the only positional shift to occur though and, as we mentioned earlier, the beauty of *Cholo*'s wingers in this setup lay in their flexibility and versatility, allowing for multiple different shifts sometimes even in a single game. Of course, there are many different possibilities to shift the personnel across positions alone, but in the next segment, we will look at one of the major tactical shifts that the wingers are responsible for.

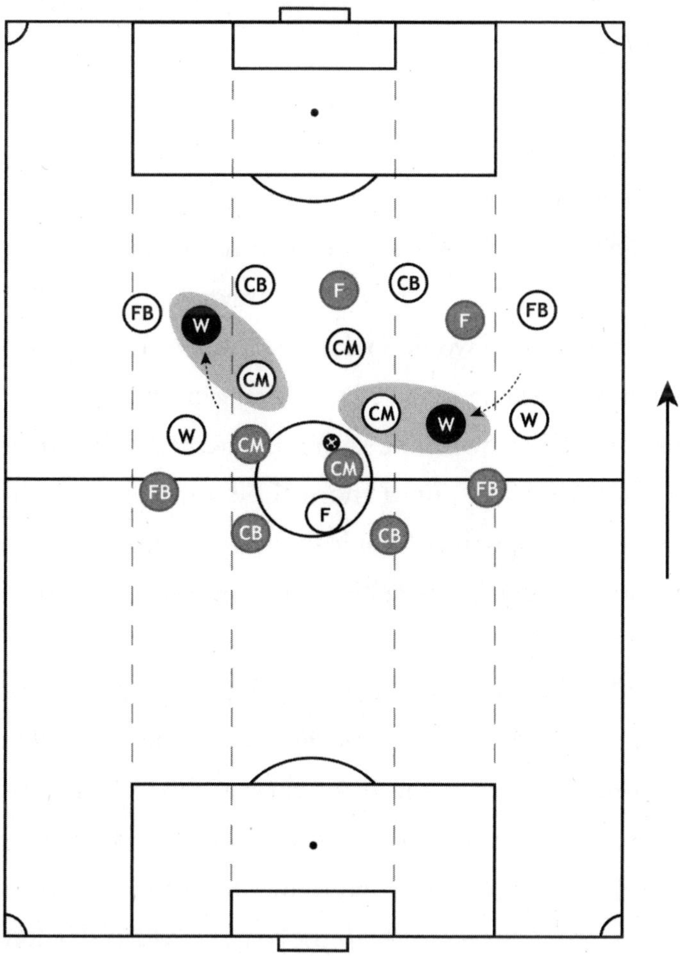

***Fig. 22** Wingers shift to create a 4–3–3 formation*

Instead of just one winger shifting into either the attacking or midfield line at a time, Simeone would go on to come up with a tactical iteration where both the wingers would move into different lines at the same time, creating the 4-3-3 shape shown in Figure 22. This would then open up multiple possibilities for Atlético in possession.

Although used at times in the early years, this 4-3-3 shift would become more prevalent as the seasons went by, with Atlético keener to build up when in possession of the ball. As we know, this does not mean that they would look to play complete possession-based football, but that the side would look to start their direct attacks from midfield as opposed to kicking it long from the back like they had done earlier. This meant that their midfield now required more time and space in the centre of the pitch to be able to pick out the best passes forward, which is what this change in formation would look to address.

The shift itself is fairly simple, with one winger dropping to the side of a midfield three, while the other moved up to form the front three. This could come about in two ways, with either the ball-side winger dropping into midfield while the other pushed up, as shown in Figure 22, or with the roles being fixed before the game, with the same winger dropping regardless of which side the ball was on. Koke would serve as a prime example of the second case, and he would usually be the man to tuck into midfield to make use of his technical ability to progress the ball.

The most notable difference with the 4-3-3, as opposed to the 4-4-2 or 4-2-2-2, is Atlético's willingness to play more centrally when in possession, using the now three midfielders to pass and move through the middle third of the pitch. They could still cause the wide overloads as they had done before by shifting across, but the main benefit would still lie in the central progression. Also, the advanced winger would now provide another last line presence, ensuring that the opposition back line had to deal with three players attacking the spaces in between them. Together, the movement of the wingers to the different lines would also drag the opposition central midfielders out of position, and we will once again turn back to Figure 22 to dive deeper into this.

With their movement, the Atlético wingers now attack different spaces in the opposition lines, with the advanced player getting in between the opponents' full-back and the centre-backs, and the deeper one getting in between the opponents' central midfielder and winger. The latter has now naturally engaged the opposition midfielder, moving into his vicinity and leaving him with the choice of either covering this winger or stepping out to press the ball carrier. Now, for the advanced winger, it is important to understand that while his final positioning sees him engage the back line, his initial position was closer to that of an opposition midfielder, and hence his movement to push forward leaves that midfielder with a similar choice as well.

As a result, if the opponents' midfield is not disciplined or prepared enough to deal with the movement of the wingers, they could be left in total disarray and end up allowing ample space for the player in possession. It is understandably not easy to prevent these shifts either, so, more often than not, the more organised sides willingly concede this space anyway in order to prevent their midfielders from committing too high up the pitch and allowing Atlético to play the ball through the lines fairly easily. Hence, Atlético's midfield can take their time to pick out their pass forward while also having extra support in the middle and on the last line for direct passes.

Specifically for the wingers, this shift would allow them to showcase their individual strengths, and rather than just acting as off-ball creators who could open up spaces with their movement and provide support for long balls, they could now display greater technical ability when on the ball. The winger who joins the front three has the option of receiving the ball in wider positions and taking on the full-back, using his technicality to drive at opponents and create chances for his side further up the pitch. Meanwhile, the winger who has dropped deeper can receive in time and space before showcasing his passing range to distribute the ball across the pitch.

Having different roles for what is technically the same position on the opposite side allows for an interesting (and asymmetric) team dynamic, and Simeone can effectively use different profiles of players for the same position. We mentioned in the beginning that the winger is a hybrid between a modern winger and an attacking midfielder, but to find a player capable of balancing both roles perfectly is certainly a difficult task and also possibly explains why many wingers have struggled or adapted to different positions after joining the club. It is also a reason why Simeone often sticks to a player when they do fit as well, but in order to avoid an over-dependence, this shifting of balance between the two players then allows for one to be more of a modern winger while the other can act more as an attacking midfielder, which now makes it easier for players to adapt and fit into the system.

With multiple roles in attack, let us not forget that this is still Simeone's Atlético Madrid, meaning that the wingers are bound to play a key role in the defensive phase as well. After all, they are the two players who are required to provide their central midfielders with support in order to ensure that the side's shape remains centrally compact and forces the opposition out wide. While it can be argued that the defensive role of the wingers is far more straightforward than their attacking duties, it is by no means easier, and in this following segment we shall take a closer look at how the pair work out of possession.

In the chapter on the midfielders, we touched upon the formation of a V shape in the middle of the pitch using the central midfielders, but, in Figure 23, we shall take a look at the role of the wingers in this shape.

The point of the V shape is to ensure that the players who are stepping up towards the ball have their team-mates covering for them, with the player furthest from the ball alone positioning himself slightly higher than his closest team-mate. To explain this using Figure 23, we see how Atlético's right-winger has stepped up to apply pressure on the opposition full-back with the aim of causing an overload. As we saw in the earlier chapter, the midfielders would then take up a staggered position, with the ball-side midfielder stepping up and his counterpart covering the depth. Following this, Atlético's left-winger, who is the furthest from the

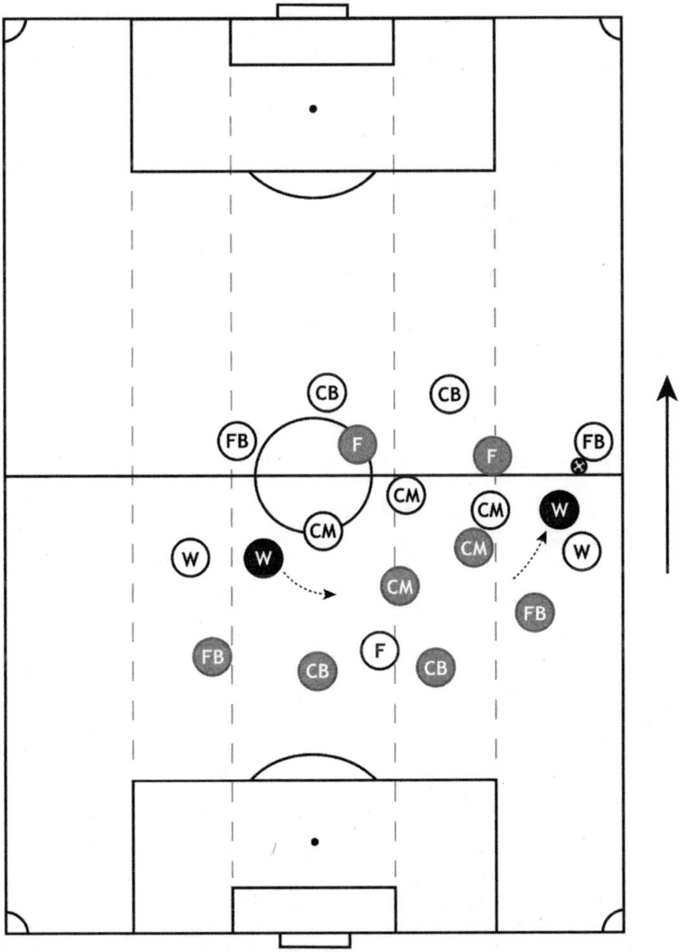

Fig. 23 *Wingers shifting to form V shape out of possession*

ball, shifts centrally but takes up a position slightly higher than that of the midfielder closest to him, forming the V.

The individual roles of the wingers in this situation are fairly simple. The ball-side winger has to step out to engage the opposition's wide player, initiating the wide overload for his side and, having been given the freedom to press, he can get in and tackle to win back possession. His movement to press should also look to force the opponent towards the touchline, enabling the line to act as an extra defender for his team. As for the winger on the far side, his primary role is basically to shift across along with his colleagues, effectively acting as cover for his central midfielders should they step out. If they do step out, he then acts as a central midfielder himself and looks to defend in the middle of the pitch.

The secondary role, however, is a bit more interesting. Though we had mentioned that it is best to cover for a team-mate by staying slightly behind them, the far-side winger does the opposite, and has been stationed slightly ahead of his nearest midfielder. Of course, there has to be a valid reason for this, leading us to consider the case of the winger taking up the deeper positioning. When the far-side winger is behind his nearest midfielder, he does offer better cover, but what he also does is open up a disproportionate amount of space down his flank. The midfield has now formed a diagonal shape that closes the space down the ball side, but opens up a huge amount of space down the far side for opposition wingers and full-backs to occupy and provide the option of a switch out to them.

In such a case, the winger's now-deeper positioning means that he has to cover more ground to close down the opposition players and in return, his midfield teammates would also have to cover more ground to create the same diagonal shape down this flank. However, if the winger is instead positioned ahead of his nearest midfielder, as is the case, he is now in a much better position to step out and engage an opponent should a pass be played out to his flank. Moreover, his initial positioning complicates such a pass in the first place as no opponent would find themself truly free in space, as they would be close enough for the winger to mark and track.

Should the winger step out and engage, the V shape would also be easier to replicate down his flank, rather than having to move into the diagonal, and his side can regroup with quick movement over shorter distances rather than having to cover more ground. The shifting essentially becomes a sort of rocking motion, with the players swaying from side to side in this shape, as opposed to a weirder and counter-productive seesaw-like motion to form the diagonal shape that we discussed instead.

Hence, using the wingers, Simeone is able to provide his central midfielders with the necessary support through the middle, while also equipping his side with the right armour to deal with wide attacks. Combined with the actions of the midfielders that we saw in the previous chapter, Atlético's wingers have fundamentally set up a 'pressing trap', which means that they have invited the opposition to play through a certain zone that at first looks vacant but underneath the surface is actually fairly well guarded, hence trapping them in that zone. In this case, they close out the ball-side and central area, forcing opponents to move to the opposite flank, which initially seems vacant, before moving across to 'trap' them there. What makes it harder for opponents is the fact that, even if they do want to stay away from such a trap by forcing their way through the central passages, Atlético have fully committed to blocking them out, meaning that they might as well try to beat the trap instead.

This is not to say that Simeone's side always succeed in this though, and we have mentioned that an opposition's best way of beating the defensive setup is to be sharp and quick with their passing, ensuring that they make the most of the minimal gaps that they can find. In such a case, the wingers may not always be able to step out to press, or shift across to engage, leaving their full-backs exposed to the opposition winger. While this is still somewhat ideal in the sense that the attack is out wide, it means that there is a one-v-one down the flank, with high chance that an opposition forward or midfielder can move in to support and create an overload. This is certainly not ideal, and Atlético's defence is now not only stretched as a result of the full-back having to step out, but is also relying on the tackling ability of the full-back to prevent the winger from getting past him into space.

Such a situation certainly puts Atlético on the back foot, at least momentarily, and while they were proactive in their defending before, they are now forced to take a more reactive approach to put out this fire. That does not mean that they toss everything out and switch into panic mode though, and instead they focus on engaging in a different kind of shift, with the wingers once again being given crucial responsibilities to protect and support the defence.

For a side that focuses on being as compact as possible, having a player drawn out and isolated is perhaps one of the worst things that could happen. To allow this without any cover or support would turn out to be an even bigger disaster though, and it is this calamity that Atlético look to avoid by using their wingers as a defensive plug. As we have mentioned, and shown in Figure 24 (next page), an Atlético full-back has been drawn out wide, leaving a gap between him and his centre-back, which has allowed an opposition

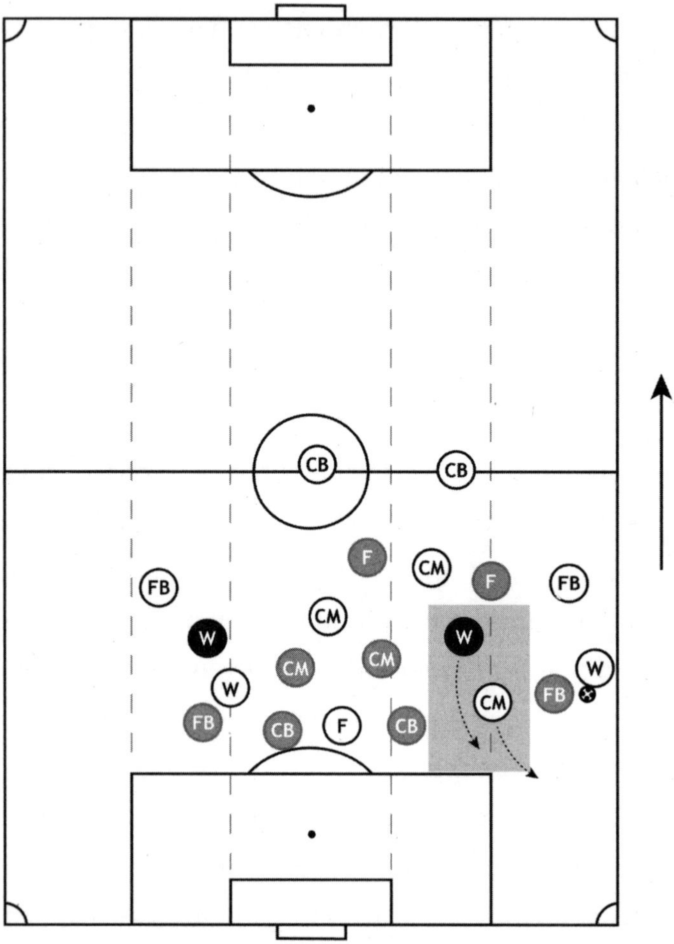

Fig. 24 *Winger covering the space between the centre-back and full-back*

central midfielder to dart into the channel to create a two-v-one against *Los Rojiblancos.*

With a simple through pass, the opposition winger can play his supporting team-mate into space around the penalty area for him to then pick out an attacker centrally, or the winger can beat his man and push into the space himself, while simultaneously having the support to make it four attacking players in the box. It is not possible for Atlético's full-back to consistently handle this, hence his winger drops in behind him to cover off the run of the opposition midfielder, making the option of a pass more difficult and allowing the full-back to focus on his own defensive duel. While not exactly a shift like the ones that we have seen earlier, this movement from the winger sees him plug the gap in the back line and track a potentially dangerous opponent in a threatening area of the pitch.

What it also does is make it a two-v-two situation, and the winger provides the necessary cover that the full-back needs. Should the full-back be beaten, the winger can engage his opposition counterpart, while his full-back can recover and mark the opposition midfielder, essentially seeing the two players temporarily swap roles in order to maintain the two-v-two and keep their opponents out wide. It is by far the most basic defending that you might see at the highest level, with team-mates covering for one another, but the fact that the wingers are available in their narrower position to seamlessly drop into this gap is what makes this sequence work so well. Moreover, it also ensures that the rest of the back line can remain in and around their optimal positions to deal with any crosses or passes into the box without having to entirely shift across or concede space between each other.

If anything, the winger's role revolves around space and the consistent exploitation and defending of that space. For a position associated with skill and flair, Atlético's wingers need more than just that, with awareness and effort just as important as any neat pass. This is not to say that the more technically gifted bunch would struggle though, and to assume as much would be a grave injustice to the plethora of talented wingers who have starred in the red and white kit. Remember, the technicality is not masked, but instead used to elevate the position beyond its tactics to make for better execution, and in this next segment, let us take a closer look at some of these wingers who have kept Atlético ticking through the years.

* * *

Jorge Resurrección (Koke)

'He has been marked out as the conductor of Spain's orchestra for the next ten years,' said Xavi, heaping praise on a then 22-year-old Koke. This was not just a sign of things to come though, rather an acknowledgement of the boy's talent that had captured the world.

Born and raised in working-class Vallecas, Koke might just embody Simeone's Atlético Madrid down to a tee. They are 'humble, working-class people, who live their lives with plenty of value', Koke says describing the people of Vallecas, but he could be describing Atlético itself with the same sentence. After all, having joined the club aged just eight, they are his people too.

Known for his passing, physical ability and vision, Koke could not be further away from the description of a modern winger. Take nothing away from his technical brilliance or his dribbling though, but for long it was assumed that the midfield role was more natural for the Spaniard, having played there right through his youth teams. Under Simeone though, he would be put out of position, often down the left wing but he was fairly comfortable on the right as well. After all, Simeone's midfielders were tenacious tacklers of the ball, and Koke was a creative gem. Movement, awareness and excellent combination play in tight spaces, however, would see Koke thrive in this role under Simeone, forming the ideal profile for a winger in Simeone's system.

His illustrious career would start with a senior debut way back in September 2009, aged just 17, and despite just a handful of appearances that season, his involvement would only increase over the next few campaigns. By January 2011, he had become a regular member of the matchday squad, continuing to make league appearances alongside Europa League games with the arrival of Gregorio Manzano later that year. His transition to the core of the first team would take place under Simeone though, and in the second half of the 2011/12 season Koke would see his minutes significantly increased.

Starting every knockout game until the semi-finals of the successful Europa League campaign, Koke would become an undisputed starter across all competitions from the 2012/13 season, at the age of 20. It almost seemed like everything in his career was fast-tracked, because by 21 he had made his 100th appearance for the club and, at 22, he was a La Liga champion, having played a key role in the league and Champions League as well. It had been 16 years since Koke had entered the fold of the club, and he had already achieved more than most, but his career still had a long way to go.

He would finally shift back to central midfield for starters, not without a couple of seasons of trying and testing without any real change, and where his passing and movement had created attacks further ahead, they were now vital in building up the play for his side. 'He feels more and more like the master of the play,' said Simeone after finally deeming Koke to be ready for the central role, and it would be just a matter of time before he would be ready for yet another, that of captain.

First leading the side in a Champions League knockout game in March 2015, Koke was the natural successor to the likes of Gabi and Diego Godín, with there never being any doubt that the armband would be passed to him. After all, he was mature well beyond his years and his leadership was evident every time he stepped on to the pitch, setting an example with his energy and effort to work defensively as much as he did in attack.

He would officially become the club captain after Godín's departure in 2019, but in truth there never was really any change and Koke continued to lead the side as he had done for years.

He would get the chance to do the same for his country as well, captaining them in a friendly against the Netherlands, and despite not initially turning into the conductor that Xavi had envisioned, Koke is already a veteran of two World Cups (2014 and 2018), with the 2022 finals set to be the latest addition, and he also featured at Euro 2016 before starting every game in Spain's run to the semi-finals of Euro 2020. He did go two years without a cap between 2018 and 2020, but has since taken his place back in midfield for *La Roja*, making it his own.

Back at Atlético, he would set personal records, taking second spot in the club's all-time appearance list during their title-winning 2020/21 campaign and, at time of writing, is just a few matches away from Adelardo Rodríguez's record of 553 games. It has always been a matter of when, and not if, Koke would break this record, and in the modern era where players rarely remain at one club and at the highest level, it is only right that the physical personification of Atlético itself takes the top step.

That 2020/21 triumph is perhaps his greatest achievement as captain as well and a fair reflection of the man. Chasing a title that seemed to be slipping away despite being well ahead of the pack for most of the season, even as others lost hope Koke never faltered. He knows that nothing ever comes easy, and he is willing to work for it, echoing the sentiments of the club in his own words,

'We are Atlético. If we don't suffer, we are not ourselves.'

* * *

Arda Turan

Now remembered as an outcast at Barcelona and for antics on and off the field that seem straight out of a soap opera, it is easy to forget just how good Arda

Turan used to be. He was, and perhaps even is, arguably the greatest footballing talent that Turkey has ever produced and this boy from Istanbul once had the world at his feet.

A product of Galatasaray's youth team, Turan shone for both club and country by the time he was 21, having played a key role in Turkey's run to the semi-finals at Euro 2008 and being named captain of his club, a responsibility which he would undertake until 2011. That was when Atlético came knocking to make him the most expensive Turkish footballer of all time for a fee of €12m, which saw him join Gregario Manzano's side. Despite a shaky period for the club, Turan would still register three goals and eight assists in all competitions before Simeone took over, and his career would only take off after the Argentinian's appointment as he seemed to be a perfect match for the incoming system.

Known for his excellent ball control and dribbling, he would be used as a more creative outlet, complementing Koke down the opposite side as Atlético went on to win the Europa League in his first season. In fact, Turan's skillset was so unique at the club that there was virtually no player who could replace him at the time, at least not as a whole, making him crucial to the foundation of that early Simeone side. He would continue to put in influential and game-changing performances, especially in the famed 2013/14 campaign, unfortunately coming off early with an injury in that last-day draw at the Camp Nou, keeping him out of the Champions League final as well. Nevertheless, he continued to fill his trophy cabinet with many of Europe's top prizes, bagging a UEFA Super Cup, Copa del Rey and a Supercopa de España in addition to the accolades above, with his performances marking him out as one of the best wingers in world football at the time.

There were, however, some signs of his bad temperament and, while the winger was always intense and aggressive, one of the things that suited the side, he had his occasional outbursts as well. In 2015, he famously threw his shoe in the direction of the assistant referee after failing to be awarded a foul in a Copa del Rey fixture against Barcelona, and back home his reputation was quickly going downhill. Once hailed as a golden boy, Turan was suddenly being viewed as someone who personified the evils of fame and success, turning into an egotistical and confrontational figure, no longer the humble boy with Midas touch.

While Turan himself dismisses any such changes in personality, and maybe even rightly so, his career from then on would fall off a cliff in unprecedented fashion, with little justification for his actions which left him well off the heights that he had previously reached individually. Barcelona would snap him up for a deal totalling close to €40m, but Turan would have to wait close to half a year to make his debut due to the club's player registration ban, before entering a star-studded side led by the famous MSN (Messi-Neymar-Suarez) trio, leaving him with limited game time. He still had a fairly decent role for a couple of years under Luis Enrique though, with a 20-minute Champions League hat-trick against Borussia Mönchengladbach turning out to be the biggest highlight as he went on to win all the domestic competitions and the UEFA Super Cup in these two years.

However, with Ernesto Valverde's arrival in 2017, he was quickly cast into the shadows and would never play for the club again, initially spending half a season without a game, before being loaned out to İstanbul Başakşehir for the remainder of his contract. A move to his home country would not rejuvenate his career though, and setting aside his rather average performances, his relationship with fans back home had turned even more sour as well. An alleged assault of a journalist on a flight after Turkey's Euro 2016 had seen Turan retire from international football, and more recently in 2018, he received the longest ban ever handed out in Turkish football for pushing a linesman during a league encounter.

While serving the ban, matters would only get worse, and a nightclub brawl with a famous Turkish pop star ended with Turan firing an illegal firearm at the floor of a hospital where he had supposedly gone to apologise. Such a bizarre incident naturally led to a suspended court sentence, which proved to be the final straw for Başakşehir, who promptly terminated his loan and sent him back to Barcelona, where the club would pay him to do nothing while he ran down the remaining six months of his contract. He would move back to Turkey with his boyhood side Galatasaray once the contract did expire in the summer of 2020, but the now 35-year-old (at time of writing) has never really grabbed headlines for anything other than turning up overweight to games.

Turan has seen his career marred by the sheer number of peculiar incidents that dot it, serving as an elaborate distraction from the fact that he was at one point an extremely good footballer, and a once beloved *Colchonero*. The affection has since waned in Madrid, but for those few years where his talents came together he experienced a peak like no other, and few footballers can claim to have reached the same heights. A high that turned out to be beautiful, followed by a fall from grace that was anything but.

* * *

Of course, with the introduction of the 5-3-2 formation, Simeone's use of wingers would end, with their duties reassigned to other positions instead. While it lasted though, it was a position that would break the mould, having little resemblance to that of Europe's elite and yet able to challenge them toe to toe every season. It would be an injustice to refer to these wingers by their positions, and a better definition of their craft would be given by their roles, which saw them create an efficient link between the midfield and the attack, seamlessly dropping and shifting into both throughout a game.

The wingers were not wingers at all, proving to be a handful for anyone who dared to classify them as such. They would defend the wide areas and attack the central ones, forcing opponents over the touchline just as much as they would drift between opposition lines. They were a special breed and, as many would discover, it was not a shoe that could fit just anyone.

A system without wingers. Some might call it lifeless, devoid of any excitement or thrill and, while they might have a point, a certain Argentinian clearly disagreed.

To him, it would be the definition of success.

6

Shape Shifters: Full-Backs

'You always adapt to the place you live'

'THERE'S ONLY two things for a full-back, you're either a failed winger or a failed centre-back. No one wants to grow up and be a Gary Neville!'

Gary Neville himself is on the receiving end of yet another playful jibe from Jamie Carragher, with the pair appearing on English television in 2013 and discussing the role of full-backs as Liverpool prepare to take on Swansea City. Carragher, while he had been a centre-back himself, has had his experiences at full-back on occasion and, while intended as a joke, his words are quite thought-provoking. How many people actually dream of becoming a full-back?

This is not to say that the role is less vital than any other, and neither is it short of legends to idolise with Roberto Carlos and Paolo Maldini serving as excellent examples, but the fact remains that most people have a natural inclination towards other positions on the pitch. Maybe the full-backs do not catch the eye enough. After all, Carlos is best remembered for his stunning free kick in 1997 for Brazil against France, which seemingly defied every law of physics, and his general attacking exploits rather than anything actually to do with the left-back position, and while Maldini is hailed as one of the best defenders of all time, perhaps it is easier to want to be a centre-back instead.

But why do people not dream of becoming a full-back? There is nothing inherently wrong with the position (rather it remains extremely crucial) and, if anything, it has become one of football's most talked-about roles in recent times, with revolutionary players coming to the fore. Perhaps it is just one of those things that does not really have a sound explanation, or maybe this entire premise is false and there are thousands of kids waiting to become full-backs, but that number must be far smaller than those wanting to become forwards for instance.

And when Trent Alexander-Arnold, one of those revolutionary players, mentions this again on live TV, it does keep you thinking. 'Obviously there was the famous saying, "No one wants to grow up to be a full-back or a Gary Neville,"' he says referring to Carragher's earlier statement. 'As a pair, we want to change the way the position has previously been thought about. We want to bring in a different way of thinking.'

Alexander-Arnold is referring to his well-known Liverpool team-mate Andrew Robertson, and the pair's exploits need no introduction, having been one of the world's best full-back combinations over the past few years. The change in style for a full-back to become a creator rather than a defender would work wonders for reputation, with the two of them battling it out for assists on the way to a Premier League title and Champions League success. A few miles across the north-west of England, Pep Guardiola would try to match this, coming up with his own full-back pairing of João Cancelo and Kyle Walker at Manchester City to follow on from his pairing of Dani Alves and Jordi Alba at Barcelona. The latter duo probably hits closer to home in the context of this book, and while they revolutionised the game in their era, the former pairing is the one that the modern game is tilting towards.

Does this then make the full-back position underrated? We have probably asked more questions than we have answered, but for a position that is so crucial to success, it has surely been overlooked multiple times in terms of its technical importance on the pitch. In an era where direct attacks are predictable and more intricate systems are needed, full-backs have risen in prominence as the keys to unlocking sides and the 'different way of thinking' that Alexander-Arnold hoped for has started to creep in. Most of the top managers have already understood this though, and as for Diego Simeone, he was well ahead of the curve.

'If you have great full-backs, your chances of winning a football match significantly increase. With great full-backs, it's easy to figure out the rest of the players,' Simeone said in an interview back in May 2019. It must sound odd at first, because none of Simeone's full-backs would ever be hailed as revolutionary and, in typical Atlético fashion, would only be remembered most for their defensive contributions. However, by this point we know better than to take the side at face value and so let us dig a little deeper.

In the same interview, *Cholo* went on to explain why the full-backs are so crucial, stating how they need to defend and protect their centre-backs, while also getting forward and providing crosses if needed. He was allowed to get technical and would then go on to talk about different tactical combinations that come about based on how the full-backs are used, mentioning the basic underlap and overlap among others, but, somewhere in the middle, he dropped a certain word that catches the attention. A word that would perfectly define a full-back in his system, 'Great full-backs can **adapt**.'

For a position that is thrust into the bottom corner of the pitch, a full-back's game is truly a tale of two halves. In their own half, they are often far more reserved, keeping their passes simple and staying resolute in defence. In the opposition's half though, they become more expansive, looking for incisive passes and making bombarding runs forward to attack space. The key to successfully performing these two polar-opposite duties lies in their adaptability when faced with different situations, and this would prove to be even more crucial for Simeone's Atlético.

As we already know, the balance of duties is tilted in favour of the defence, with Atlético preferring quality over quantity in attack. While this may mean that the full-backs are often in their own half, the key to optimising their attacks lies in their ability to spot an opportunity and act accordingly or, in other words, adapt. Despite football being about repetition and trying to consistently work to a set tactic to break through opposition defences, it is not always that a side focusing on direct and incisive attacks is presented with the exact same scenarios over and over again, meaning how they act in that specific moment will go on to define the game.

While adaptability is something that depends on a player's mindset, it is also a trait that needs to be coached in order for players to recognise and train accordingly for different situations. For example, we saw how Gregorio Manzano struggled with the same set of full-backs, asking them to cover an improbable amount of ground to adapt to different scenarios in the game. When Simeone entered, he needed to break this philosophy and reconstruct it in order to ensure that it became easier for his players to adapt to different situations. This cannot happen overnight, and *Cholo* would begin to implement his own blueprint in phases.

The very first thing that Simeone did with his full-backs was to ensure that they were much closer to the centre-backs, almost having equidistant spaces between the four defenders. The aim of this was to minimise the width of the back line as much as possible and, with the full-backs on either end, they would become responsible for maintaining this short distance. We know that Atlético like to be centrally compact anyway, but the extent to which the back line would remain compact is important here, along with the phases where this is implemented. In order to further explain this, let us consider the situation in Figure 25.

The situation shown is similar to ones that we have seen earlier, with the opposition looking to build up

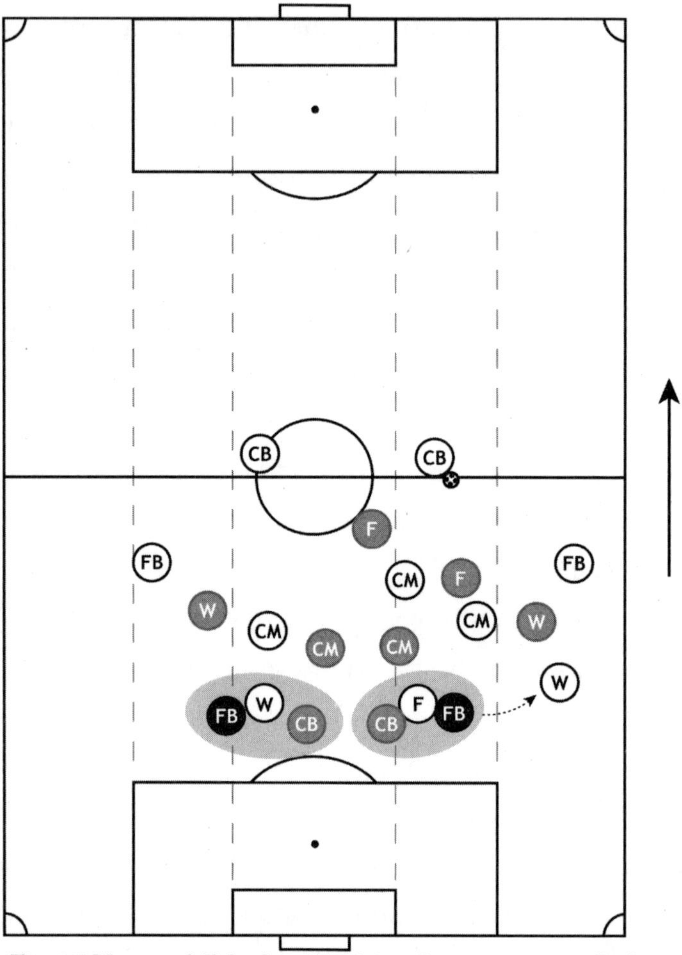

***Fig. 25** Narrow full-backs minimising distance to centre-backs*

from the back and Atlético looking to force them to the wider areas. We know that the midfield line is ready to shift across to overload and cover for each other, while also staying aware of any potential switches to the opposite flank. To go into greater detail, the ball-side winger and a central midfielder would move out wide to cause the overload, with the other two covering and creating the V-shape in the middle. However, there is still one more point to account for in such a situation and that has to do with the extent to which the midfield line can shift across.

As much as Simeone wants the lines to be compact, in such a situation it is difficult to ask the midfield line to remain overly narrow as they would end up with too many players on the ball side. The V shape would practically be rendered useless since it does not really lessen the distance for the far-side winger to cover in case of a switch and Atlético could quickly become vulnerable. As a result, the midfield needs to spread across to some extent to ensure that, while they are still compact, they can get across quickly if need be. It is a fine line to tread as the gaps need to be small enough to prevent opponents from sneaking through and also large enough to prevent them from easily going around the block, and this is where the positioning of the full-backs provides some much-needed support.

By keeping the back line extremely narrow, Atlético can effectively plug any gaps that the midfield leaves, not by adding players but by simply making central passes more difficult. First of all, as shown in Figure 25, the full-backs are more naturally poised to cover the space between themselves and their centre-backs, effectively cutting out any opposition runs into these spaces. This is probably the most threatening pass that the opposition can look to play, bypassing both Atlético's midfield and defence to play their attackers into space. However, with the two-v-one created in favour of Simeone's side across any space between the back line, these passes are now easily cut out.

Should the opposition still want to play centrally though, their attackers now need to drop ahead of Atlético's back line to receive the ball to their feet instead. By forcing the opposition to do this, Simeone's side has now limited the number of lines that can be bypassed with a single pass to just one, with the midfield line being the only that is slightly vulnerable. Such a situation is not as threatening as the one we saw earlier, and especially using the full-backs, it is much easier to defend against as well. This is because Atlético can still maintain a numerical advantage, and should a pass be played into one of these dropping forwards, they can be crowded out easily as they have two defenders in their vicinity with the recovering midfielders also stepping closer to engage them. This essentially means that with the narrow positioning of the full-backs, Simeone's defenders not only cut out the first situation and force the play to be in front of them, but they are also better positioned to deal with this second situation as well.

All this once again forces the opposition out wide, but as we shift the focus to the full-backs in Atlético's defensive setup we notice something quite interesting. In the earlier chapters, we saw how the wingers and midfielders would be ready to get in and close opponents down after pushing them out wide, but for the full-backs, it is the opposite. With a very compact back line, the full-backs have now made a load of space available out wide for the opposition to exploit and, as seen in Figure 25, there is a winger positioned down the flank to take advantage of this space. This then leads to the full-back's actions in the next phase of play.

If we were to look at some of the earlier diagrams from the previous chapters, we would see that the full-backs have been positioned wider than has been given here and would be covering this winger. The difference in positions in this situation is not an error though, but rather this position is a precursor to the situations that we had seen earlier. By this, we mean that the full-back looks to shift out in phases before finally arriving at the wider position to cover the winger. Getting back to Figure 25, we have already seen that to initially force the play out wide, the full-backs stay narrow in order to prevent the two central passes that we covered earlier.

Once the play moves though, the side needs to shift across and this is when the unmarked winger becomes the responsibility of the full-back.

The full-back cannot simply step out on his own, however, as he would then again allow spaces through the middle and hence the entire back line would first shift across to ensure that he is closer to the unmarked winger while not being too distant from his centre-back. After this, the full-back only engages the winger once a pass is being played to him, stretching the back line for the first time in this sequence. The central space is then covered by the winger, which is something that we saw in their chapter earlier, and the full-back has all the freedom to challenge his winger and force him over the touchline. This shift has basically alternated the compactness of the midfield and the back line, making the former narrower and the latter wider in order to first open up the pass to the winger before closing it down. Hence, the opposition's attack in the next phase has been snuffed out as well.

One caveat regarding this setup is that it restricts the ability of the team, and especially the full-backs, to press higher. It relies on the different lines simply spreading and contracting horizontally, but should an opposition winger drop deeper to receive, the full-back cannot follow him to maintain the overload in the wider areas. This is crucial to Atlético's defensive plans and hence, Simeone would move on to the next stage of his full-backs' transformation.

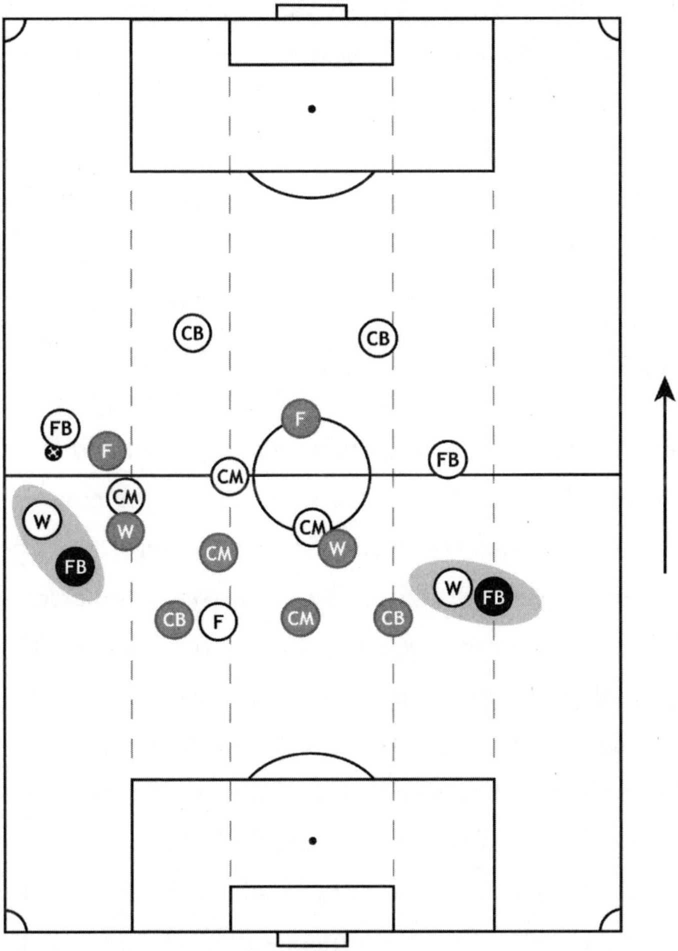

Fig. 26 *Full-backs allowed to mark and track wingers*

While the use of an extremely narrow full-back, almost as a wide centre-back, allowed *Cholo* to immediately correct the issue of conceding goals by having an extremely compact and solid back line, it did have some issues as we stated, such as the inability to track a dropping winger. Moreover, though it does allow for a good structure in deeper areas, it prevents the team from pressing higher as the amount of space allowed wide and in behind would be far too great a risk for the defending side to take. As a result, Simeone would have to build on this initial setup to ensure that his players could push on and press higher if need be.

The simplest ways of achieving this would be either to shift the back line across with the full-back leading, similar to how the wingers lead the midfield shift, or to spread the back line out and increase the distance between the defenders as the full-back steps out. The second scenario would not be ideal, with compactness key to the defensive tactics and, as for the first scenario, a simple shift would open up too much space down the opposite flank for the opposition to switch into. Hence, Simeone would come up with a solution that effectively tweaks his midfield setup to cover for his defence as well.

As we can see from Figure 26, one central midfielder has dropped into the back line to allow them to spread across while maintaining their overall compactness. This does seem to go against the midfield V shape that was a feature of the side, but it should be said that this exact setup would come about in the later years of the 4-4-2 where we had seen Atlético operate with a midfield 'destroyer'. Prior to this, the midfielder would be stationed slightly ahead of the back line maintaining the V shape, but also ready to drop in between the centre-backs and still allowing the full-back to step out and press. This press has become much easier for the full-back as well since he does not need to worry about any space in behind him and his focus lies only on his winger and causing the overload.

The ball-side full-back is not the only one to benefit though and, looking at Figure 26, we see that the far-side full-back has also been allowed to get wider and track the winger on his side. This full-back is now not as vulnerable to runs behind him or players receiving crosses behind him either since he will not be dragged as centrally as he was before. What this also does is keep this full-back in prime position to deal with any switches of play, since he can very easily step out in such a case and cover the space to the side of his midfield. Hence, moving on from the narrow structure, Atlético are now able to defend both flanks using their full-backs.

This would not complete the evolution of the full-backs in the back four though, and the next step was to get them forward in attack. Despite most of the initial attacking play stemming from balls into the channels for the forwards, Simeone understood the importance of the wide areas for ball progression and, in order to create more sustainable sequences of possession as the side evolved, he would once again build upon the role of the full-backs.

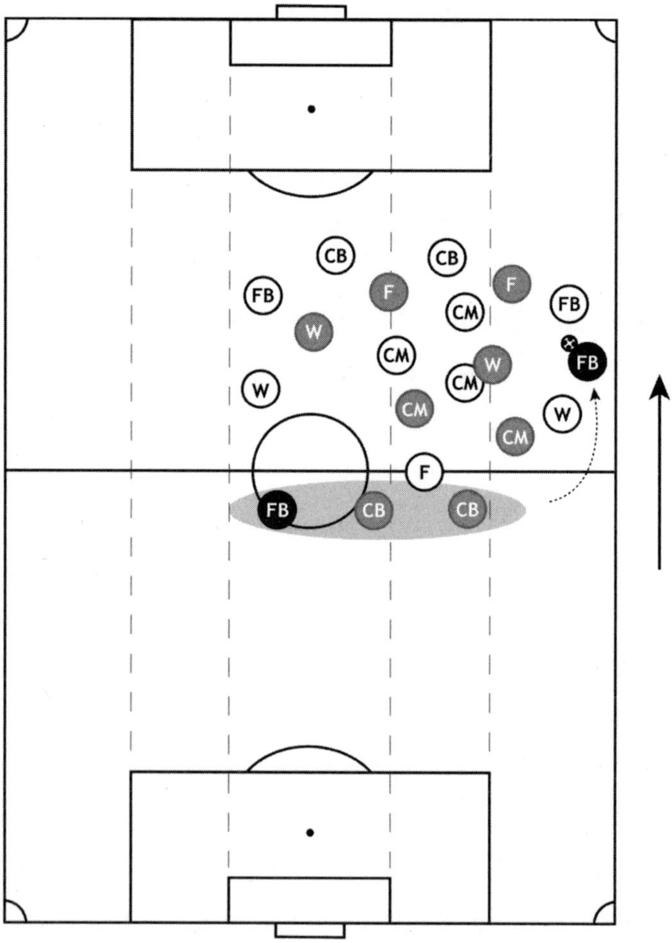

Fig. 27 One full-back progresses the ball, while the other tucks into defence

The tactical evolution of Atlético to develop better patterns in possession meant that the full-backs, who were primarily engaged in defensive duties, now had to get involved in attack. While this is not really a ground-breaking development considering the fact that full-backs at the time were already doing this, it was still relatively new for Atlético's wide defenders who had to be fairly reserved for most of the initial stages of the 4-4-2. This is not to say that they were incapable in possession (this was quite the opposite as they had experience of playing as wingers even), but rather that this would be the first time that they would consistently get to showcase their ability on the ball in Simeone's setup.

So, what exactly is their role in possession? Well, we have already seen in previous chapters that the Atlético wingers take up narrower positions, meaning that the full-back is responsible for providing the width in attack. This means that the full-back needs to step out of the back line and get forward to take up a position down the flank, which results in the situation shown in Figure 27. Once again, we see how Atlético maintain their overload in possession, keeping the central midfielder as the deepest of the four players out wide to cover for the advancing full-back.

This overload is crucial and it forms the foundation of the team's wide build-up, allowing for neat short passing combinations and wide rotations to progress the ball up the pitch. If we were to consider that the full-back is in possession of the ball, like in Figure 27, we can see that he has two good short passing options to his forward and his winger, allowing him to link up with them and possibly play one of them in behind the opposition full-back. The Atlético full-back himself can pass and move to get higher up the pitch as well and, in case he is closed off, he still has the option of playing the ball backwards to the central midfielder or his back line. Having all these options available to him, he is easily the most important player in this situation and now a primary creator of wide attacks.

Such responsibility requires a good amount of attacking freedom though and, despite having the central midfielder for some cover, the full-back has put a considerable distance between himself and his back line. The centre-backs could quickly become vulnerable in a defensive transition, and the far-side full-back has to play a crucial role in maintaining compactness and allowing his team-mate to get forward freely. Looking back at Figure 27, we see how the Atlético left-back does just this, tucking into defence alongside his centre-backs and forming a back-three structure. This now means that, should there be a turnover in possession, the defence essentially consists of three centre-backs and the ones on either side (the left-back and right-sided centre-back) can step out to engage opponents and cover for the absence of the right-back while being supported by two defenders behind them.

Atlético now have a fairly good way of consistently progressing the ball down the wings using a full-back, but looking closer at Figure 27, we see that this attack is now heavily tilted to one side of the pitch and there are large spaces left down the opposite flank. These areas can potentially be very useful considering the amount of space on offer, but unfortunately there is no player that can currently access it to provide an option for a switch. Hence, to maximise the attacking potential of the side, Simeone implements the final phase of his full-back tactics.

While Atlético like to funnel attacks down a particular side and make their playing area as narrow as possible, they know the crowding issues with this as this is what they themselves do to their opposition when out of possession. Their first step to avoid being crowded out down the flank is to overload it themselves, using one full-back to be the widest player as we saw earlier, allowing them to take control of play down the wings rather than being forced out of play. By doing this, Atlético then have the option of taking a second step, which is to move out of the flank and switch the play.

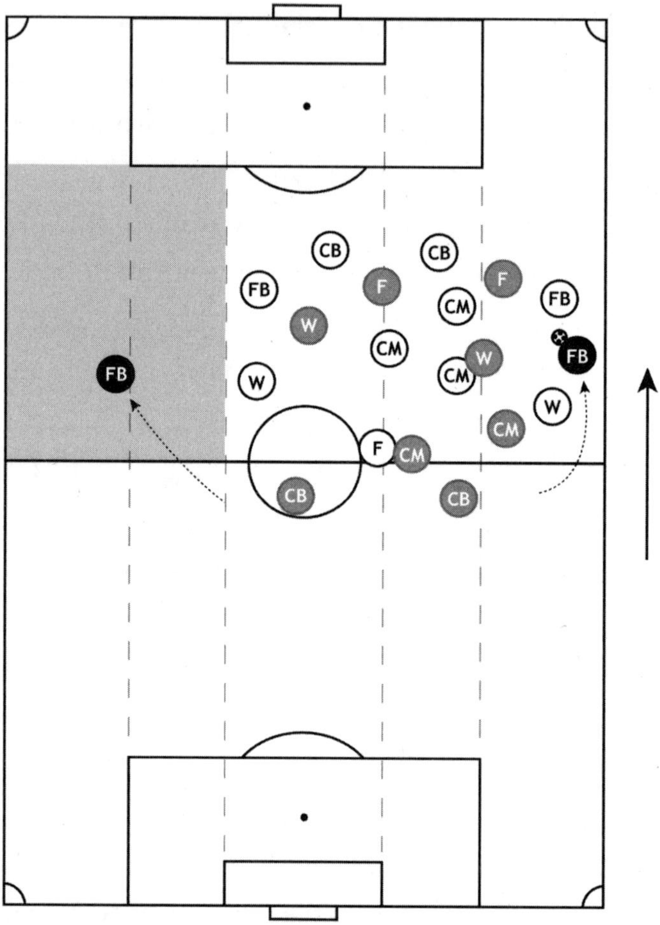

Fig. 28 *The far-side full-back steps out to exploit vacant space down his flank*

When defending, this switch is something that Atlético prevent simply because of the pressure that they apply on the ball side, but considering the fact that they have the numerical advantage even in possession, the crossfield pass becomes a viable, and dangerous, option. Having bunched up the pack towards the centre using the forwards and wingers, all Simeone needs is for a player to make use of the vacant space down the opposite flank, and for this he uses the far-sided full-back. As seen in Figure 28, this is perhaps the most advanced and attacking form that the full-backs have taken, with the pair of them being much higher up the pitch now as compared to the initial phases of their roles. However, that naturally comes at the cost of not supporting the centre-backs, so let us take a deeper look into how this works.

Now, it is important to understand that this situation follows on from the one we saw in Figure 27, where the full-back tucked in to form a back three. This means that the left-back does not immediately venture forwards once Atlético gain possession of the ball, but instead starts from his deeper positioning alongside the centre-backs only when they are in control of the ball and have sustained possession. In this way, he is able to offer the basic defensive support to free the right-back before taking on his own attacking duties. His movement forward is then fairly straightforward and he positions himself on the far side to freely receive any switch in play.

With both full-backs in attack, Atlético now need a player to provide support for their centre-backs just as the left-back had done. We already know that one central midfielder has engaged in the wide overload and is covering for the right-back, but he does not offer direct support for the centre-back due to his higher positioning. Hence, it is the other central midfielder that has to drop slightly deeper than before to readily split the centre-backs and form a back three. This situation is similar to the one in Figure 26, where the central midfielder had dropped into the back line to allow the full-backs to press higher and, in this case, he is allowing the full-backs to get forward in attack.

The two full-backs are now the widest players in attack, and after having restricted the playing area to just a small zone, Atlético are now suddenly stretching their opponents across the pitch by forcing them to defend against the second advancing full-back. The rest of the attacking players are now afforded space centrally to attack the channels and drift between lines as well, which adds to the opposition's problems. Interestingly, this setup has begun to resemble that of a more possession-based side, but where those sides may look to use it much higher up the pitch after steadily forcing the opposition backwards, Atlético use it much earlier as they look to maintain a more direct and incisive approach from the back.

Especially with this latest structure, Simeone knew that he was on to something as a result of being able to open up multiple attacking opportunities by stretching the play rather than just compressing it as he had done before. Again, it was by no means a novel approach, but after using his full-backs merely as specialist defenders in the initial stages to stem the concession of goals, he had now found a way to get them involved as crucial players in the attacking phase in order to unlock opposition defences. However, he knew that this was still not the finished product either as it still had some issues that needed ironing out.

The biggest issue was the fact that this advancing of full-backs had to take place in stages, rather than being able to get both of them forward together to stretch the opposition at once.

Since the latter was compromising the defence at times, Simeone was slower to transition into such a setup and, while his method did allow the second full-back to find more space when he moved forward, such a sequence also allowed the opposition to deal with the attacks separately, meaning that they could first shift across to deal with the first full-back, before moving back across once the switch is played to handle the second full-back. They would still be stretched, but since they were not having to deal with multiple issues at once, they could be better prepared and organised to thwart the attacks.

The fundamentals were there though, and this certainly provided a different kind of attacking threat than the usual counter attacks through the middle. Simeone had realised the benefits of spreading his back line to consistently reach the wide areas and this was not only useful in possession, but also out of it as well. By allowing his full-backs to step out and defend the flanks with greater liberty, Atlético were able to control the flow of the game and ensure that they could always dominate the wings and suffocate opponents near the touchline.

The phase-by-phase development of the full-back role would also provide food for thought, as a position that had been an extension of the centre-backs had now transformed into a more complete profile that could hold its own defensively while also serving as a creator in possession. The position now demanded its freedom to thrive, with and without the ball, and with an eventual shift to a 5-3-2 formation, Simeone would finally oblige.

With a change in formation bringing about a back five setup, the full-backs would undergo a positional change to become wing-backs. This meant that they could stretch the play more naturally than they had

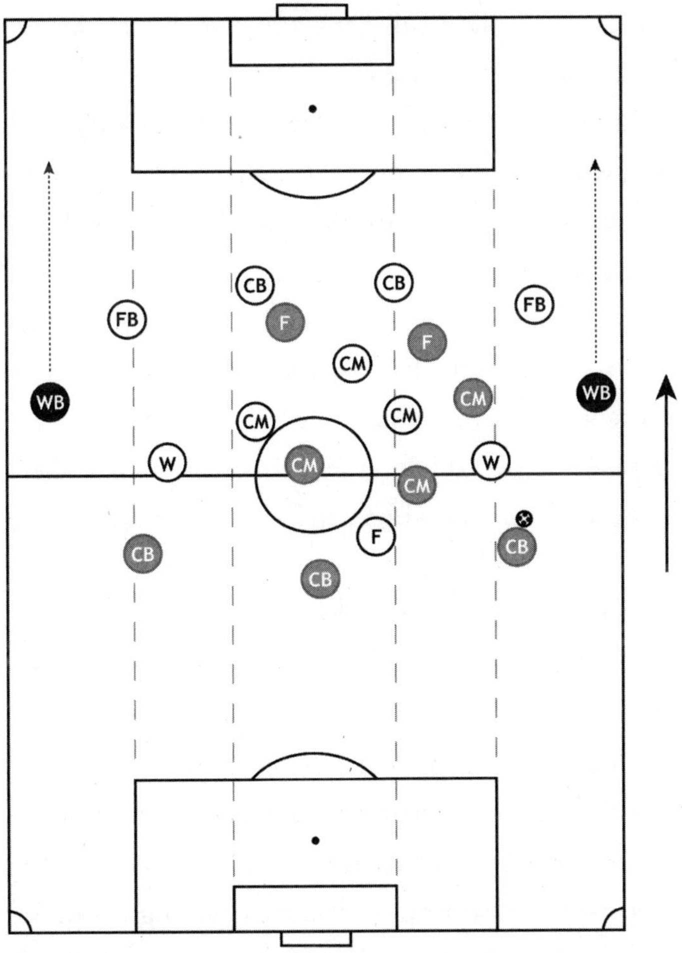

***Fig. 29** Wing-backs now stretch the play together with their natural positions*

been able to and that their starting positions could be higher as well. Before we move on further to understand the intricacies of the new role, however, it is first important to understand how exactly a wing-back differs from a full-back and, for that reason let us take a look at Figure 29.

As we mentioned earlier, the wing-backs are stationed much wider and higher than a standard full-back and this directly affects their duties in and out of possession.

For starters, wing-backs generally take on a more attacking role than a full-back because they have more than enough cover should they be caught higher up the pitch. Especially in systems like the 5-3-2 where there are no wingers either, the attacking threat of the wing-backs is crucial to ensure that chances can be created from the advanced wide areas and, as shown by the arrows in Figure 29, the pair need to consistently advance down the outside.

This is not to say that they do not have to do any defending, but the extent to which it becomes a priority has lessened when compared to a full-back and the wing-back is also responsible for covering a smaller area as well.

By having five defenders instead of four and being stationed wider, the wing-backs are better positioned to defend near the touchline than a full-back and they can focus only on these narrow stretches out wide, with an extra player sharing the load of covering space across the pitch. This is in stark contrast to the defensive duties of the full-backs that we saw earlier and they had to ensure that they step out of their defence with the right timing to avoid opening up spaces in between the back line.

In their tactical evolution, all these changes would be welcome at Atlético as the side needed to adapt to the modern game and find a system that best suited their current group of players. We have already spoken a little about how the club itself had been looking to evolve and expand its global reach and, while Simeone wanted to ensure that the playing style did not massively shift away from direct, counter-attacking football, the old rugged methods could not simply be carried over. The modern full-back boasts attacking intent and this needed to be unleashed, with the back five helping to achieve just that.

The attacking duties of the wing-backs would still be very similar to that of the full-backs though, and the improvement going forward would largely be down to execution more than any outright change in tactics. Of course, a new setup does open other possibilities with respect to modes of attack but primarily the goal would be the same, to get high and wide. This naturally means that the switch of play is still an important weapon and in this next segment, we will see how this plays out with the wing-backs.

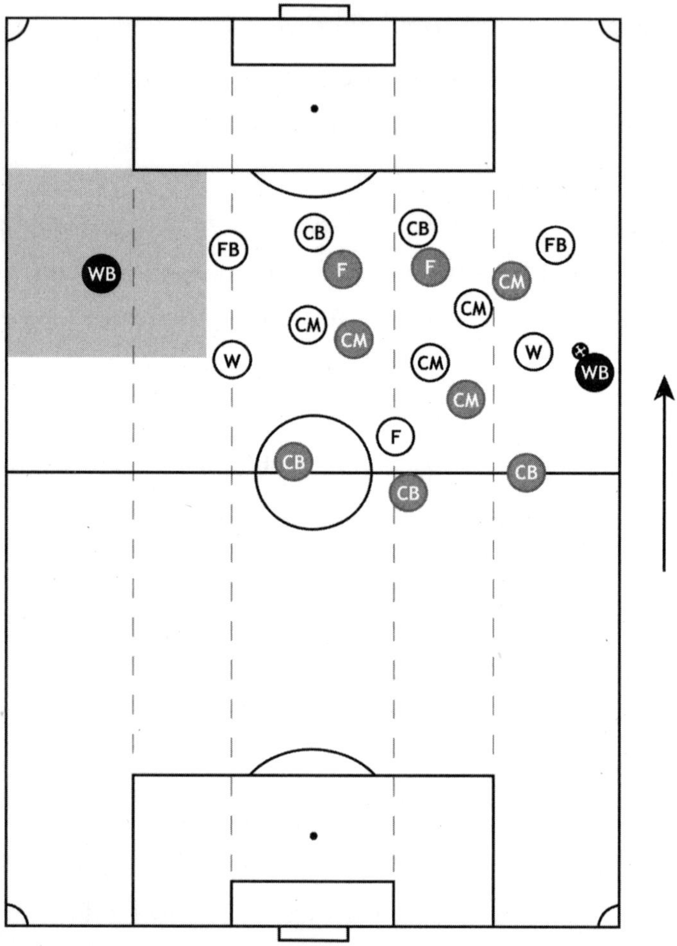

Fig. 30 Wing-backs can receive the switch in a more advanced position attacking the back line

Looking at Figure 30, with three centre-backs already present for cover, the far-side wing-back does not need to worry about offering defensive support for his counterpart and is given the freedom to attack the wide areas from the beginning. Not only is his starting position much higher than what it was for the full-back, but, instead of moving forward into midfield like before, he can now move further forward to directly attack the back line, having been given this liberty to push forward. In doing so, the opposition defenders are stretched by the initial positioning of this wing-back alone and they cannot simply shift across to deal with the ball-side wing-back like they had done earlier.

There is, of course, more to this and, without the presence of the wingers to compress the play in this formation, we have already seen how the midfielders take on this responsibility by continuing to overload the flanks and draw the opposition to the ball side. However, a major difference, and potential hindrance, is that there is no player to directly engage the opposition full-back anymore, which technically means that he is now free enough to simply move across and mark Atlético's wing-back. Should this happen, the switch is not as effective an option unless the pass is particularly incisive since despite the back line being stretched, the far-side wing-back can immediately be put under considerable pressure to prevent him from receiving the pass cleanly.

Fortunately for Atlético though, the positioning of the wing-back prevents this from happening. By being stretched from the beginning, the opposition has allowed larger central spaces than in the case with the full-backs for example, meaning that they simply are not as compact as they would like to be to deal with the ball-side threat. Their focus is then to nullify that threat, which means that they would rather not allow more central space caused by pushing their full-back wider.

Moreover, looking closer at Figure 30, the forwards are occupying both centre-backs and effectively in one-v-one situations with them. We also saw earlier how the ball-side centre-back has to deal with any potential run into the channels as well, meaning that the other centre-back needs to be prepared to shift across. In such a case, if the full-back does not do the same and is instead marking the wing-back, it leaves room for the second forward to make a free run into the box. Hence, when faced with the choice of having to decide between allowing either this or the switch, the opposition would prefer to stay compact rather than opening up their back line.

With the wing-backs, Simeone is now able to effectively exploit the spaces between the last line of the opposition defence by not only having one wing-back ready for a switch to take him in behind, but by also having the same player create central pockets for his team-mates to attack. Seeing the potential of using this player as even more of an attacking force, *Cholo* would then get the idea of once again tilting the balance of duties among the players in the role, meaning that one would have to shoulder more defensive responsibility while the other advanced. This would then alter the shape of the side, leading to multiple positional shifts and more dynamic attacking sequences, which we will now look into.

With three central midfielders and a full-back joining the front line, the 4-3-3 formation is one that, despite not seeming to be the most natural, becomes easy to shift into. This setup is rather interesting because in general, when sides do play with wing-backs, the position is often occupied by attacking full-backs (i.e. players that are actually full-backs but play as wing-backs due to their attacking strengths) who push forward from the back line. The back five easily becomes a back three, with the wing-backs moving into midfield, creating a 3-4-3 or 3-5-2 shape more often than not. Simeone, however, would go for something different.

The wing-back position itself is slightly different in that most players who play in the role are not wing-backs by nature, but they are players who have been adapted to suit this role after usually having developed as full-backs. However, in Atlético's case, instead of an

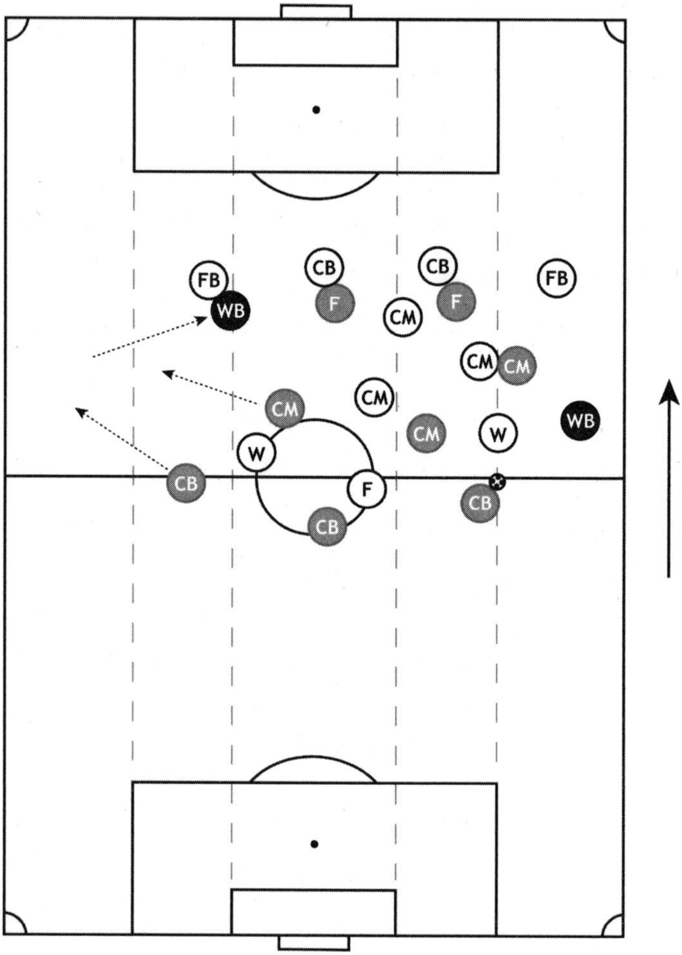

Fig. 31 *Wing-backs shift to create a 4–3–3 shape in possession*

attacking full-back occupying the wing-back spot, *Cholo* would switch things up and opt for a 'defensive winger' to play on one side. But what exactly is a 'defensive winger'? Simply put, we have classified this as a winger who has been positioned in the wing-back spot rather than a full-back, meaning that this player is originally an attacker that has now been asked to defend, rather than the opposite.

While both wing-backs would need to attack, Simeone wanted one of them to be a real force going forward and, in typical *Cholo* fashion, he concluded that it would be easier to teach a winger to defend than to teach a full-back to attack in the explosive manner that he wanted. Of course, he would certainly do both to ensure that either wing-back was good enough going forward on their own, but in dividing the duties among them, he knew that there had to be one player that shouldered the extra attacking responsibility. This naturally fell on the winger and, with this setup, shifts like the one in Figure 31 become far more natural.

Having moved into a 4-3-3, the 'defensive winger' (who is usually the left wing-back) joins the front line and takes up a position which is far more befitting of the player, allowing them to act as a standard winger. The forwards also move across, with one of them becoming a winger on the opposite side and, to accommodate this change in the front line, the other wing-back has become a standard full-back as the back line shifts across, with the left centre-back now becoming a makeshift left-back to cover the flank. It is a fairly simple shift to take up a fairly common formation, but in the context of

Atlético's tactics, this shift in the game causes multiple issues for opponents to deal with.

It is first of all important to understand that this shift, as any other, cannot be taken in isolation as it involves the movement of players from a prior position. Any such movement then results in Atlético, and the opposition even, behaving slightly differently than they might if they were to simply start out with whatever setup that they were shifting into. To be more specific with respect to this case, just because Atlético are moving into a 4-3-3, it does not mean that their players are directly acting how a player in a standard 4-3-3 would, and it also does not mean that the opposition is positioned to defend against this 4-3-3 right from the beginning.

By initially starting in a 3-5-2 that spreads across the pitch, the opposition are wary of a potential switch between the wing-backs as we had seen earlier. They have also already been drawn towards the ball side, which they might not have done to the same extent if they were to be defending against an outright 4-3-3. As a result, when Atlético make this shift, the opposition are momentarily caught in an awkward shape as they look to adjust to the new setup.

As we see from Figure 31, the 'defensive winger' has shifted centrally to attack the inside of the full-back, as opposed to the outside space near the flanks, and has pinned this full-back to his position. Down the opposite side, the other wing-back has dropped to receive the ball from his centre-back, in turn drawing an opposition winger towards him, while his team-mates also draw the opposition's central midfielders towards the ball side as well. At this point, the opposition central midfielders are focusing on preventing wide overloads and runs into the channels, meaning that they are willing to commit themselves towards the ball side in order to prevent Atlético's first phase of attack.

In a way, the opposition then expect Atlético's front line to stretch the play once the pass has been played out to the dropping wing-back, and hence their shape in midfield has remained compact to prevent any gaps centrally, while allowing their wingers to drop and form a midfield five of sorts to cover the wide areas as well. However, since Atlético have moved into the 4-3-3 instead, it is their back line and midfield line that has starting stretching the play, meaning that instead of the 'defensive winger' finding space out wide, it is now the furthest centre-back (makeshift left-back) and central midfielder who have found themselves in neat pockets of space.

The makeshift left-back is pretty much afforded the space to get forward like a normal full-back and, while this would be a threat, it does defeat the purpose of having the extra centre-back as cover, meaning that he remains behind simply as an option to switch the ball across the back line to recycle possession. The far-side central midfielder, however, has worked himself into an excellent pocket of space towards the side of the opposition midfield and behind their winger, with the freedom to get wider and act as a winger to receive a switch in play. With the opposition full-back being pinned, he can receive in space and he then has excellent passing options all across the front line, with the 'defensive winger' also darting into the channels. The awkward shape of the opposition has left them exposed now as they have tracked the wrong spaces, allowing Atlético to take advantage.

With a slight variation of this shift itself, Simeone could also look to restructure his setup once again, this time even by reverting to the old 4-4-2 formation.

One of the major benefits of using the 'defensive winger' is the fact that this player can shift across any line seamlessly. This is, of course, very useful for enabling a dynamic shape and, having pushed him forward to create the 4-3-3, Simeone can also pull him back slightly, hence creating a 4-4-2 reminiscent of the older times. We do, however, know that a positional shift may not always function exactly as the fixed

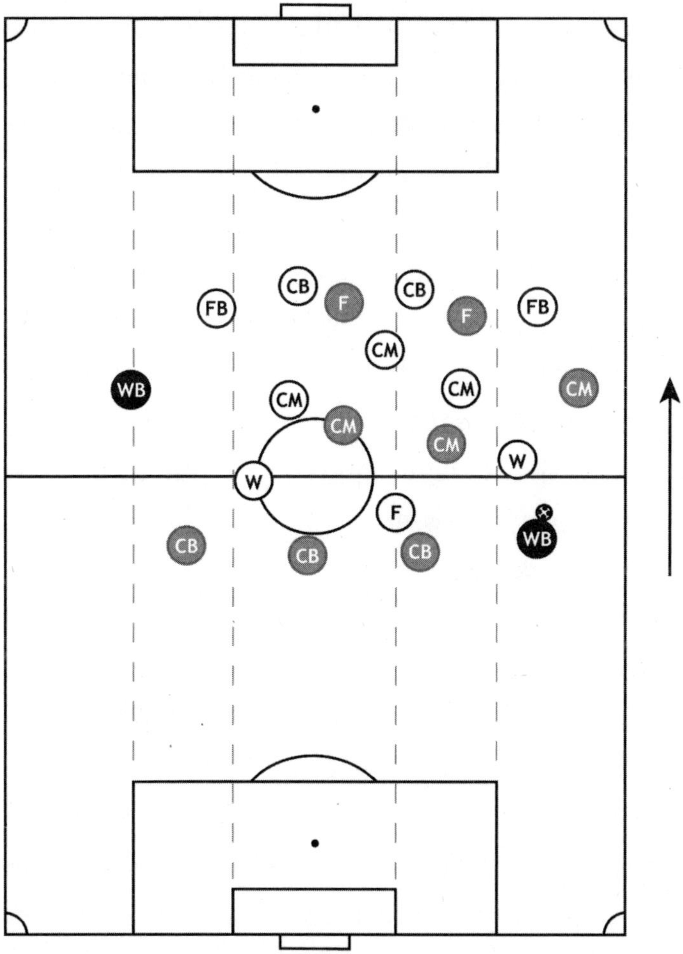

Fig. 32 *Wing-backs shift to create a wider 4-4-2 formation*

formation and this would be the case here as well, with a major difference between this shift and the earlier fixed 4-4-2 being the width of the setup.

In the 4-4-2 of early years, we have seen how the wingers take up central positions and basically form a

4-2-2-2 structure rather than a flat 4-4-2. As for this positional shift though, the 'defensive winger' needs to hold his width while the rest of the midfield move towards the ball side, meaning that his fellow 'winger' (furthest central midfielder) is also holding width down the opposite flank. In such a case, the opposition can overload the midfield considering the fact that Atlético will have just two central midfielders there, but as we saw in the earlier shift, they are not reacting directly to this new formation but rather to the change in shape from the previous setup.

If we look at Figure 32, Atlético's right wing-back has dropped into the back line in the build-up to help the side progress the ball from the back. To provide a passing option and carry on in their style of progression, the midfielders and forward line shift across to the ball side, creating an overload and drawing opponents towards them. Such a situation is largely similar to the usual 3-5-2 build-up that stretches the play, but the interesting move here is that, with the wing-back's deeper position, one of the central midfielders has moved to the flank to become a makeshift winger rather than staying central and allowing the wing-back to move forward.

As for the opposition, they are still reacting to the initial 3-5-2 formation, meaning that as the wing-back

On the hunt! A throwback to Diego Simeone's playing career in the colours of red and white. He would soon be back at his beloved club, this time hunting for some of the biggest prizes on offer.

Start of something special. Diego Simeone poses with club president Enrique Cerezo and sports director José Luis Caminero at his first press conference as manager of Atlético Madrid

It has only been five months, but Diego Simeone already has his first trophy as manager and here he is celebrating winning the UEFA Europa League in 2012.

Diego Simeone lifts the UEFA Super Cup after a convincing 4-1 victory over Champions League winners Chelsea, his second major trophy in eight months.

'Madrid is Red and White', reads the back of Diego Simeone's shirt. The Copa del Rey victory in 2013 ended a 14-year wait for victory over their city rivals in stunning fashion.

Soaring high! Diego Simeone is thrown into the air by his players as they win their first La Liga title in 18 years after a hard fought 1-1 draw away at fellow contenders Barcelona. His second league title at the club and first as manager.

Completing the domestic set. Diego Simeone gestures to the fans after winning the Supercopa de España, securing all major domestic honours in a span of one year.

The rest of the band. Diego Simeone celebrates winning the UEFA Europa League in 2018 with his coaching staff. 'Mono' Burgos (far right) and 'Profe' Ortega (second from right) would form a crucial part of the backroom.

Seventh heaven. Diego Simeone holds up his fingers to show just how many trophies he has won in as many years after beating Champions League winners Real Madrid in the UEFA Super Cup. Every time he has won the Europa League, he has gone on to win the Super Cup!

Champions of Spain once more. Yet another hard fought away game sees Atlético Madrid come from behind to win the match and seal the title on the final day. Diego Simeone is duly tossed in the air again.

In his sights. The elusive Champions League trophy remains the only major honour that Diego Simeone is yet to lift with Atlético Madrid, and two final losses in three years against Real Madrid have been hard to digest.

'Paseo de los Melancólicos, Manzanares, how much I love you!' Atlético Madrid bid goodbye to their famous Estadio Vicente Calderón.

External view of the stadium situated right on the river bank, with the M-30 motorway passing under the main stand.

All that remained for a while was the main stand, and soon parks and residential blocks will replace the historic stadium with a thunderous matchday atmosphere.

Atlético Madrid have since moved to the modern Metropolitano stadium, currently sponsored by the Wanda Group, and their facilities rival some of the top clubs across Europe.

With extra seats and an atmosphere like this one, the new stadium is truly a spectacle on matchdays. Definitely not a nice experience for an away side!

Entertainer, crowd conductor, manager. On another one of his trademark celebratory runs, his passion for Atlético Madrid visible for all to see. Diego Simeone is not done yet, and he will never stop giving the biggest clubs a run for their money.

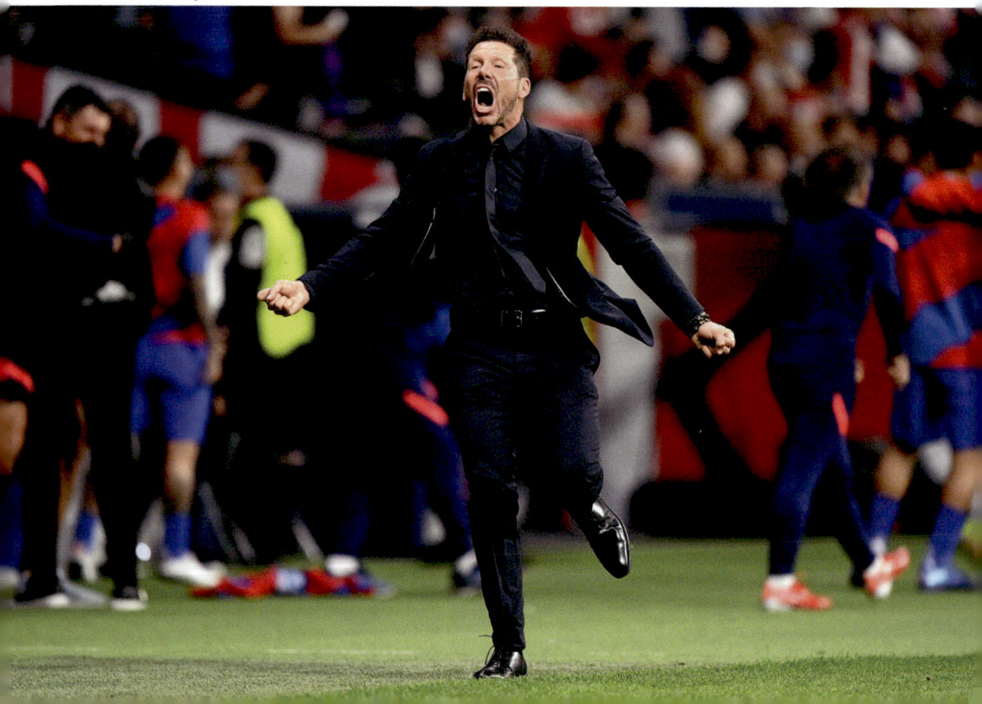

drops and midfielders shift, they too are drawn across in order to continue tracking their men. With the back line shifting across due to the dropping wing-back, the 'defensive winger' is then naturally pushed further up the pitch and he now finds himself in free space out wide, almost identical to the sequence with the 3-5-2 setup itself. However, while the end goal remains the same, the use of an alternative method to reach it does provide Atlético with some dynamism in their attack. Should an opponent find it relatively easy to spread across and defend against the 3-5-2 formation, the dropping wing-back can shift to the 4-4-2 to first draw them across before switching the play and finding his team-mate down the other flank.

Interestingly though, while serving as an effective means of alternating their method of progression, the 4-4-2 shift would continue even out of possession at times, with Simeone rolling back the years despite having the five defenders at his disposal.

When Atlético shifted to a back five, most people expected their structure to become even more defensive when out of possession. They now had the extra man permanently in defence, after previously using a central midfielder to drop in, and all signs pointed to a stiff back line that would sit deep and cover the width of the pitch. However, while this would still be true, it became

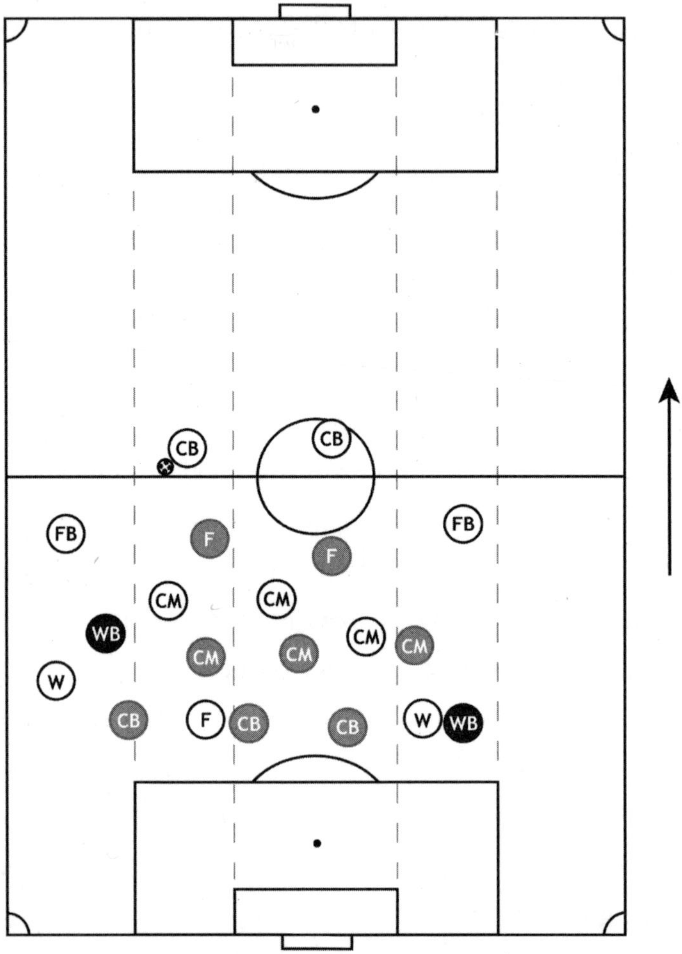

***Fig. 33** Shifting to a 4-4-2 shape out of possession with wing-back remaining in midfield line*

more and more apparent that this would not be the only way that the side would defend.

One of the key principles of Atlético's defence has been to control the flanks after forcing the opposition to the wide areas. Despite the use of wing-backs, however, the 5-3-2 formation is not the most effective way of covering the wings though, owing to the fact that the midfield and forward lines are usually too central, meaning that it is harder to cause overloads without completely drawing the side across. As a result, by maintaining a back five, Simeone is only able to defend the flanks much closer to his goal and cannot effectively apply pressure higher up as the side had previously done in the 4-4-2.

The most obvious solution then is to shift back to the 4-4-2 when looking to press higher, and as can be seen from Figure 33, this is exactly what Atlético would do. By once again using the left centre-back as a makeshift left-back, the wing-back can push out to cover the wider areas beside the midfield, creating the 4-4-2 shape out of possession. This shift usually involves the 'defensive winger' pushing up into midfield, mainly due to the fact that he can then press and defend just as a winger would do in higher positions, allowing him more leeway for error. Should the opposition play the ball down the opposite side and away from the 'defensive winger', this player does still step up into midfield on his side, allowing the midfield to shift across, with the right central midfielder now acting as a winger instead.

From this position, the defending is similar to that of the original 4-4-2 that we saw earlier, with Atlético cutting off the central passes as shown in Figure 33 and leaving the opposition full-back as the clearest passing option for his centre-back. In this case, the ball is played down the side of the 'defensive winger', who can then step across and close down the full-back, while his midfielders and forward support him in creating the overload. Possibly the only major difference between this and the earlier 4-4-2 structure would be the positioning of the opposition themselves, as they may have structured their side to exploit the spaces of the 5-3-2 instead. This usually means that they might initially have some numerical superiority in the spaces to the side of Atlético's midfield, but with the 4-4-2 shift, these areas are now well defended.

Eventually, it is also easy to shift out of the 4-4-2 and fall back into the natural 5-3-2 structure, or any back-five setup for that matter. The 4-4-2 shape serves its purpose as a structure that enables higher pressing, allowing Atlético to control the flow of the opposition's first phase of attack, which is the build-up. However, as the opposition progresses, active pressing becomes secondary, with Simeone then prioritising a solid defensive structure that can sit back, with the back five offering just that.

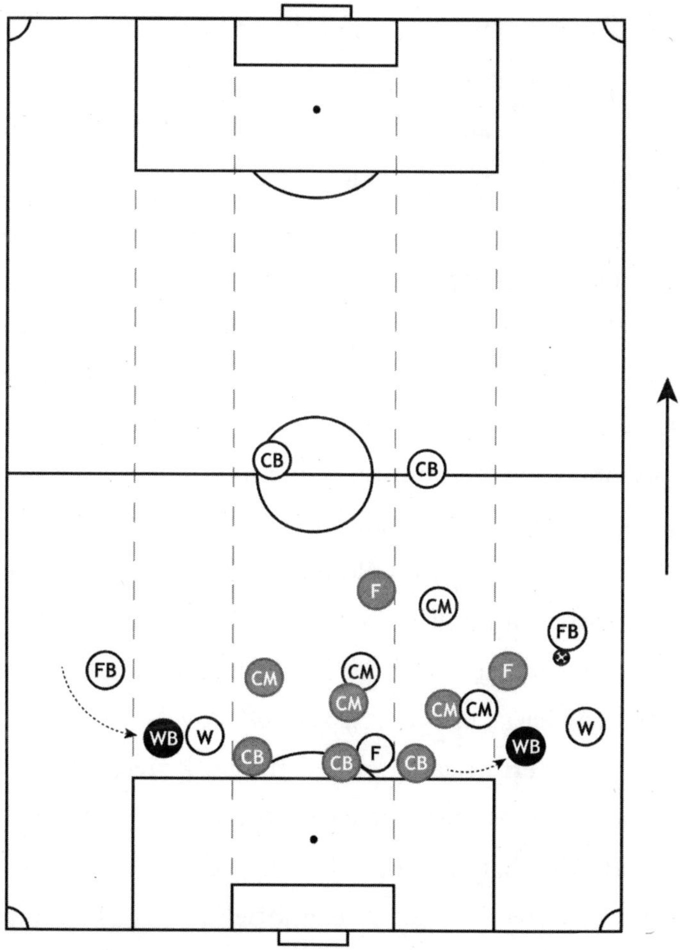

Fig. 34 *Shifting into the back five as the opposition progresses*

The simplest way of shifting into the back five is to just have the wing-back drop back down the ball side as the opposition work their way down the same flank, but in Figure 34, we will consider a slightly different scenario to better understand the different ways in which such a shift can occur. Here, we shall consider that the opposition have opted to switch the play down the opposite flank, possibly after not finding much success down the other side.

In this case, Atlético's shift occurs rather smoothly as, instead of simply falling back vertically and scampering to get into position, the team changes formations while moving back and across in a fluid motion. The initial four defenders drop deeper to account for the opposition's territorial gain, before sliding across to close down the ball side as usual. The 'defensive winger', who had been part of a midfield four, can now do the same and neatly slot into the spot left for him on the far side of the defence. It is nothing spectacular, and in fact it is extremely basic, but yet it is very effective.

Having effortlessly formed the back five, Atlético can then choose how to set up their other two lines, considering that one player has moved out of midfield. With just the three central midfielders, they cannot possibly hope to minimise the spaces on either side on their own and, in Figure 34, it is the forward who drops into the side of midfield to maintain a line of four. This is not always the exact situation though and the forward may move centrally, but in general the forward will drop somewhere into midfield and either he or a central midfielder (the one who had become a makeshift winger) shall take on the responsibility of covering the wide areas. If we also consider the case where the ball was not switched but rather played down the same flank, then the central midfielder closest to the 'defensive winger' may take on this role of covering the wide areas instead, once again highlighting the flexibility of the players within the system.

There would be more derivations as well and, in a spectacular variation of this shift, Atlético even resorted to a 5-5-0 formation when playing away against Manchester City in the first leg of a 2021/22 Champions League quarter-final. 'In pre-history, today and in 100,000 years, attacking a 5-5 is very difficult. It is that there is no space. Apart from the fact that they are very competitive and defend very well, there is no space,' Pep Guardiola would say after the game, where, for 90 minutes, his side struggled to create clear chances, hitting the target just twice, with one of those just being enough to score what would eventually be the tie-winning goal. The use of the word 'pre-history' would cause a stir back in Spain, but the fact remained that Atlético's flexibility to shape-shift throughout a game could baffle even the very best of coaches.

The flexibility is brought about by the wing-backs, who have built upon all that their full-back predecessors have done and more. What would Atlético be without these wide defenders and, more specifically, what would Atlético be without these below players to follow?

* * *

Juan Francisco Torres (Juanfran)

'Hola Atléticos, I have asked the club to address all of you with this letter to tell you everything that I feel.'

It had only been a couple of days since the 2016 Champions League Final, where Atlético had faced city rivals Real Madrid at this stage for the second time in three years. This game would go even further than the last, with 120 minutes of action not enough to separate the two sides. Atlético would go second in the penalty shoot-out, matching their opponents for the first three penalties before Sergio Ramos scored the fourth for Real, neatly slotting the ball into the right-hand side of the net, pumping his fist to the supporters in white behind the goal. The onus was on Atlético to reply, and up stepped Juanfran.

The rest, as they say, is history. The ball would ricochet back off the post, allowing Cristiano Ronaldo to seal the trophy with the next kick and rip off his shirt in celebration as Real won their 11th Champions League title. The white half of Madrid erupted, but on the other end, it was the Atlético fans with a standing ovation, applauding a tearful Juanfran who had his arms outstretched, asking for forgiveness. Two days later he would pen a letter to them, opening with the lines above, pouring out his feelings and thanking them for their affection. In the minds of the supporters, however, he did not need any forgiveness because, after all, it was he who had provided the assist for the equalising goal in the first place, allowing them to dream of greatness. And besides, one penalty miss, no matter how important, would not change his legacy in their eyes.

To remember Juanfran's time at Atlético by this one incident would be nothing short of a travesty, but rather this would serve as a moment that encapsulated his connection to the club and what he meant to all *Colchoneros* around the world. Rocking up to the shores of Atlético in January 2011, he was an unassuming, old-fashioned player stuck in the modern era who only knew how to give 100 per cent and more every time he stepped on to the pitch. His journey, however, was anything but ordinary and, just to prove Jamie Carragher's point, he would not start out as a full-back either.

Growing up in a family full of Real Madrid supporters, his father even being a club member, Juanfran's development actually began as a winger in the academy on the other side of the capital, idolising Portuguese and Real great Luís Figo. Juanfran himself would never go on to shine at the Bernabéu like his idol did, and even though he did replace Figo for an appearance in a Copa del Rey game, the Spaniard would in total amass just ten more down the flank before being loaned out to RCD Espanyol for a season starting in 2005.

He would score just once but featured heavily in a campaign where Espanyol narrowly avoided relegation and, upon his return to Real Madrid, he would join the long list of prospects deemed surplus to requirements. Aged 21, he would be sold to CA Osasuna where he would stay for four and a half seasons, even scoring a goal in a final-day victory against his childhood side in 2009 to help the club avoid relegation that year. He would largely contribute to mid-table finishes for the rest of the years though, with his goal contribution tally never even crossing ten in a single season.

He was, therefore, a rather uninspiring signing when he moved to Atlético in January 2011, but it was here that his transition would begin. After Gregorio Manzano had used him as a right-back owing to injuries in that department, Simeone would make the switch in positions permanent, fine-tuning Juanfran's skillset with the extra work and training required to play the position. He would himself put in the extra effort and reportedly get to training early to ensure he could be the best version of himself in this new role, and it eventually worked, with Juanfran cementing his place on the right of defence. A committed and passionate fighter, he fitted Simeone's mould perfectly and, with 355 appearances over eight years and with seven trophies to his name, Juanfran would undoubtedly be a success.

He would eventually leave in 2019, aged 34, to finish his career in Brazil, but in spite of closing out his chapter at Atlético as a player, he has already sounded out his intentions to return to the club in some capacity in the future. 'I want to be the sporting director at Atlético Madrid,' Juanfran said in an interview with *MARCA* in 2019 after previously saying that he would 'return soon to try and make [them] better' during his emotional farewell from the club. Real Madrid by birth, Juanfran could not be more Atlético by nature and his unwavering passion for *Los Rojiblancos* is evident in his letter all those years ago.

'I also want to thank you for always believing in us and, above all, for proving that being an Atlético is something very special, different, and that our heart beats stronger than any other. I love you very much and *AUPA ATLETI*.'

* * *

Filipe Luís Kasmirski

Most players usually describe the best moment of their lives as the time when they won a major trophy, signed for their favourite club or maybe even their wedding or birth of a child. For Filipe Luís, though, this moment came at the famed Royal Albert Hall in 2015, at the premiere of the movie *Interstellar*. Sat in a box beside the president of Warner Europe, Thierry Henry and legendary actor Michael Caine, he would recount the event as 'the best thing [he] had seen in [his] life', even engaging the latter in conversation about cinema. What could he possibly know about it to speak to such a seasoned professional, you may ask, but in truth, Filipe Luís knew a lot, and not just about cinema.

Apart from being an avid cinephile, Filipe Luís loved astrophysics and science so much that he held discussions about the universe with club doctors. He had wanted to be a doctor himself, but his father had talked him out of it (in stark contrast to the norm), and he also has a proper understanding of finance and even once solved a Rubik's Cube while speaking to the host during a television interview. Filipe Luís is certainly not your average Joe, and this is even before we talk about his football.

Originally of European descent (he gets the 'Kasmirski' part of his name from his Polish roots, but that's a whole other story), Filipe Luís was born in Santa Catarina, Brazil, and though he did consider representing Poland at international level later on, Brazil was where he felt at home. After all, his upbringing had been traditionally Brazilian and after initially finding a place at a futsal club, he would eventually end up about two hours away from home when signing for Figueirense, who, at the time, could only afford food and lodging at the club's residence without any remuneration. It would prove to be a tough period, but it was in the youth academy there that Filipe Luís's career trajectory drastically changed because, for the first time, he was played at left-back. His mercurial dribbling skills had meant that he had joined as an attacking midfielder, but when all the left-backs were unavailable for a training session, the naturally left-footed player was made to fill in the spot (add another one to Carragher's list). He was just 17 at the time and, within a couple of years, he found himself at Ajax.

It was an uncomfortable transition into European football, however, and despite training with the likes of Wesley Sneijder and Rafael van der Vaart in the academy while learning about the tactical side of the game, Filipe Luís struggled off the pitch. The club had placed with him with a Dutch host family to settle in, but having become used to living alone by then, the Brazilian was out of there within a week and moved into his own apartment. Far away from home and faced with a language and culture that he did not understand, the defender spent most of his time drinking and had begun to go astray. His father eventually set him back on track though and following a year at Ajax, where he never featured for the first team, he moved to Uruguayan side Rentistas before being loaned out immediately to the B team at Real Madrid.

He was now more mature and ended up having a good season in Spain, playing the second-highest number of minutes for the side, and might even have been signed permanently had Rentistas lowered their asking fee. He would, however, stay in Spain, on loan at Deportivo La Coruña before signing permanently for them after a couple of seasons. Filipe Luís was starting to catch the eye the more he played and he would even have a minor flirtation with Barcelona, with Pep Guardiola particularly impressed by his talent. Once again though, his club would not budge on transfer fees and he would be denied a promising move. More bad luck would hit and in January 2010 he would suffer an awful leg twist that kept him out for the majority of the remaining games that season.

The Brazilian recovered very quickly, but Deportivo suddenly had doubts on whether he could hit the same peak that he had before, and were now seemingly willing to offload him for a lower price. In came Atlético with Quique Sánchez Flores, having just won the Europa League that year. However, a disappointing first season from the club as a whole, followed by a disastrous start to the next under Gregorio Manzano, meant that it took over a year before Filipe Luís would begin to find his feet at the top level under Simeone. It was an unlikely but perfect match, and the left-back would flourish, winning a trophy in each of their three seasons together.

Just after the famous La Liga win, however, the Brazilian would depart for Chelsea in search of a new challenge. His wish was to come true and Filipe Luís would be challenged throughout that season both by his manager, José Mourinho, and César Azpilicueta, his direct competition for the spot. It was not one that he would win though, and after just a year (which was still successful with a Premier League and League Cup double), he would re-join Atlético, with Simeone even having messaged the defender asking him to return. 'He knew every centimetre of my brain,' Filipe Luís says, explaining how it was only ever Simeone that got the best out of him as he went on to make 333 appearances in total (over both stints) for *Los Rojiblancos,* before eventually departing for good back to Brazil with Flamengo.

Despite not having retired yet at the time of this book, he too has already taken strides towards coaching and, much like the others before, has his eyes set on a possible return to Atlético. Having lost the Champions League Final twice, he says that he has unfinished business and would love to get his hands on that elusive trophy. His playing days at the side would be remembered fondly after his rough start and in his own words, the transition was quick.

'I was a left-back lacking confidence in December and the best in the world in January. One month.'

From the first moment that he linked up with Simeone until the very last, Filipe Luís would stay right at the top.

* * *

Yannick Carrasco

One of the most creative and dominant players in Atlético's current squad, Yannick Carrasco's affection for *Los Rojiblancos* started way back as a kid after a relative gifted him and his brother a kit. This was all the way across in Belgium, in Vilvoorde where Carrasco was born, but for the dreamy-eyed child not everything was pretty. His father had left the family when he was still very young, leaving his mother to raise him and his brother, and her two youngest children, all on her own. It is from her that he gets his Spanish roots, and even though he initially debuted with the name Yannick

Ferreira-Carrasco, he would drop his father's name shortly afterwards.

He attributes his success to those early days with his mother, but at the age of just 11, Carrasco would move out of his neighbourhood to pursue his footballing dream. It was an incredibly huge step at such a young age, but as people would find out, he was mature beyond his years. Arriving at Genk as a street player who had spent most of his time in the park learning his silky-smooth skills, Carrasco was faced with a totally new environment, one where he did not even understand the language. Back home his family had spoken Flemish, and he found it difficult to communicate and adapt to living with his host family. Still, his belief was unwavering and, in a famed academy that had nurtured the likes of Kevin De Bruyne and Thibaut Courtois, Carrasco began to find his feet.

Such was his versatility that at the time, the Belgian could play all across the attack and even use either foot, with his coaches stating that all they had to do was refine his game and iron out a few issues. The boy himself was sure of his ability and loved having the ball at his feet and, by the age of 17, he had Spanish and French clubs vying for his signature. He would move to the French Ligue 2 in 2010 with Monaco, and the next five years would see him slowly make it to

Europe's biggest stage. Initially starting in the academy, Carrasco's talent was evident and within a couple of years he was in the first team, helping the side win promotion in his first full campaign.

Large investments were made and there were doubts over Carrasco's ability to perform at the top level, but the manager at the time, Claudio Ranieri, was impressed and rewarded him with appearances in Ligue 1. He was relatively unknown before his debut, but with each passing game he was staking a claim to be the best player in the side, which was quickly gaining fame across Europe. By 2014, Monaco had made it to the Champions League with Carrasco himself scoring a crucial tie-winning goal at Arsenal to push his side past the round of 16, and it was clear that their brightest talents were soon to be taken away from them.

It would not take long either, and in the summer of 2015, Carrasco arrived in Madrid. Despite an initial settling-in period, the Belgian quickly had the fans chanting his name, capturing them with his grace and skill on the pitch. At the end of that first season, he would even score in the Champions League final against Real, only increasing his popularity among supporters and catching the eyes of many around the world. He would have an excellent start to the 2016/17 season as well, but unfortunately, the hot streak would not turn into anything consistent, especially in the following campaign. Carrasco could dominate some games but become nearly invisible in others and this slightly frustrated the Atlético faithful who could see the talent, but not always reap the benefits. Simeone seemed to lose confidence as well and he was no longer starting as often, with rumours of a falling out that the manager was quick to deny.

A surprise was on the cards though, and arguably at his peak at the age of 25, Carrasco would leave Europe entirely and move to China, signing with Dalian Yifang (now Dalian Professional), a club owned by the Dalian Wanda group, who had a stake in Atlético themselves. The move came out of the blue, and while Carrasco stated that he needed a change of scene away from the spotlight, he still kept himself in the European scene, having made himself a crucial member of the Belgian national team by that time. By December 2019, however, the Covid-19 pandemic had already begun in China and over the next few months it would spread to the rest of the world, with football being halted all around. Having had his season stopped early, Carrasco had already signed back on loan for Atlético in the January 2020 window to continue playing, but with the Spanish authorities going on to suspend their league shortly after, he was again without a game to play, but at least he was back in Madrid.

With the resumption of football later that year, Atlético would then make his signing permanent in September 2020 and there was no doubt that Carrasco had now come back an even more mature player. All this time, he had been a winger, but with Simeone's 5-3-2 he found himself as the perfect candidate for the 'defensive winger' role, making the position his own and leading Atlético to their second league title under Simeone, scoring crucial goals against rivals Barcelona and towards the end of the season as the side battled to keep hold of top spot. The Belgian was back where he belonged, at the pinnacle of European football, and despite an injury-hit 2021/22 season he remains a crucial part of this Atlético side.

Aged just 28 at time of writing, Carrasco has already come a long way, and only time will tell how much more he can achieve.

* * *

Kieran Trippier

Very rarely do English players travel abroad, let alone to Spain, to play their football. In fact, only 20 Englishmen have ever moved to the Spanish top flight and just a fifth of those, a grand total of four, have managed to lay their hands on the league title: David Beckham, Steve McManaman, Laurie Cunningham and, finally, the only full-back on the list, Kieran Trippier. How he got there, though, is yet another fascinating story.

Born in Bury, England, Trippier grew up in a household full of Manchester United fans, watching the Neville brothers, Gary and Phil, who were from just down the road and playing for his favourite club. Maybe he did want to grow up being a Gary Neville, and after kicking the ball around in the garden with his brothers, Trippier joined Blackburn Rovers at the age of eight and even trained with United as well. However, a year later, he would decide to join his friends in moving across town to train with Manchester City instead. Envisioning himself taking free kicks like David Beckham as he grew up, Trippier stayed in the blue half of Manchester until he was 21, with a couple of loan stints at Barnsley at the end, before he moved initially on loan to Burnley in 2011.

It is there that he would link up with Eddie Howe for the first time, playing every week, and when breaking into the XI at City proved to be difficult, he would make his move permanent in 2012. His first season would end well, with Trippier going on to win the Burnley Player of the Year award, and with the arrival of Sean Dyche as manager he would only get better. He was now far more defensively solid and would be named in the Championship PFA Team of the Year for consecutive seasons before sealing promotion to the Premier League in 2013/14.

Burnley would go straight back down and, while they would bounce back up immediately, Trippier had already had a taste of the top flight and stayed on in the Premier League, with Tottenham signing him up. Mauricio Pochettino was the manager then and Kyle Walker's consistent performances meant that it took a while for Trippier to firmly become the first-choice right-back. He would get good chances when Walker was faced with injury during 2016/17 and, when the latter left for Manchester City at the end of the season, Trippier would continue to get game time.

All this would earn him a first call-up to the England squad for the 2018 FIFA World Cup qualifiers, but the defender is remembered more for his exploits during the World Cup itself. Trippier would consistently create chances from right-back and prompt comparisons with Beckham owing to his set-piece delivery, even scoring a crucial free kick to give England the lead in the semi-final against Croatia. His side would eventually lose 2-1, but Trippier broke records again, ending a run of 12 years without the nation scoring a direct free kick at a World Cup, while simultaneously becoming only the third Englishman to have scored in the semi-finals of the tournament after Sir Bobby Charlton and Gary Lineker. He would eventually make it to the Euro 2020 tournament as well, the final of which England would lose on penalties, but that period in 2018 was certainly the right-back's purple patch.

Trippier did start to fade away in the season after this, hampered by injuries, but he would still play for Spurs in the 2019 Champions League final defeat to Liverpool. Rumours circulated that chairman Daniel Levy was offering him to other clubs by the end of the season and, after 114 appearances for Tottenham, he left England behind and moved to Atlético in search of a different challenge. The move did raise a few eyebrows, with the defender being Atlético's first English player in 95 years, and Trippier himself could not speak a word of Spanish, but he settled in exceptionally well, establishing himself as a key member of the squad. Communication was seemingly not a problem and Simeone, the man who Trippier referred to as 'mister', would work individually with the defender and even message him when he was in bed to talk about football.

After building on the 2019/20 campaign, Trippier and Atlético kicked off 2020/21 in outstanding form, stretching their lead at the top to double digits at one point. However, he would be slapped with a ten-week ban following a breach of the English FA's betting regulations concerning private messages regarding his transfer, and despite the defender and his club proclaiming his innocence and appealing the decision to FIFA, the punishment stuck. Atlético started losing ground and, by the time Trippier returned, it was a frantic finish to the line. 'I felt more hurt because I felt it was my fault,' he said, but fortunately for him and Atlético, they managed to bring the title home. By now, Trippier was much loved by all the *Colchoneros*, and he had the first trophy of his career at the age of 30.

Trippier was the perfect right-back for Simeone's side, complementing Carrasco down the other end and using his versatility to shift from wing-back to full-back and keep the team ticking. His absence only highlighted his importance to that title-winning side and he would total 83 appearances for *Los Rojiblancos* over two and a half years, eventually moving back to England with Newcastle United in January 2022, a decision that he put down to his family and wanting to be closer to home. He was the first signing of Newcastle's new Saudi-led era.

Under Simeone, though, Trippier played some of his best football and showed the world that he was nowhere near the finished article some people had claimed him to be. He had achieved what he wanted and had sparked his career back to life, leaving the Atlético faithful with a gift of the league title.

* * *

Despite a change in formation seeing a complete revamp of the full-back role, turning them into wing-backs by definition, Simeone's emphasis on the position never changed. These needed to be players he could trust, who could provide crucial contributions in defence and in attack and, most of all, who could adapt to everything that was thrown at them. As much as Simeone likes solidity, he also desires flexibility, and for this the full-backs are crucial.

Maybe not everyone wants to be a Gary Neville, but Simeone needs his Gary Nevilles. To him, the full-back position is almost like the skeleton upon which the flesh takes shape, for whatever the figure it is that these defenders have outlined, the team fills it to complete the entire structure.

Patrolling down the sides of the Atlético Madrid pitch, far before the modern era truly understood their worth, Simeone put the full-backs at the centre of all his ideas.

7

Great Wall of Madrid: Centre-Backs

'The weak don't interest me'

FOOTBALL IS a fairly simple game. For the most part, the rules are fairly straightforward and in order to win all you have to do is score at least one more goal than your opponent. Agreed, this is easier said than done, but that is all it takes, just one goal. On the flip side, however, if you concede a goal more than you have scored, you leave the game empty-handed. There is hardly ever a prize for just turning up and, once again, it all boils down to just a single goal.

Depending on the end at which the ball goes in, one solitary goal can be the difference between winners and losers on the day, and adding up the games it could even be the difference between surviving relegation or winning a championship. Of course, this is a largely simplified version of the sport itself, ignoring the financial power of clubs, the qualities of the players and any tactics involved, but at the end of the day, it only takes one goal to be the difference.

This then leads us to an interesting question, at which end is the goal more significant? The great Sir Alex Ferguson famously said that 'attack wins you games, defence wins you titles', but in 2017, Sky Sports reporter Adam Smith did a bit of digging to find out if this was indeed true. He would find out that, since the 1995/96 Premier League season (the first after the competition had been cut to 20 teams), the champions have had an average ranking of 1.4 for goals scored but only an average rank of 2.4 for goals conceded, meaning that they have generally outscored their competition on the way to the title. Moreover, out of the 22 teams that had won the league up until that point, 14 had the strongest attack, with only nine having the best defence in that period (not all teams had the best attack or defence, and some had both).

This firmly puts the ball in the opposition net, but could there be even more to this? For the sake of argument, let us consider a different scenario, taking a team at the very beginning of the season. Excluding all the cups and taking only the league into account, to ensure that each game arrives at some result at the end of 90 minutes, we shall go over two hypothetical paths which the season could go down. The first way would be that the side scores at least one goal a match, but can concede any number of goals, varying from game to game. In this case, the attack is firing consistently while the defence remains inconsistent. The second path would be the inverse, and we shall imagine that the team does not concede in a single game, but the number of goals it scores varies every week. The defence is now consistent and the attack is inconsistent.

While there are then many permutations and combinations within each situation itself, if we look at it as a whole, we get two contrasting seasons. With a consistent attack, we increase the chances of winning with the goals themselves, but at the same time, are open to virtually any possible result, win, lose, or draw. With a consistent defence, however, we eliminate one result entirely as without conceding a goal, it is not possible to lose a game. You may draw some where the attack fails, but when they do score, you are guaranteed a win. The attack is still key here since you cannot hope to win the league just by drawing every game, but suddenly the defence becomes far more important simply to avoid defeat.

Of course, we do admit that this argument is based on highly improbable situations and offers far less insight, if any at all, compared to Smith's factual findings, but it does certainly put things into perspective regarding how managers might view a season. Ideally, they would like to defend and attack to equally high levels, but some are obviously far more adventurous while others make no secret of their conservative nature. As for Diego Simeone, it is clear which half of the pitch he prefers.

Cholo, despite his seemingly brash and loud facade, is a cautious man, meticulous in all that he does. To him, everything is an intricate process, one that needs to be followed carefully and only then can success be attained. In fact, his whole match routine is a process as well. As Guilherme Siqueira, the left-back who played for Atlético between 2014 to 2017, revealed in an interview once he had left, Simeone always sat at the same spot, always had the same list of music playing on the bus and changing room and, after the warm-up, he would always bounce the ball on the ground with his hand before making the captain do the same. He would also famously always ask for a square table for his side wherever they went, so that everyone could sit facing everyone else, with no one ever too far away. You could go as far as calling him superstitious, and while that may be true, he certainly left nothing to chance.

And for someone so diligent with their pre-match routine, you can bet that he was not leaving the game to chance either. Everyone wants to win, and to say that

Simeone wanted it more would be a cliche, even though it might be an apt one. However, he understood that winning a game came down to the individual moments, much like the single goal at either end that we saw earlier. If you picked the right moments and executed well enough, the ball was in the opposition's net and the points were in your bag. If you missed these moments, as does happen at times, then you might find the ball in your own net, the solitary goal sealing victory for the opponent.

This second situation, however, was not one that he was willing to take a chance on.

Just as much as Simeone likes winning, he hates losing, and to him the first step on the way to winning was simply not to lose. However absurd this might sound, we have already seen with our earlier argument that avoiding defeat and searching for victory can in fact be two different things, and Simeone understood how important it was not to concede a goal in order to completely remove, or at least significantly lessen, the possibility of a loss. Like the stubborn kid at the playground taking their ball back home when they are losing, if he could not win, no one could.

For a long time, there would be a cliche about Simeone's Atlético, that each game would follow the same gruesome process. The opposition would dominate possession, play the ball out wide, cross the ball in, and Atlético's centre-backs would clear. The opposition would regain possession, pass the ball out wide, play the ball into the middle, and, well, you get the idea. Eventually the ball would fall to an Atlético player, or the centre-back may find the ball at his feet, and within the next few seconds they would be at the other end and one of the attackers would have slotted the ball into the net: 1-0 to Atlético.

Often criticised for playing for a draw, Simeone's style of play is not exactly one that plays for a point but rather one that looks to prevent the opposition from taking three. Atlético conceded goals far too easily and were letting games slip past them when Simeone first walked in, and from that point onwards he decided that there needed to be a change. He needed a team that was capable of repelling even the most potent attacks, and a defence that not only suffered themselves, but piled the suffering on to the opposition as well. And at the heart of this suffering, he needed his centre-backs.

While most people come away stating that Atlético are hard to play against, fewer people understand exactly how hard it is to play in such a system. The unwavering focus and determination that Simeone demands requires large amounts of effort all throughout the game and only the strongest of players in terms of mentality could go through this process every game and every week. While all the players knows their roles, the buck eventually stops with the centre-backs, considering that they are the final piece of this outfield jigsaw that has to block off everything that dares enter the penalty box. Not for one second can they switch off, and not for one second can they think of giving anything less than 100 per cent. For a team like Simeone's Atlético, the centre-backs simply can not be weak.

Despite painting the picture of a bloodied mercenary, there is of course more to this than just last-ditch defending and unending bravery or aggressiveness and, in this chapter, we shall dive deeper into one of the most important positions in Simeone's system that laid the groundwork for years of success to follow.

While the centre-back position has also undergone changes over the years, we shall start off with their role in the initial 4-4-2 formation, before understanding how they have gone on to evolve. Following on nicely from the previous chapter on the full-backs, Figure 35 highlights how the centre-backs functioned in the extremely narrow back line structure. Including the full-backs, the four defenders had been nearly equidistant from each other and held a flat line when the ball was slightly further away, but when the opposition progressed closer down the flanks, it was the job of the

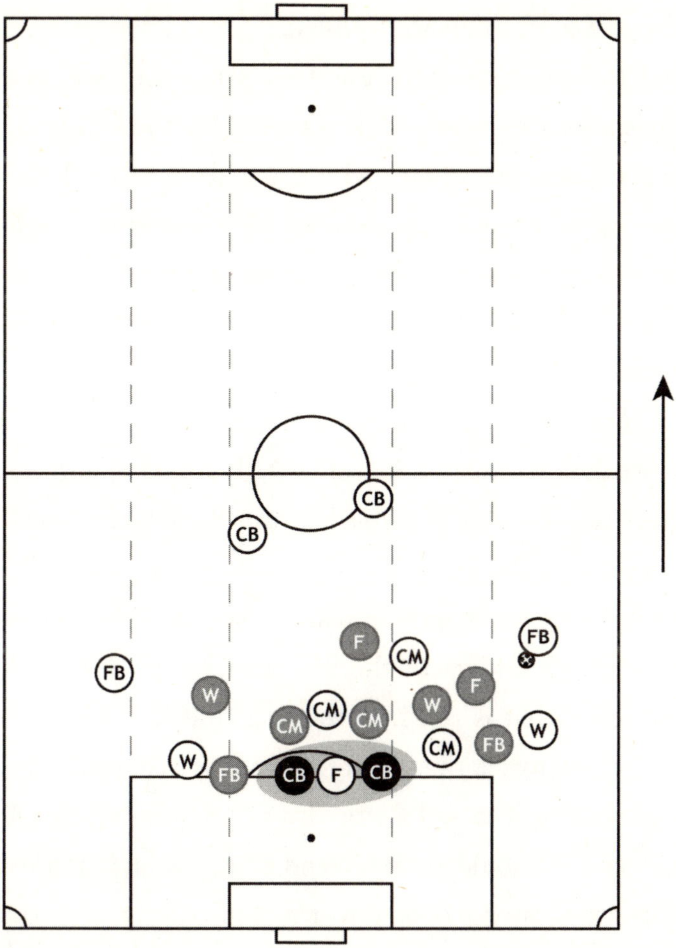

Fig. 35 *Narrow centre-backs minimising space between them*

full-back to step out and engage. It is here that the role of the centre-back starts to take prominence.

In most back lines, once the full-back gets drawn out wide it would be the duty of the closest centre-back to shift across and cover the space behind them with the rest of the defence following suit. However, with Atlético we have seen how this is not the case, and instead of the centre-back covering for the full-back, it is usually the winger who drops deep to track any opposition run into the channel. While neither is right or wrong, Simeone opts for the second method as his focus is to primarily keep the centre-backs in the middle of the box.

With all of his prior tactics forcing opponents towards the flanks, *Cholo* effectively limits opposition attacks to crosses or cutbacks from the wider areas, if not for long shots from outside the box. As a result, the majority of his defensive plan is based on the notion that his defenders in the box are able to deal with anything that is put into the area and it is then not surprising to see that most of Simeone's centre-backs, especially in the 4-4-2 era, are tall, strong and good in the air. Should these defenders not be able to deal with crosses or passes into the box consistently, the entire basis of the plan can come apart very quickly since Atlético would end up forcing the opposition to exploit their weakness.

Moreover, if the Atlético centre-back is not in the optimal position to deal with any passes into the box, it renders his profile useless as the system is not making the best use of his attributes. This scenario would occur in a case where the centre-back is the one tasked with covering for the full-back, as he would get drawn out to the channels and be much wider than he needs to be in order to deal with potential crosses. His fellow centre-back would also need to shift across to minimise the space between them and prevent opponents from exploiting it, and he too could end up being in a suboptimal position or simply having to deal with too many opponents on his own.

Hence, Simeone keeps his centre-backs in the manner shown in Figure 35, where not only are they staying central and covering any crosses or passes into the middle of the box, but they are also suffocating the forward in between them to prevent any runs in that space since these could easily lead to excellent chances if not tracked properly. This now proves to be an effective setup that suits the style of defence that *Cholo* has opted for, but what is even more interesting is that this narrow centre-back unit shows its usefulness even outside a settled low block.

One of the most important parts of the centre-back's game is the manner in which they defend in transition as it involves quick decision-making and the covering of a large amount of space. Being a side that likes to attack in transition, Atlético know just how crucial the centre-backs are in preventing such counter attacks, and

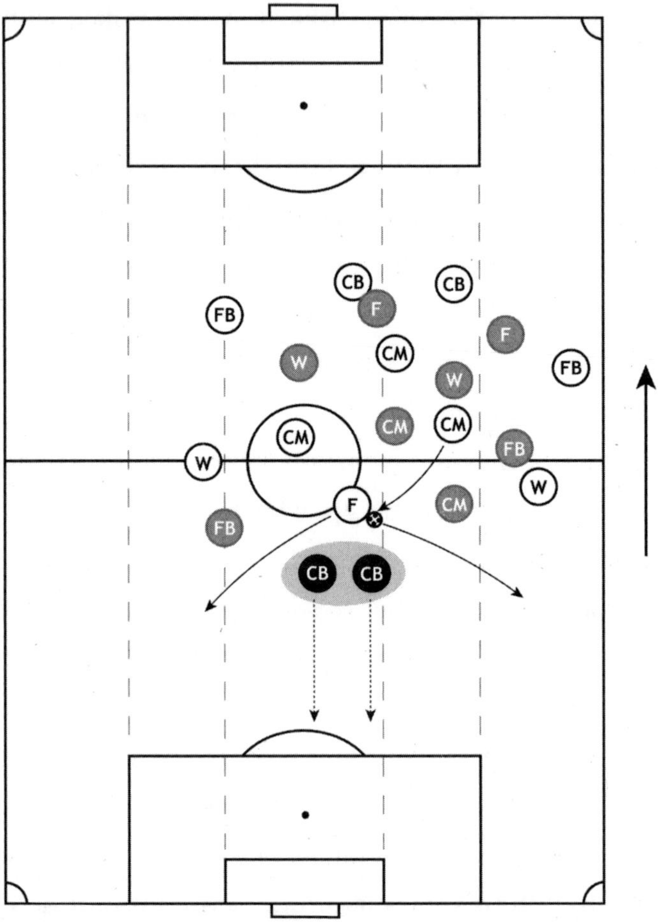

***Fig. 36** Centre-backs maintaining narrow structure as they drop deeper in transitions*

hence it is important that they are given the right set of instructions in order to thwart transitions. Looking at Figure 36, we can visualise these instructions and, interestingly, we see some similarities to the earlier structure as well.

The first thing that we notice is the fact that the centre-backs maintain their extremely narrow shape in the middle of the pitch even when faced with transitions. Usually, considering that their team-mates are caught higher up the pitch and hence leaving them with the entire width to cover, centre-backs maintain some distance between each other to ensure that they are not leaving too much space towards the flanks which opponents can look to get into and exploit. As for Atlético, however, the centre-backs stay close to each other and form their own unit down the middle.

So how exactly does this help? Well, the obvious benefit of this unit is that the opposition cannot drive through the middle and are forced to wait for support down the flanks before playing the ball out wide. This has always been the basis of Simeone's tactics as well and, in this case, it buys time for the other defenders to drop back in to deal with any balls played back in from the wider areas. The ball carrier cannot simply drive at either centre-back and attempt to take him on either since it would always end up being a two-v-one in favour of the centre-backs, and with this option made difficult, a pass out wide would be the straightforward option.

There is no denying that a pass out wide can still be dangerous, especially when afforded the space in transition, but this is where the next benefit of this structure comes into play. If we consider a scenario where the centre-backs are relatively spaced apart and looking to cover some width as well, then as the ball carrier drives centrally, the centre-backs need to make movements from out to in, or in other words, they need to engage the ball carrier starting from their wider positions. In this case, the ball carrier can use this to his advantage by drawing the centre-backs closer before laying the ball off out wide, meaning that the centre-back has now committed centrally and cannot recover quickly enough to deal with the wide player.

The narrow structure serves to mitigate this, and instead of an out-to-in movement, the centre-backs are engaging or stalling the ball carrier with their starting positioning itself before moving from in to out to engage the wide player once the pass is played. The setup allows for a more effective and natural movement to deal with this wider pass should it be played and therefore it allows for an effective means of at least stalling opponents until backup arrives.

But what happens when the opposition then looks to specifically exploit the spaces around the centre-backs instead? For this, we will turn our attention to Figure 37 on the next page.

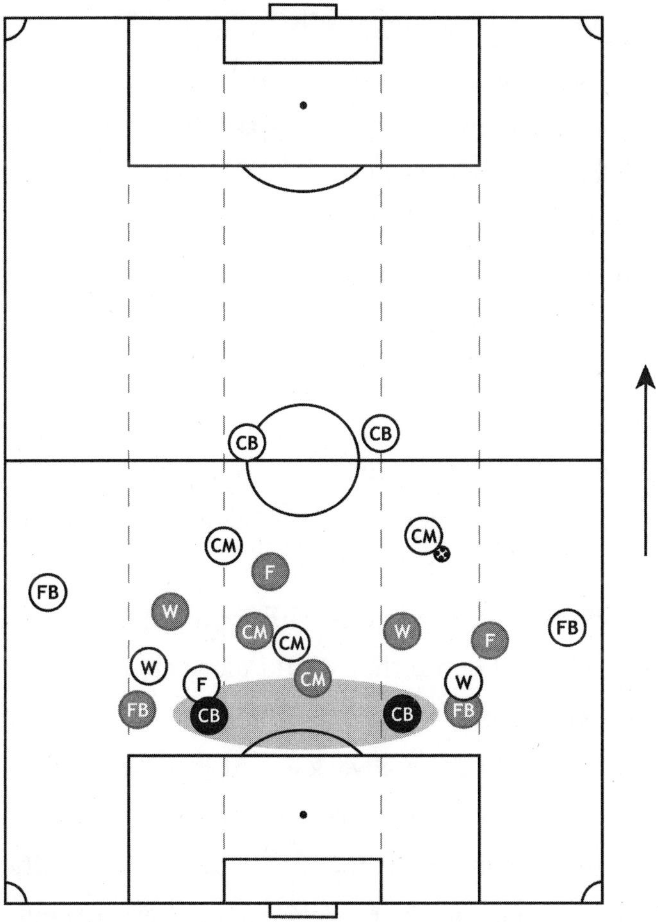

***Fig. 37** Centre-backs wider to defend half-spaces*

Considering the fact that the Atlético centre-backs are often positioned close to each other to block out a forward, some teams then looked to attack the channels by making use of the space between the centre-backs and full-backs when the ball went out to the wide areas. Their plan would revolve around quick passing combinations to attack this space before a winger could drop in and theoretically find space in between the defenders. However, here is where the awareness of the centre-backs comes into play.

In order to maximise their chances of attacking the channels, opponents would either push their forwards into the half-spaces (left half-space in Figure 37) or have their forwards drop into midfield in order to engage them and prevent them from dropping to fill in gaps in the defence. When this happens, a narrow structure only results in the centre-backs defending relatively unthreatened space while opening up gaps on either side, and hence they would move closer to their respective full-backs as shown in Figure 37.

This way, Atlético always had at least two players in the channels to ensure that they were not overloaded there and, instead of the full-back tracking the opposition's winger, their own winger or forward could do so instead. If ever the opposition did manage to cross the ball in, Simeone's side could simply move in to fill the central space either with the centre-backs moving back to their narrow shape or by having a midfielder drop into the space instead. This tactic worked wonders against newly crowned Champions League winners Chelsea in the 2012 UEFA Super

Cup, where Atlético kept their opponents at bay on their way to a 4-1 victory.

Chelsea had attempted to get the likes of Juan Mata, Eden Hazard and Ramires into the channels and exploit the spaces between the centre-backs and full-backs, first attempting to stretch the back line in order to do so. However, with their forward – and ex-Atlético man – Fernando Torres Fernando Torres often having to drop deeper or move into the channels himself, *Los Rojiblancos*' back line did not find it especially difficult to stretch across by ditching their narrow centre-back structure in favour of a wider spacing between the two central defenders. Moreover, in this case, the defensive-minded Mario Suárez started in midfield, often dropping into the back line to fill in the space between the centre-backs if needed.

Despite having a narrow and rigid centre-back structure, Atlético could very easily change it up and adapt to the tactics of the opposition. Awareness plays a key role in this process of adaptation as well, since a poorly tracked forward could easily slip into the space between the centre-backs and find himself unmarked. Of course, the shift in formation to use the deeper midfielder can cover this and, noticeably, this is similar to the one that we had seen earlier in the chapter on the full-backs. Additionally, as the years went by, we have seen how this midfielder becomes the 'destroyer' that easily falls into the back line to create a makeshift back five as well. This splitting of the centre-backs then takes us to the next phase of their role, which sees them having to defend more than just the central areas and repel crosses.

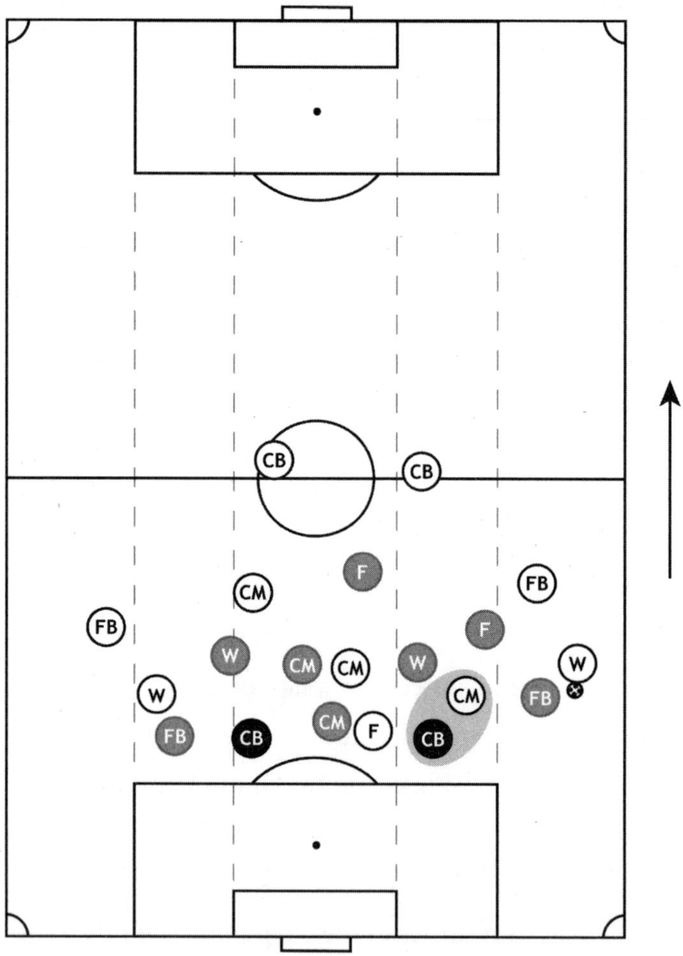

Fig. 38 Centre-back covers for full-back with a deeper midfielder ('destroyer') dropping into the back line

As teams started developing better ways to break down a low block, most notably by packing the last line of defence, Simeone understood that a narrow centre-back pairing could quickly come undone even with the slightest of errors. Opponents had started to attack the channels more often and most top sides around Europe were not simply crossing the ball into the box but rather using intricate passing combinations to slice through defences, leading to Atlético's back line having to spread across just as we had explained in the previous chapter. Given the tempo which opponents were looking to play at, the winger could not always be tasked with tracking runs either, and hence it only made sense that the centre-backs took on this responsibility.

This newer role is certainly in stark contrast to their previous one and, looking at Figure 38, we see how the right centre-back is now positioned to track the run of the opposition central midfielder. Apart from this, we can also see how the spacing between the two centre-backs and the deeper midfielder covering between them allows the side to defend more space at the back, instead of having just the two players to deal with any central crosses or passes as we saw earlier.

While this setup would eventually lead to the 5-3-2 formation, where the deeper midfielder becomes another centre-back, it also signalled a clear change in how Simeone had started viewing his centre-backs. Having first used them as a reactive force that would rather hold their position and wait for the ball to be played towards them before dealing with it, they were now being used increasingly as defenders with more freedom to step out and engage, taking on a more proactive role at the back. They had the flexibility of stepping out and covering a larger area, tracking opponents that might drift in position and, in general, they were not as rooted to the middle as they had been before.

Interestingly, their positional profile itself did not change much, with Simeone still largely preferring centre-backs who were tall, physical and good in the air, but along with this, agility and speed over distance were also becoming more prominent attributes. However, among all these, one major attribute of the centre-backs that often went unnoticed, though it would later come to the fore, would be their passing. Often lauded for their contributions in scoring from set pieces, especially in their first title-winning campaign, the Atlético centre-backs were involved in creating attacks just as much as they were involved in finishing them off.

For a team always looking for quick and direct football, the fastest method of getting the ball forwards was to bypass the entire midfield, playing it long from defence into the attackers. Of course, this is ignoring goal kicks and, despite not usually being attributed with this, such long passing would become a feature of the Atlético centre-backs who were certainly no less effective on the ball than they were off it.

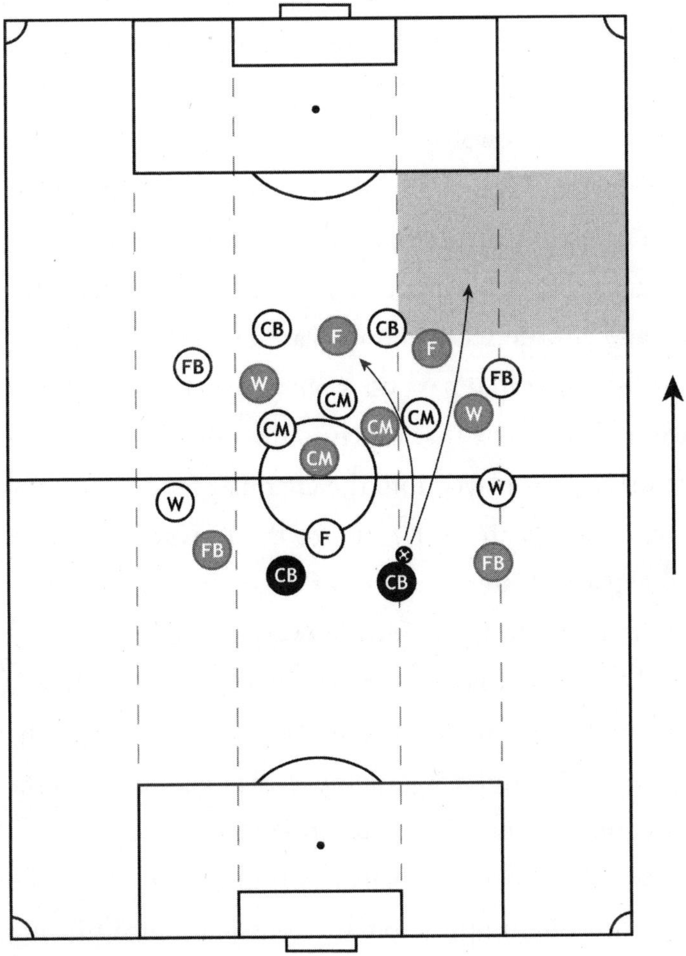

Fig. 39 *Centre-backs progressing the ball to start attacks*

Ball progression would resemble 'route-one' football, as it would come to be known in the English game, wherein this exact term is used when centre-backs go long to a target man who can bring the ball down or lay it off to a team-mate, completely bypassing the build-up phase. Atlético's specific way of progression would slightly differ, as while they did aim for a target up front, what they were also trying to do was to hit the right spaces as well.

Taking Figure 39, we see that the centre-back in possession of the ball now has two main passing options. His team-mates ahead of him have bunched up and crowded the central areas to win the second ball in case the initial pass does not succeed, and this pass can either be one that is played directly to the forward or one that is played into the channels for a forward to chase. While the intricacies of the forward's role will be explained later, the basis of these passes all revolved around the same thing, which was territorial gain.

In this manner, the centre-backs are almost like quarterbacks in American football, initiating the forward play and using their passes to gain yards in the direction of the opposition goal. Simeone's aim was always clear, to get the ball away from their own net and push it as high up the pitch as possible, since this not only gave them something to feed on in attack, but it also minimised their chances of conceding at the same time. These were more than just glorified clearances though, and with the minimal possession that they had, each pass was all the more valuable.

As a result, Atlético's centre-backs needed to be good passers and effectively break lines with their passing in order to get the ball in to the attackers. We have seen that the first method involves finding the target man, with the centre-backs often chipping or lobbing the ball up to the forward, who can then lay the ball off to his supporting players before running in behind to receive. As for the second pass, it requires even more precision to break all the lines ahead of the centre-back, playing the ball into the channels for the forward to chase and receive in behind. Both methods would turn out to be primary outlets of attack, and while opponents could look to defend against this method of progression, what made it trickier was the fact that Atlético were operating so much narrower than most other teams, meaning that they could immediately press and close down their opposition should the pass not succeed.

The centre-backs had now become the unlikely creators, and despite all the talk of them being nothing more than old-fashioned defenders, Simeone had clearly developed in them attributes more befitting of the modern era. Eventually, with the shift to the 5-3-2, the addition of another centre-back would bring about a total shift in the way Atlético wanted to play out from the back and, with greater freedom on the ball, each centre-back could display these attributes more consistently.

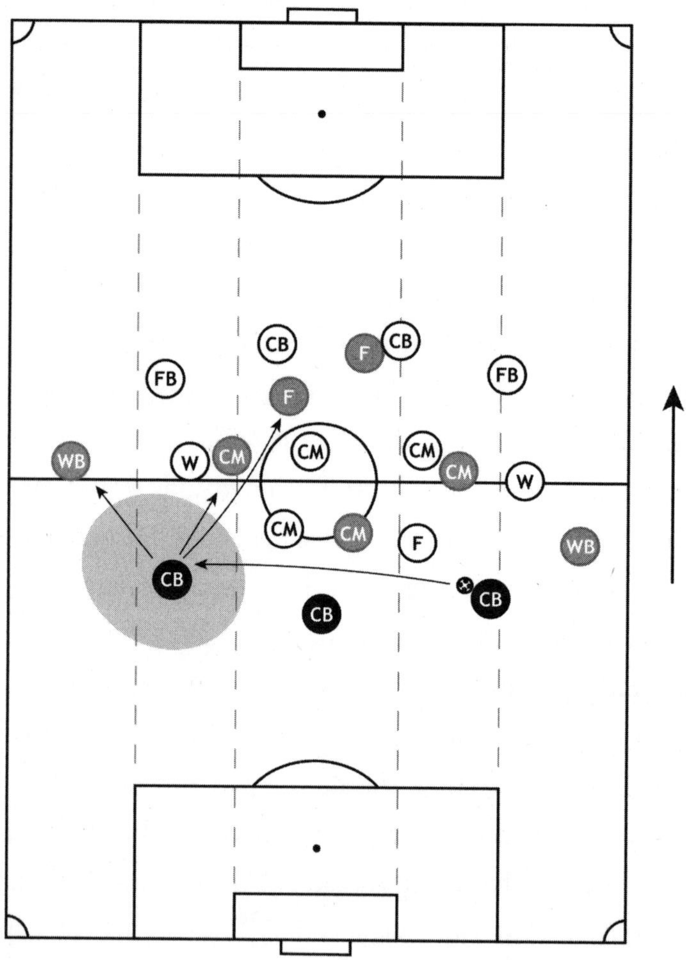

Fig. 40 *Wide centre-backs in a back three having more freedom in possession*

One of the very first things that we notice when attempting to analyse the three centre-back setup is the fact that the back line is now far more spread out in possession. Naturally, due to the addition of a centre-back, the three players can spread across a larger area as compared to the two centre-back system that we saw earlier and, while this allows the wing-backs to get higher, it also allows each centre-back far more time and space on the ball. By examining Figure 40, we will see just how this helps Atlético in the build-up.

Usually, when teams attempt to press with their front line, very rarely do we see any more than two players committing to a central press up front. By this, we mean that, more often than not, only one other player (usually a midfielder) would accompany the forward in stepping up higher through the middle in order to press the opposition centre-backs and cut out passing lanes, while the wingers take the full-backs and the deeper midfielders cut off any other central players. In the context of a back four formation with two centre-backs, this situation is now a two-v-two in the build-up phase, where the centre-backs need to deal with two opposition attackers in order to progress the ball. However, when in a back three as shown in Figure 40, the same situation is a three-v-two in favour of the side in possession.

What this three-v-two does is that it generally prevents opponents from pressing too aggressively with their front line as they cannot effectively cut out every pass from the back. For example, considering that the right-sided Atlético centre-back is in possession at the start of the build-up, the opposition can cover his forward passes to his wing-back or central midfielders, or they can cover his lateral passes to his other centre-backs, but not both. They are doing the former in Figure 40, but should they attempt to step up aggressively and close down the other centre-backs as well, the Atlético central midfielders can easily drift into space to receive, and hence bypass the first line of pressure with just one simple pass. As a result, opponents typically prefer to cut off the forward passes instead, allowing the comparatively unthreatening passes among the centre-backs themselves.

However, these same passes can soon become very dangerous. We mentioned earlier about how the back line is able to spread out more owing to the addition of a centre-back and one of the major benefits of this can be seen when the right centre-back opts for a pass to his left centre-back on the other side. In this case, with the opposition's first line of pressure having moved closer to the right to cut out the options for the right centre-back, the left centre-back finds himself with ample time and space upon receiving the ball, with the opposition quickly looking to shift back across and apply the same pressure.

The pass, of course, travels faster than the movement of the opposition, meaning that there is a window of opportunity present to the left centre-back, where he is afforded the possibility of making multiple passes that are not only threatening, but also fairly simpler to play due to the slightly unsettled shape of the opposition. Moreover, having played around the first line of pressure by receiving in his wider position, the left centre-back can also look to break further lines with his passing and, in this specific case, we shall explore three of his passing options.

Of the three passes, the simplest one available is the pass out to the wing-back who finds himself in plenty of space out wide. We have already seen how by operating with wing-backs, Atlético are able to position their wider players closer to either touchline and not only stretch the opposition but also create space for themselves as well and, due to this, there are usually unmarked passing options down the flanks. By playing this pass, the left centre-back can bypass the opposition's midfield and allow his wing-back to take on the opponent's full-back, effectively starting a quick attack down the wing. Alternatively, the wing-back can also engage in passing combinations and wide rotations in case he does not opt for the direct approach, instead passing it around in attack to find an opening in the defence.

The other two possible passes for the left centre-back are more central ones, with the distance covered by each pass being the only difference. The first of these would be the ball to the central midfielder, who, in this instance, is being tracked by an opposition winger and, similar to the previous pass, this also aims to break through the midfield line of the opposition. This pass is also made more effective owing to the positioning of the wing-back, since the opposition winger has to make a decision on which player to track, and should they get caught being indecisive, then the pass to the central midfielder can very easily penetrate the midfield. Upon receiving, the central midfielder then has the option of turning into space and driving at the opposition as well, taking on the last line of defence and linking up with the forwards or the advancing wing-backs to create chances.

As for the third pass, this is one that is played directly to the forward, meaning that the midfield line is completely bypassed without any additional movement and this too is a ball that is available owing to Atlético's structure. The gaps opened up through the middle are a result of the team looking to stretch their opposition, and with the involvement of a third centre-back, natural passing angles are opened up in order to pierce through these openings and efficiently progress the ball. With the forward finding space between the lines, he can simply drop to receive the pass before turning and taking on the back line, creating a two-v-two against the opposition centre-backs with support arriving as well. The forward can also opt to play with back to goal instead and upon receiving the pass, he can link up with the central midfielders or even play the ball out wide before getting forward himself as an alternative means of progressing the attack.

Each of these passes is effective in its own right and they all result in the same thing, which is effective ball progression. However, with the amount of time and space on offer, it would be a shame if the centre-backs were limited to these passes from deeper positions, and hence Simeone builds on this once again in order to allow his centre-backs to carry the ball forwards as a means of progression as well.

One of the biggest benefits of a three centre-back setup is not just the cover and support that the midfield and forwards have, but it is also the cover and support that each centre-back has himself. Should a centre-back need to step out in a back four, either in possession or out of it, there is only one other centre-back covering

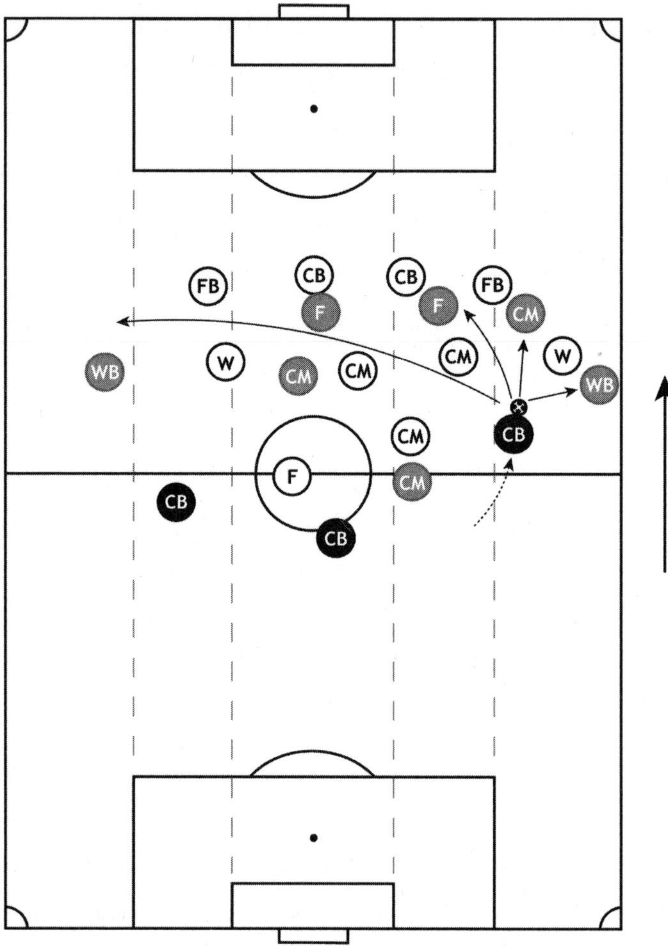

Fig. 41 *Wide centre-back allowed to step out and carry the ball forwards*

the space in behind and ideally a midfielder would have to drop into the back line to offer additional support. In a back three, however, this problem does not arise since the supporting player is already in the back line and should a centre-back step out, there are still two centre-backs (and possibly an extra midfielder) who adequately cover the space in behind, just like they would when in a back four.

This proves to be extremely handy when it comes to progressing the ball and, following on from the methods of progression we saw above, we can now see how the wider centre-backs can create a new dynamic by stepping out as well. Having been naturally offered space towards the side of the opposition's first line of pressure, the Atlético centre-backs can push forwards and carry the ball into midfield, opening up newer passing angles from this advanced position. As we see in Figure 41, the passes to the wing-back, central midfielder and forward all remain, but due to this higher positioning, their exact angles and even their threat level has changed.

While the pass to the wing-back remains the safer option, it is no longer as progressive as it was earlier and is almost a lateral pass now, which helps in maintaining possession down the wide areas as opposed to getting the side forward with limited passes. As for the pass to the central midfielder (we have seen how one darts into the channels), this midfielder is now in a more advanced position almost having joined the front line, meaning he can look to get in behind with the pass or he can simply receive just ahead of the opposition back line, just like a forward might. The pass to the forward itself remains largely similar to the one before, but the reduced distance and change in angle does mean that he too can be played in behind far more easier than in the previous scenario.

In addition to these three basic passes, however, another important pass is opened up, which is the switch from the centre-back to the far-side wing-back. By stepping into midfield, the centre-back has only added to Atlético's numerical superiority down the ball-side of the pitch, meaning that the opposition are more likely to be drawn towards that side in order to add numbers and minimise gaps. When this happens, we have already seen how the wing-back down the far side finds himself in space and, in this specific case, he is an open passing option for the centre-back in possession. Moreover, the centre-back is under minimal pressure as well since the opposition needs to cover his more attacking team-mates, meaning that he has the time and space to accurately play this longer pass as well.

As a result, by simply stepping out from the back line not only does the centre-back make his forward passes more incisive and threatening, but he also opens up other passing angles that add to the attacking options the team possesses, giving them multiple ways to progress the ball forwards. In fact, this would not be all either and, with a simple positional shift, Simeone could flex his versatility once more.

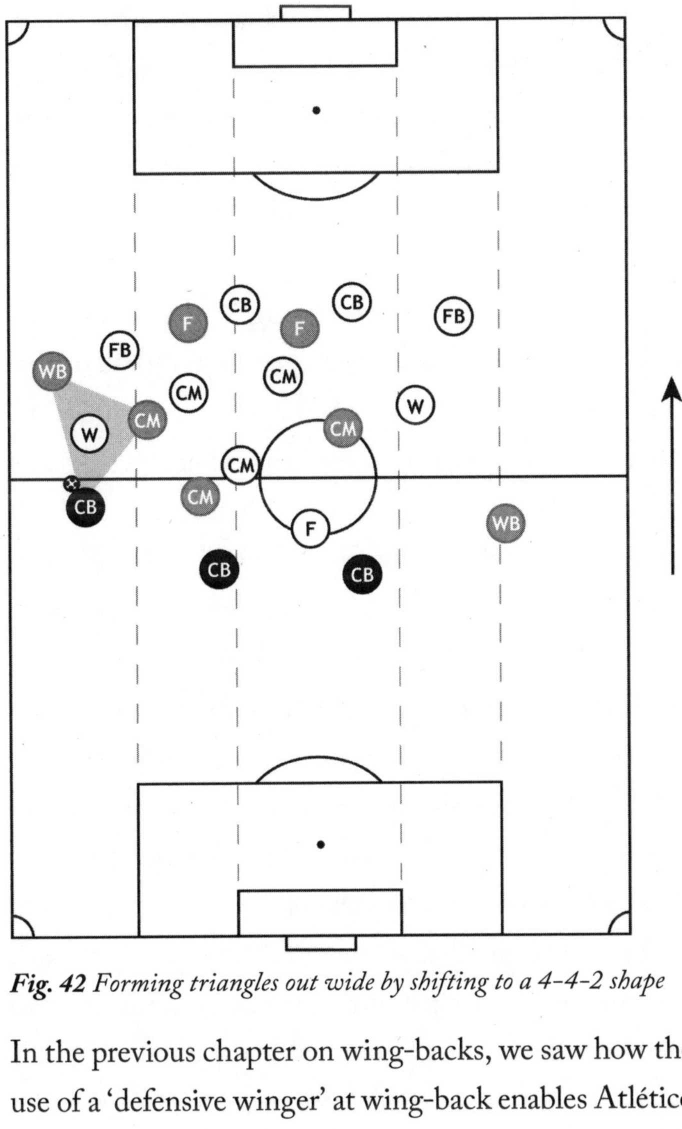

Fig. 42 Forming triangles out wide by shifting to a 4-4-2 shape

In the previous chapter on wing-backs, we saw how the use of a 'defensive winger' at wing-back enables Atlético to comfortably shift between formations both in and out of possession. However, when this player moves out from the back line to join either the midfield or forward line, the back five now becomes a back four, and the centre-back closest to him is now tasked with providing cover down the flanks. Hence, such a shift not only results in the wing-back becoming a more natural winger, but it also sees a wide centre-back take on the role of a full-back in a back four.

This is particularly interesting in possession and, looking at Figure 42, we can see how Atlético have moved to a makeshift 4-4-2 shape when building up from the back, with the left centre-back acting as a left-back in this phase. What this does, apart from allowing the wing-back more attacking freedom, is that it naturally creates a neat passing triangle down the flank, where the wing-back and the centre-back are joined by a central midfielder to form this trio. In general, these kinds of triangles are conducive to quick passing combinations in order to progress the ball and, in this specific case, it also enables Atlético to create their wide overload in possession.

Having formed this triangle, the left centre-back now has two clear passing options to the other two members in the triangle and, while the opposition full-back and central midfielder can move to track them, it is only the opposition winger that is capable of blocking out a pass completely. The math does not add up as one player cannot possibly block out both passes, but another issue is the fact that, even if the winger directly cuts out one passing option, the Atlético centre-back can indirectly play the ball to the same player. For example, should the winger cut out the pass to the wing-back, the centre-back can simply pass the ball to the central midfielder who then has the open passing lane to play the ball in to the wing-back, taking the longer route but eventually reaching the intended player.

This way, progression down the flanks becomes fairly simple and the wing-backs can get much higher up the pitch since the centre-back now acts as the wide player in the build-up. Moreover, even if the opposition commits numbers to the flank to prevent the overload, the centre-back will have the option to switch the ball to the opposite wing-back who can then look to exploit the space on the other side, again allowing for multiple points of attack. The build-up phase has now been massively overhauled compared to the earlier 4-4-2, and perhaps the most important change has been to tweak the player profiles and encourage the centre-backs to showcase their on-the-ball attributes more often. This new setup simply cannot function if the centre-backs are poor with the ball at their feet or do not have the required passing range, and hence it becomes important to have skilful players in this position.

However, do not for one second think that the defence has become any less important, and with an extra centre-back in the back line, you would imagine that Simeone is licking his lips at the prospect of being able to defend more solidly at the back. Having already got some insight into how this works, we will now take a deeper look at some variations that are brought into play by this three centre-back setup.

Naturally, the role of the centre-backs is linked to that of the wing-backs, and hence a lot of what these centre-backs have to do depends on the shifts of the wing-backs that we saw earlier. We have already seen how the addition of an extra centre-back serves the same purpose as a defensive midfielder dropping into the back line, and while we have understood how the central midfielders and wing-backs shift to create various structures, in this section we shall take a closer look into how the centre-backs behave in accordance with these changing shapes.

Starting off with the basic back five in a deeper block, the duties of the three centre-backs are similar to those of the centre-back pairing from before, to defend the central areas and minimise the gaps between them. The obvious difference between the two, however, is

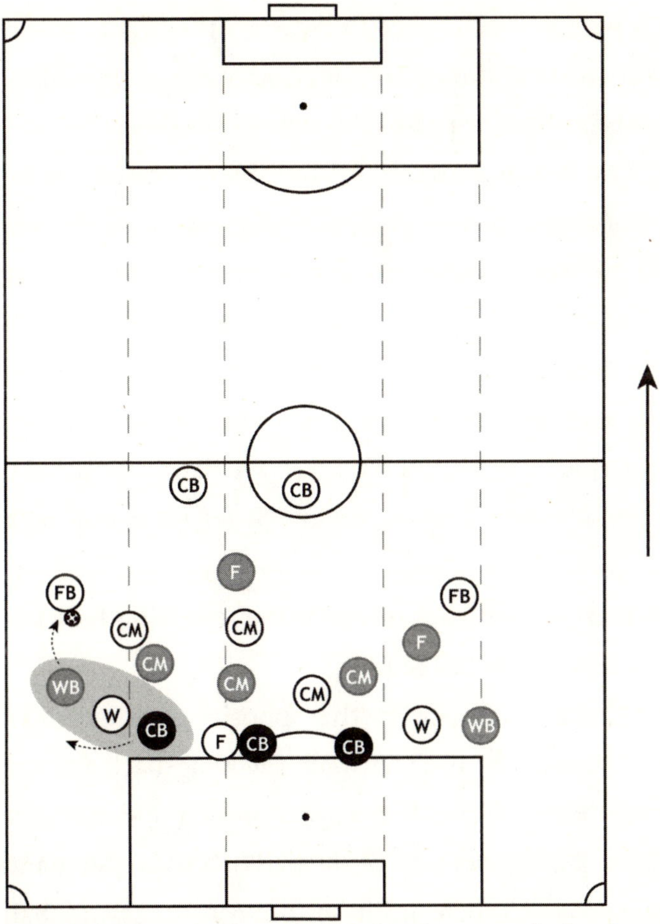

***Fig. 43** Defensive duties and shifts of a centre-back when out of possession*

that with an extra centre-back, there is now a wider distribution of players in this middle portion of the back line while maintaining the smaller spaces between each centre-back. This means that the centre-backs can now comfortably defend the channels as well without having to leave too much space in between them, and it also gives them a numerical superiority when defending against crosses or passes through the middle.

The change in role, however, occurs when attempting to press higher, with the wing-back moving into midfield to leave a makeshift back four, almost like the structure that we had seen in possession, but this time in defence. In this case, the left centre-back needs to operate as a left-back again, and to understand this we shall look at Figure 43. Here, we have considered a situation where Atlético are in a 5-4-1 formation with a forward having dropped into midfield, but with the ball carrying full-back relatively free, the wing-back has to step out and engage him.

When this happens, the opposition winger now finds himself in space between the wing-back and the centre-back, making him a good passing option for his full-back as he can receive the ball down the flank and get into an excellent position to cross or pass the ball towards the middle. The responsibility for preventing this then falls to the left centre-back, who tracks his man out wide as Atlético now start to form a 4-5-1 shape. This does not mean that the attack is stopped, though, as the opposition still have a forward that has crept in between the centre-backs and, after this shift, he finds himself in space in the channels. As a result, the middle centre-back has to shift across along with this man, as does the right-centre-back in order to maintain the right distance, eventually causing a complete shift to the 4-5-1 formation.

While these increased spaces could be exploited fairly easily in such a scenario, the fact that this is something that Atlético are prepared to do means that they are more capable of dealing with it when it occurs. Instead of the side being opened up by opponents that look to draw the wing-back out and stretch the back line, Atlético have already rehearsed such a situation, allowing them to seamlessly carry on with their defence without much fuss. Of course, the centre-backs play a crucial role in this and in essence, regardless of the formation ahead of them, the centre-backs are ready to shift between a back four and back five comfortably, with the wide centre-back having to be especially familiar with defending down the flanks.

This is certainly not an easy task, but it does allow for a lot of variations when done right and, in order to nail this, it is not entirely uncommon for Simeone to play a full-back as one of the wide centre-backs either. The benefits are plenty and most noticeably it allows for a more natural defence of the wide areas when shifting to a back four, while also proving to be useful in the wide build-up as well. Moreover, this player also has the necessary defensive cover offered by the other two centre-backs, meaning that any shortcomings in this regard do not affect Atlético as badly as it might if he was instead played as a centre-back in a back four.

As a result, it once again makes for interesting viewing to see Simeone take players out of their natural positions and field them in seemingly uncomfortable ones, but considering the specific duties assigned to these different roles, it is almost a match made in heaven and not only does it get the best out of the player, it also creates a well-oiled machine that functions to the best of its capability. This is now a unit that consists of a lot of moving parts, in stark contrast to the rigid centre-back pairings of old and along with impeccable judgement and awareness, adaptability and versatility have once again come to the forefront of *Cholo*'s setup.

These are all tactical attributes, but an often-overlooked aspect is also the mentality of these centre-backs as they tirelessly carry out their roles every single week. Despite football being a team game, the onus is on the centre-backs to keep that clean sheet intact and for a side that defends, defends and defends, this is not only physically tiring but mentally draining as well, for most players at least. Try telling this to Simeone's centre-backs, however, and they would probably laugh you off, because if there is one area that they never fall short in it is their mentality. Of course, the same could be said for the entire team, but in the case of these cold-blooded warriors who would become the face of a defensively astute Atlético side, they simply had to be stronger. In every era, in every formation and in every single game, their character could never be faulted.

In this regard, Atlético have seen some truly tenacious characters take their place at the heart of defence, who rightfully warrant a place in this book.

* * *

Diego Godín

'Sometimes a fall helps you to reverse just enough to come back with more momentum,' Godín says in an interview, and for a man who for the entirety of his career, and even his life, would rise above the rest against all odds, there might not be a more fitting quote.

In fact Godín's fighting spirit was to become visible right from the young age of four, when the Uruguayan fell into a river while trying to catch some fish and found himself getting carried away by the waters. Here was a boy who did not know how to swim, but by the time his sister was able to fetch her parents and stage a rescue attempt, he was pulling himself back to shore with nothing other than his raw survival instinct to guide him. Fight and survive: the young child had his motto for life.

Fast forward to the age of 17, two years after leaving his hometown of Rosario behind and relocating to the capital city of Montevideo, Godín was now an attacking midfielder, who, unfortunately, had begun to see his footballing dreams crashing down before his eyes. The year was 2003 and Defensor Sporting simply did not think he was good enough, sending him packing just a few weeks before the new season had been set to begin.

Godín almost gave up, but as we would come to realise, he did not understand what that meant and after a short break he would get back to Montevideo with Club Atlético Cerro.

There was one caveat though, as Cerro did not play with an attacking midfielder, so Godín would feature as a right-sided midfielder for their fifth-tier team at the time. He somehow had his first break, and determined to make the most of it, he would suck it up and do as he was told even when he was shifted to centre-back to cover for injuries and suspensions. To say that he did so willingly might be a stretch as Godín wanted to be the man scoring goals, but with his tall frame he was a natural filler in defence and he knew better than to complain as well. For someone who initially figured that he would be of no use in that position, Godín never looked back.

Still 17, he understood his position and learned his trade so quickly that in the same year he was pushed up to the third tier and eventually the first team, rising up to Uruguay's first division in a matter of months. Godín would be handed the armband as well soon after, and three years later in 2006 he would take the next step and depart for Nacional, one of the country's top two teams. He had fallen, and now he had risen to the top, but his journey was just about to begin.

After a year at Nacional, Godín would arrive in Spain, signing for Manuel Pellegrini's Villarreal aged just 21. He was understandably a backup option at first, but after a debut in a UEFA Cup game, followed by a short cameo off the bench in the league, the central defender would go on to make 16 consecutive starts on his way to a total of just about 2,000 minutes of first-team action in his debut season. It was a firm success as well, and having racked up the seventh-highest amount of playing time in the squad, Godín had played a crucial part in Villarreal's record league finish, seeing them end as runners-up.

The following season would see the Uruguayan get his first taste of Champions League football and he would start it with an impressive clean sheet away from home against eventual finalists Manchester United in the first group game. Another impressive performance against Arsenal in the quarter-finals would unfortunately end in a loss for his side, however, with Godín being incorrectly adjudged to have committed a foul in his own box, giving away a penalty that effectively ended any hopes of a fightback. He still marched on though, and his performance levels rarely dropped as Villarreal finished fifth in the league, followed by seventh the next year, having lost Pellegrini to Real Madrid.

The downward trend would continue for the Yellow Submarine, but following an impressive 2010 World Cup Godín would jump ship and land in the Spanish capital with Atlético Madrid. His debut came in a 2-0 victory over Inter Milan in the UEFA Super Cup, but as is already well documented, the club would enter a difficult period yet again with Gregorio Manzano failing to take Quique Sánchez Flores's side forward. Through no real fault of his own, Godín was falling and, when Simeone arrived, he took it upon himself to get *Los Rojiblancos* to rise again. Everything about the setup suited the now 25-year-old and, despite not being the quickest centre-back, his positioning, composure and awareness were impeccable, not to mention his aerial prowess that helped dominate both penalty boxes. Scoring goals was on his mind when he shifted to the centre-back position, and now he had found a way to score from there too, especially when his team needed it the most.

Roll on to 17 May 2014 and the last day of the La Liga season. Atlético Madrid trailed against Barcelona at the Camp Nou, with Alexis Sánchez's shot having crept into the top corner after about half an hour. Had the game ended then, the league title would have slipped out of the hands of *Los Rojiblancos* and fallen into the grasp of their opponents, who had started strongly in what was effectively a final. Atlético looked meek, and as the minutes trickled on towards half-time it only looked like the game was headed one way. Four minutes into the second half though, everything would change.

As Gabi wandered over to the corner flag and set the ball down, the odds were stacked heavily against *Los Rojiblancos*. Diego Costa and Arda Turan both had to be taken off in the first half owing to injury, and just like that Atlético were without two of their main attackers who had got them this far. They needed a goal, and as the captain swung the ball into the box, one man knew where it was coming from. Godín would rise majestically above the rest, reaching out with his head to send the ball into the back of the net, the score now reading 1-1. Fight. Survive. Win.

For the next 40 minutes, the centre-back would battle to overcome wave after wave of Barcelona attack but much like he had done all those years ago, he kept his head above water and pulled his side to victory. Godín was a La Liga champion. He would almost repeat the heroics the following week in the Champions League final, where he once again rose to meet a corner and put Atlético within seconds of winning the trophy, but as we all know, it was not meant to be. Nevertheless, Godín's time with *Los Rojiblancos* would last for nine long years, with the Uruguayan winning eight major honours, seven of them under Simeone. He had the complete domestic set in Spain and, barring the Champions League, he had won every major European club title as well.

Godín would also become a legend for his country, holding the record for the most appearances in the national side with whom he has won one Copa América title and made three consecutive World Cup tournaments starting in 2010, reaching the semi-finals, round of 16 and quarter-finals respectively, while also claiming the captain's armband along the way. He would do the same at Atlético, taking on the role after Gabi's departure, but for a player with natural leadership ability it never really mattered if Godín had the armband or not. He would hand over the captaincy to Koke upon his departure in 2019, leaving as the foreigner with the most appearances for *Los Rojiblancos* and joining Italian side Inter Milan.

By now, Godín was 33, and in his only season at Inter, he would play a part in the side that would finish just a single point behind eventual champions Juventus, also scoring a goal in the 2020 Europa League final defeat, and becoming only the sixth player to have scored in the finals of Europe's top two club competitions. He would stay in Italy with Cagliari following that season, now well away from the limelight of European football, and in January 2022 he would move back to South America to join Brazilian side Atlético Mineiro.

As he prepares to lead his nation out in what would be his fourth World Cup at the 2022 edition, Godín will undoubtedly go down as one of the finest centre-backs to have played the game. After all, it is not every day that a player in his position gets nominated for a Ballon d'Or, let alone for it to happen twice, but that was what made him special. Whatever the odds against him, Godín was prepared to bet on himself and his illustrious career will always be a testament to the warrior that he is. That four-year-old fought for his life, and after making it out alive, he never stopped fighting.

* * *

Miranda

While most Brazilians are known for their flair and skill on the ball, often playing attacking roles during their younger days, Miranda was someone who willingly played in defence, though the back story to this is a bit solemn. The youngest of 12 siblings, Miranda was just six years old when his eldest brother, Vicente, passed away due to an accident at his workplace, where he had plied his trade as a technician for an electric company in order to help provide for the family. Vicente, however, had also been a popular and excellent defender among the amateur leagues of their hometown Paranavaí and, following his passing, Miranda would set out to honour his brother and carry on his legacy.

With little memory of the incident itself, Miranda came up through the youth ranks of Coritiba, in his local state championship, and in 2004 he would move into their senior team, becoming a regular as a 19-year-old and helping them win the state championship as well. By this time, he had also received an offer from Sochaux to play in France, but with the sudden passing of his father and his wife expecting a child, Miranda reached a point where he seriously considered his mother's advice to stay behind and even pondered giving up the sport altogether. Big decisions had to be made by a boy who was just out of adolescence, and he would take the leap to move to France.

Unfortunately, the decision proved to be a wrong one and the Brazilian found it difficult to settle in the new environment, making only around 20 appearances as Sochaux ended the season with a mid-table finish. Interestingly, Miranda never even had an agent at the time either, but sensing that a move back would be the best option, he committed to a loan offer from top-division side São Paulo which saw him return home in the summer of 2006. It was here that his career would take off domestically and Miranda would win the league title in his first three seasons at the club, even featuring in the Team of the Year in 2007 and 2008 as well. No more team honours would follow in the next three years, however, but further Team of the Year appearances in 2009 and 2010 would highlight the centre-back's consistency and, eventually, Atlético Madrid snapped him up in July 2011.

By this time, Miranda was just about to turn 27, and he would do so before his league debut as he took his place in the heart of defence alongside Godín. The poor start to the season under Manzano did little to prove his worth, but much like most of the players to feature in this book, a link-up with Simeone would change everything. Miranda would score in the semi-finals of the Europa League on the way to lifting the trophy and later that year he would score in the 4-1 Super Cup thrashing of Chelsea as well. He and Godín had begun to develop an unlikely goalscoring partnership and, despite nearing his 30s, Atlético would renew his contract until the end of 2016.

They would soon be rewarded for this, and Miranda's best moment in the red and white shirt was just around the corner. Leaping above the Real Madrid defence in the 2013 Copa del Rey final, the Brazilian would score his header in extra time not only to win the trophy but also to end a 14-year winless streak against their city rivals, signalling a change of times in the Spanish capital. Miranda's goal would not only immediately endear him to the Atlético faithful, making it the one moment that he is almost entirely remembered for, but in his own words, it 'changed everything' for a club that was long viewed as far too inferior to the *Galácticos* across town.

The goal would also serve as a nice foreshadowing of the season to come, and a formidable defensive campaign would see Miranda become a La Liga champion at the end of it, having played a crucial part in Atlético's rise to the top. Unfortunately for him though, his time in Spain was coming to an end and the Champions League final loss would be followed by a largely inconsistent 2014/15 season, at the end of which he would move to Inter Milan at the age of 31. He was nowhere near finished, however, and he would go on to make over 100 appearances over the next four years for the Italian outfit, while also finally making it to his first World Cup finals in 2018. Though his club success had brought him international recognition, Miranda's experiences with his national side had been brief until that point, largely being overlooked in favour of the likes of Thiago Silva and David Luiz for the major competitions.

In fact, despite receiving his first call-up in 2007, his debut would come two years later and once again after a handful of appearances in 2009, he would have to wait until 2013 for his next inclusion. Miranda would also end up being left out of the 2014 World Cup on home soil despite his strong club campaign, something which the centre-back would feel sore about and it was only after the tournament, under new coach Dunga, that he would begin to feature regularly for his national side. He would go on to make 58 appearances in total, the last one coming in 2019, which would be the same year that he would leave Inter and move to Chinese side Jiangsu Suning. However, the club would dissolve just over a year and a half later, allowing the 36-year-old Miranda to return back to São Paulo in 2021, where he still plays at the time of writing.

Though he might have arrived later on the scene after spending most of his younger years back home in Brazil, Miranda would certainly blossom at the right time and, at his best, he was a part of one of the toughest defences in the world, racking up the clean sheets as Atlético began their ascent to the top. More than this, however, Miranda will be remembered by *Los Colchoneros* for his contribution at the other end, specifically that goal against Real Madrid, which still remains an important part of Atlético history and is seen as the moment where *Los Rojiblancos* finally stood up to their city rivals, giving them the courage and the belief that they could achieve so much more.

* * *

José María Giménez

Born in Toledo, Uruguay, Giménez's story would not start too far away from the legendary Godín, who had grown up just a couple of hours away although he was nine years older. In fact, Giménez would be all of six years old when Godín moved to within half an hour of his hometown to join Defensor Sporting and then Cerro, and just about nine when his countryman debuted for the national side before moving to one of Uruguay's biggest clubs in Nacional. All this would prove to be nothing more than numbers, however, and within a decade, the pair would cross paths when they shared the pitch for the first time in Madrid.

Although starting much later, Giménez's path would have some similarities to Godín's, most notably when he was rather harshly told that he 'won't play football' by the youth director of another one of the country's bigger clubs, Peñarol. 'It hurt so much because my dream was to become a footballer and I made a promise that day that I would reach the first division and prove it,' he said in the aftermath, and the youngster who left the ground in tears would find himself taking a step back, not just in terms of joining the more modest Danubio, but quite literally shifting his position from that of a defensive midfielder to centre-back.

True to his word, Giménez would make his first appearance in the top division at the age of 17, but even he was not entirely prepared for what was to come afterwards. He would later admit that he had only ever been convinced that he would make it to the first division, and not that he would turn out to be a great player of any sort, but within a few months and just about 20 senior appearances for Danubio, Atlético Madrid would sign him in 2013 for just under €1m, shortly after his 18th birthday. What seemed a rushed move would turn out to be extremely shrewd, because later that year Giménez would also make the Uruguay Under-20 World Cup squad and go on to become one of the tournament's standout defenders as his side rather unexpectedly made the final, losing only on penalties to a France side boasting the likes of Geoffrey Kondogbia,

Florian Thauvin, Kurt Zouma, Lucas Digne and the tournament's best player in Paul Pogba.

While the rest of his team-mates made the trip back from Turkey, Giménez would fly straight to his new home in Madrid just in time for some pre-season training ahead of 2013/14. By this time, Atlético were already an up-and-coming side asking questions of Europe's top teams and, under Simeone, they had just won the Copa del Rey courtesy of that Miranda header on top of their Europa League success a year earlier. Breaking the Godín-Miranda partnership was never going to be easy though, and despite making his debut alongside his countryman in September 2013 after an injury to Miranda, Giménez would feature just a couple of times more as Atlético marched on to the title and a runners-up finish in the Champions League.

The 19-year-old would watch on as Godín's headers went into the net in two of their biggest games that season, but, interestingly, the pair would feature together more often for their country during the World Cup qualifiers that year. Despite his limited game time at club level, Uruguay's legendary coach Óscar Tabárez would deem Giménez good enough for his senior debut, a game in which former Atlético star Radamel Falcao would famously claim that the youngster put him off with questions about cars, flags and even the spelling of 'September'. Giménez himself would deny these claims, though the story does sound believable enough, and later that year he would be called up for the 2014 World Cup finals in Brazil.

The two Diegos, Lugano and Godín, would be the preferred pairing considering that they were the most experienced defenders in the squad, but with Lugano ruled out due to injury after a shock loss to Costa Rica in the opening game, Giménez would partner his club team-mate, becoming the youngest player for his nation at a World Cup as *La Celeste* looked to turn their tournament around. The fixture list did not look kind though, with England and Italy to come, but the pair would concede just once in these two games as the side finished second and qualified for the knockout stages, eventually exiting in the round of 16 as James Rodríguez's famous volley, worthy of a Puskás Award, would seal a 2-0 victory for Colombia. It had only been a year since that penalty shoot-out defeat at the Under-20 World Cup, but Giménez was now well and truly in the big leagues.

Back in Spain, he was now on his way to becoming a regular, making 28 appearances in the 2014/15 season and only cementing his spot in the side from then on. His partnership with Godín would continue to grow, both for club and country, and there is no other player with whom Giménez has played more frequently either. In fact, in the six years that they would play together for club and country, they would make 166 appearances alongside each other at an average of about 28 a season, in spite of Giménez hardly featuring the first year. Of course, this is not all about Godín, and individually Giménez has staked a claim to be one of the best defenders in the world, with his pace, strength, aerial and ball-playing ability making him a complete package at the back. Unfortunately, the only thing stopping him from truly sealing a spot at football's highest table is his own injury record, and where the greatest have always had the ability of availability, Giménez has missed over 90 games since joining in 2013, at an average of just over ten per season so far.

He is still only 27 at time of writing this book, however, and as the third-choice captain, his importance cannot be understated. Giménez certainly can play football, and having entered at a turning point in Atlético's history, he continues to write his own legacy in red and white.

* * *

Football is a game of goals, and in a sport where you have to score to win, the art of defending is often taken for granted. After all, the entire foundation of this sport is built upon those moments when the ball passes through a rectangular post set at the ends of the pitch, and without these instances the very point of this game ceases to exist. That's because if every single match were to end 0-0, it becomes nothing but an exhibition rather than a competition, with there never being any winners or losers even when played to eternity.

It is, therefore, not at all surprising that the entire focus shifts to the attacking side of the game, as each team sets out to score that single goal more than their opponent to give them the victory. Again, this is easier said than done and, in truth, despite being the essence of the game, scoring a goal remains one of the hardest things to do. But if it is then so incredibly difficult to do the one thing that the sport requires you to do in order to win, how much more difficult must it be to go against everything that it is based on and prevent the game from seeing that one moment for which the entire sport lives?

Defending truly is an art, and Simeone is one of its greatest artists. To him, prevention is truly better than cure and as he looks at the green canvas from the sidelines, his hands steadily get to work on his next masterpiece. Every artist is only as good as his tools, however, and as he traces out his muse, his centre-backs complete each stroke on the pitch in front of him. This was an art form that defied the normal, and however gruesome, exhausting and even pressurising, nothing less than perfection would do.

8

Two to Tango: Forwards

'Football is like boxing, because you have to know when it is time to attack'

ALBERT EINSTEIN is a name that virtually everyone has come across, and rightly so for a man who is widely considered to be one of the greatest physicists, and in general one of the brightest minds, of all time. He really does not need any further introduction, but you might be wondering why he is introduced at all in a book that simply could not have less to do with Einstein's work.

After all, he is by no means related to Diego Simeone or Atlético Madrid and, in fact, he would be no more by the time association football came about, so it must then be even more intriguing as to what relation he has to this specific book published decades after his existence. Well, among his greatest achievements, one of the things he would do was give us an excellent place to start this chapter.

'Look deep into nature, and then you will understand everything better,' he would say, adding to an already overflowing list of theories and thoughts that he would leave behind for us to pick apart, and into nature we shall go. There is no denying that nature is beautiful, and such balance and coexistence is a phenomenon that we have always tried to understand, but at the same time, nature can be relentless and unforgiving, and truly a survival of the fittest. You only need to look at a food chain, one of nature's most basic and yet fundamental facets, to truly grasp this essential fact. Finding food is a natural instinct and every living creature needs food, but a harsh reality is that at the same time, most of them might also *be* food. At every single step of the chain, it is hunter versus prey.

'One second can change it all, but it's not just any second, it's a flash. The prey is there and suddenly then it's not. In an instant it's over, you won't have the chance again.'

Much like Einstein, Simeone too uses nature to widen his understanding, but his application is far more focused on football as opposed to physics. Stating the above in his first book, *El Efecto Simeone*, or roughly *The Simeone Effect*, he goes on to talk about using motivation as a strategy, while also showing us his interpretation of the food chain and its relation to football. In every game, there is hunter versus prey, the only difference being that the sides can alternate to fill these roles and, according to Simeone, each hunt is decided by those moments, or 'flashes', where if you blinked, you might just have missed your dinner.

Cholo is by no means a wildlife or biology expert, but this is how he saw football: a series of moments, some of which would prove to be more decisive, but all of which would be valuable. We have just come off the back of a chapter focusing on his hatred of losing, which led to a defensive structure meant to keep even the strongest at bay, and while these moments are decisive for their own reasons, the scoring of a goal surely ranks highly in terms of decisiveness as well. At the end of the day, not losing is part of the process of winning, for which the side still needs to score and, for whom, goalscoring chances do not come in abundance.

'I don't understand, with the quality they have, that they play this kind of football,' a visibly annoyed Jürgen Klopp said, following an incredible Champions League round of 16 game at Anfield in 2020, which eventually saw his Liverpool team beaten 3-2 on the night and 4-2 on aggregate by Atlético after extra time. Coming into the game with a slender one-goal advantage, Simeone's side had typically sat back and invited pressure, though this was anything but a perfect performance. The English side were the then champions and, with 11 of their 34 shots finding the target along with a further two hitting the frame of the goal, they had easily dominated even having taken the lead early on in extra time. Atlético, however, would score three in reply to win the game and put the tie to bed, with half of their shots on target over 120 minutes finding the back of the net.

Nearly four years earlier, Bayern Munich had faced a similar fate. This time it was the semi-finals of the same competition, and even though the German side went on to win the second leg 2-1 they would be knocked out due to the away goals rule. Once again, Atlético travelled away from home with a one-goal lead, again they allowed 11 shots on target (from a strikingly similar 33 shots) and again they conceded two goals, only this time Bayern missed a penalty instead of hitting the posts. *Los Rojiblancos* would miss a penalty of their own, but one of their seven shots on target would go in, meaning that even with a performance that would turn out to be far less clinical than their trip to Anfield they would progress to the final. 'Today ugly football – Atlético – played against the best football in the world. The only time they saw the ball was for the goal,' claimed a frustrated Bayern midfielder Arturo Vidal, who, in spite of providing an assist for his side's second goal, could not believe that Atlético had gone through.

In all honesty though, both Klopp and Vidal can be cut some slack for feeling a sense of wrongdoing. They certainly had not come up against a peak Atlético defensive performance and they had even managed to score the two goals originally required of them. They both had about 72 per cent of the possession and created more than enough chances to coast through to the next round. How, then, had both of them managed to lose to the same team in the same fashion almost four years apart?

Atlético had pounced in their moments, the other two had not. For much of both games, Simeone's side invited pressure on themselves with their defensive setup, their opponents regularly taking aim as the minutes ticked on, hunting and sometimes toying with those in red and white, even coming tantalisingly close to ending it all and slaying the beast that Atlético were. It was hunter versus prey all over again, and the advantage lay firmly with the hunter.

None of this, however, was against the way *Cholo* himself had envisioned the game. Despite his worrisome exterior, he knew that no matter what, the natural course of a match would lead to his side having their moments, or even just a single moment, and that was all they needed. Having lulled their opposition into a sense of dominance, Atlético knew that for a brief second the guard might drop and, in that second, they had to spring to life. The prey turned predator, and the hunter became the hunted.

The smooth execution of this hinged not only on resolute defending but also on the clinical conversion of chances, and hence after our extended lesson on biology and philosophy, we finally arrive at the forwards in this Atlético side. For years, the public consensus has been that the pitches on this side of Madrid are barren land for forwards, where goals can never sprout. Yet, year after year, some of football's most promising, or even most accomplished forwards still find themselves taking the supposed trouble of tending these lands only to discover their fair share of goals throughout their stay.

For one of the sport's most prized positions, the Atlético conveyor belt has consistently laid out diamonds and not just during Simeone's tenure either. In the late 1990s, Christian Vieri took La Liga by storm on the way to becoming its top scorer in his only season and, when he left, Jimmy Floyd Hasselbaink comfortably filled his goalscoring shoes. When he too left after Atlético's relegation, Fernando Torres began his ascent to the top of European football with his first, and better remembered, stint at his boyhood club. Upon his departure in 2007, Atlético had not one, but two able replacements in Sergio Agüero and Diego Forlán, who spearheaded the side right up until 2011, before Radamel Falcao entered the picture a few months ahead of Simeone himself. Diego Costa, David Villa, Antoine Griezmann, Ángel Correa, Álvaro Morata, João Félix, Luis Suárez and Matheus Cunha would be some of the other names to follow, adding on to an already impressive list.

Under Simeone, each time a forward was signed the move would be questioned, and most times the player would shine before being poached by a more attacking team only for the process to repeat again. There just is something interesting about the forwards position at Atlético and, because of this, we will seek to discover just what makes it so special.

You might not have needed this book to learn that defensive solidity has been at the base of everything Simeone has done at Atlético, but this then naturally points towards the forwards having less to do in their roles. This absolutely does not mean that they are less important, however, but just that the direct and incisive style of football demands straightforward tactics and neat execution as opposed to more complex setups. This

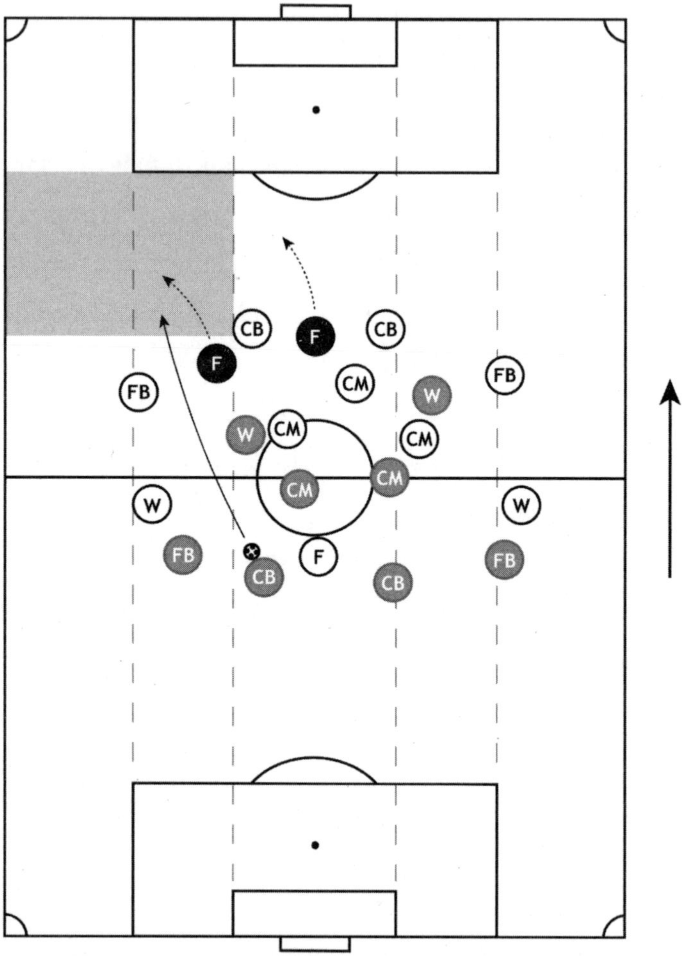

Fig. 44 Forwards run in behind and into the channels

approach is visualised in Figure 44, where we shall have a look at the attacking role of the forwards in the more direct 4-4-2 formation.

As we had mentioned in the earlier chapters, and especially in the last one on the centre-backs, the

4-4-2 shape skipped the build-up phase and would rely heavily on the ball being played forward directly from the back line.

The midfielders and wingers would support this with their positioning, allowing them to pick up on second balls or effectively press the opposition should the pass not succeed, but they were rarely the direct targets of these passes. This responsibility would fall on the forwards, who had to act accordingly in order to make the most of the long pass.

Usually when sides play out in such a manner, the forwards are tasked with receiving in two ways. The first method is by acting as a 'target man', wherein the forward uses their natural aerial ability to compete for the aerial pass and either head the ball to a team-mate or receive it on their chest and keep possession. The second method is by running in behind and essentially receiving the pass in space, almost like in a counter attack. This is often the case when sides have pacy forwards, who are often better dribblers and not as good aerially, allowing them to make the best use of their traits by running to receive as opposed to jumping. The benefit for Atlético, though, was that they had two forwards, meaning they could simultaneously use both these methods, although even then there would be a slight alteration.

While the long pass was always a primary means of progression, Atlético never really fielded players who were natural 'target men', with the exception of Mario Mandžukić, often making use of players who were quick with their feet and fast with some decent ability to compete in the air. Aerial strength when receiving was surprisingly not a prerequisite, and the focus was more on offering some competition with the aim of getting the ball in behind more often than not. The reasoning for this is actually quite simple, and it once again comes down to Simeone's preference for flexibility in his team. When you fix one forward as a 'target man' and allow the other to be more direct and get in behind, you essentially fix the players to their roles, as one forward cannot efficiently fulfil the role of the other, which is something that the opposition can realise and prepare for.

When you have two forwards capable of doing both to a fairly good degree, however, this creates some uncertainty in terms of which forward takes on which role, giving Atlético the freedom to pass to either player in different ways. Of course, they might not have been getting the full benefit of the aerial side of things, but with forwards such as Falcao, Griezmann and even Félix, the side still had players who could hold their own in the air, even if they might not have been tipped to do so considering their natural physique.

Moreover, these forwards were not expected to win headers outright in the middle of the pitch and control the ball either; rather they needed to flick the ball on either to a supporting winger or midfielder, or mostly to their fellow forward who would make the run in behind. By competing in the air, the forward was dragging his opponent out of position, creating space in behind into which the ball could be headed on in order to release a team-mate into space. Since either forward could do this, a sense of unpredictability affects the defence, who had to be prepared to deal with either option and are now more prone to errors in marking and tracking.

Admittedly, none of this is shown in Figure 44, and hence we shall now move on to the second means of progression. Now, we had already assessed this situation from the centre-backs' point of view, but shifting over to the forwards, let us now analyse how they receive the specific pass in behind as shown. Instead of challenging for the ball in the air, this pass is aimed into the channels for the nearest forward to chase and collect, allowing them to run through the back line and get into space. The main benefit of this pass is that, owing to its speed and incisiveness, it is almost like Atlético are on a counter attack even though they comfortably had possession of the ball, meaning that the pass still has the ability to unsettle the opposition's shape and at least momentarily create openings.

These moments are exactly the ones that Simeone treasures, and by having the centre-back play the ball in between the opposition full-back and centre-back, he is able to slowly draw the defenders out and create more space centrally. This happens because the opposition centre-back needs to track the forward since his full-back is now ahead of the ball, leaving space behind him which the second forward can look to exploit. Additionally, we have also seen in the chapter on wingers how the winger on the opposite side can join the front line while the forward moves wider, essentially allowing for a shift in positions to better attack all the spaces created.

In truth, this was all the forwards really had to do. Of course, they had their roles in the various positional shifts that we saw earlier, but the primary task was to make the most of these long passes and get in behind as much as possible. Once they were on the ball, they could then showcase their technical ability and look to take on defenders before finding room for a pass or shot. It would be difficult to deny that at times it was good to watch either since, after all, not many sequences get your heart racing as much as a smoothly finished transition. It certainly was not revolutionary, but it worked and that was all that mattered.

What also mattered was that the forwards also carried out their defensive duties, and these were fairly interesting as well.

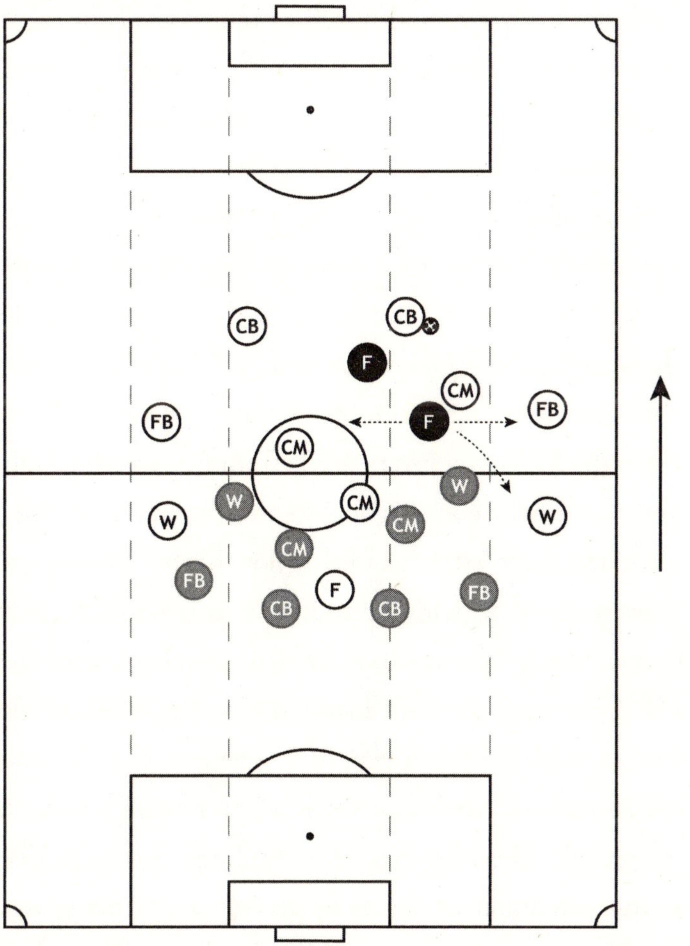

Fig. 45 *One forward covers ground while the other is relatively static in defence*

While both forwards would be given similar roles in attack to add to the unpredictability and flexibility in possession, this was quite the opposite when Atlético had to defend. We have already seen earlier on how the forwards could very easily drop into midfield during positional shifts to add numbers and defend the wide areas, but this duty was often carried out by just one of the forwards rather than both interchangeably. Players like Griezmann have always been popular with Simeone because of their ability to take on this role, but this is also a reason why some forwards have never clicked at Atletico since they do not have the versatility to do the same.

Playing with a front two meant that Simeone naturally had two players in his front line to effectively pressure opponents higher up the pitch, but having preferred to sit back in a mid-to-low block, it was more important to provide support for the midfield and prevent central overloads rather than press. Out of the two forwards, one had to remain as the outlet, while the other dropped deeper and, despite seemingly having the choice to alternate between which forwards take on which role, the roles were usually fixed primarily due to the individual attributes of the forwards themselves.

The forward position itself is not commonly associated with a lot of defending, and Simeone understood that while some of his players in this position were excellent goalscorers, they were not the sharpest defensively and were better employed in staying forward and acting as an outlet in transition should the side recover possession. This forward could then be paired with one that was more of a workhorse, capable of covering ground and shifting accordingly while also having a higher level of defensive acumen. This arrangement was crucial in accommodating players like Falcao, Villa and Suárez, who would clearly lift the overall quality of the squad but not necessarily be good fits for the defensive side of the game, with others like Adrián López, Costa and Correa covering for them.

As shown in Figure 45, these forwards would be tasked with initially being a part of the front two, but as the team dropped deeper they would then shift across behind their fellow forward towards the ball side, where they could then offer support down the flanks. This does not, however, mean that they had to cover the entire width of the pitch which would be nearly impossible to do consistently, but instead their duties would differ slightly depending on which side the ball was played. Should the ball be played out wide down the side that they are positioned, they themselves could engage and gradually drop into the midfield line almost as a winger. However, if the ball is moved to the opposite side, they certainly would not be able to get there first and, instead, they would drop directly into the midfield line, either down their side (as a far-side winger) or through the middle (as an additional central midfielder) and offer cover for the winger who would engage instead.

It surely was not light work, but once again it is fairly straightforward compared to some of the other positions that we had seen and, as far as the 4-4-2 is concerned, this was basically the essence of the forward's role. It would only be in the more expansive 5-3-2 formation where things got a bit more dynamic.

Compared to 4-4-2, the 5-3-2 formation definitely offered a more stable structure in possession and allowed for better build-up play along with multiple means of progression. Specifically for the forwards, this meant that the reliance on long passes forwards was reduced, meaning that they could offer much more than just competing in the air or runs in behind. More importantly, it meant that they could better showcase their movement since they now had greater scope for varying their positions according to different situations.

While movement is crucial for just about every position in football, this is even more so for forwards as their movement effectively decides the quality of the chances that they get. With their movement, they can

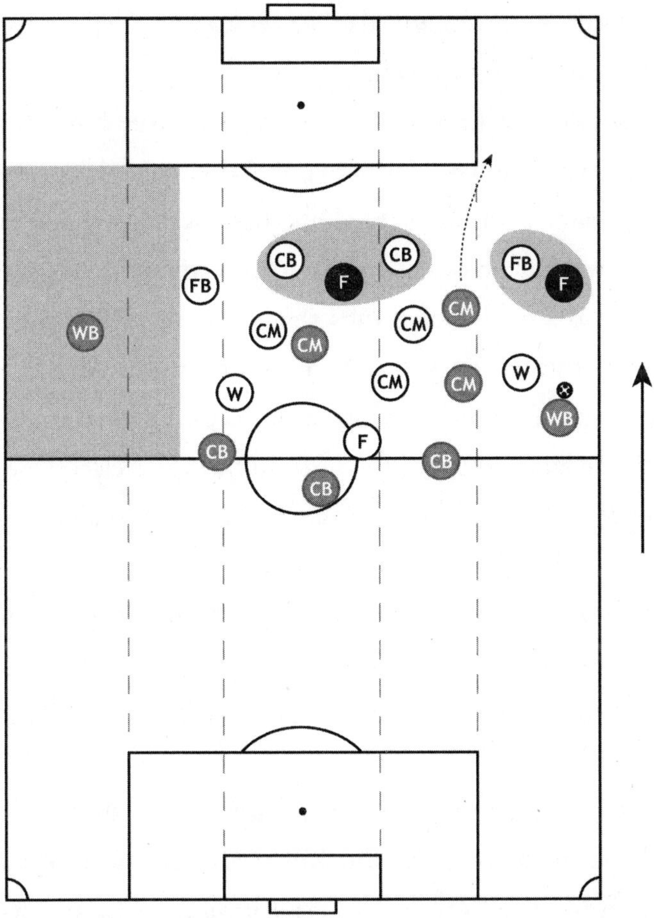

Fig. 46 *Space creation due to forwards in the 5-3-2 formation*

get themselves into the right positions to receive, be it to their feet or into space in behind, and especially in more advanced positions like in the penalty box, they can shake off their markers and find room for a shot. However, apart from just creating space for themselves, a forward's movement also serves to create space for their team-mates as well.

Looking at Figure 46, we are able to see how this works with the two forwards of Atlético, considering the greater positional freedom that they now have in more settled possession. Their movement is heavily linked to a couple of things that we have seen earlier, namely the forward run of the central midfielder and the positioning of the wing-back in space. Starting off with the latter, the two forwards in the 5-3-2 effectively behave like the wingers in the 4-4-2, compressing the play area in order to create the space out wide. However, the forwards naturally take on narrower positions than the wingers, even though they were narrow as well, and hence they shift further across in order to drag the back line with them.

In this example, one of the forwards has moved well out wide near the touchline, almost becoming a winger himself in terms of his positioning. This results in him engaging the opposition full-back and he is now contributing to Atlético's overload down the flanks as well. While this already begins to draw the opposition to the ball side, the other forward looks to compound this by putting himself between the opposition centre-backs and, in doing so, he engages both of them due to the possibility of him making the central run between them. As a result, the centre-backs have to ensure that they minimise this space while also moving across to cover for their full-back. Finally, to round this off, the far-side full-back has to follow suit and move in centrally to cover the movement of the centre-backs, eventually creating the space out wide for the wing-back.

We also saw an iteration earlier where one of the central midfielders can step up to engage this far-side full-back and pin him to his position as well, adding another last-line presence while creating more space for the wing-back as well. The switch is now on and the ball carrier, who happens to be the right wing-back in this case, can now play the ball all the way across to find his left wing-back in space down the opposite flank.

The interesting thing about this exact scenario, however, is that the movement of the forwards can create space for another player, usually a central midfielder, down the ball side as well. We have already mentioned how, especially in the 5-3-2, the central midfielders can offer an attacking threat as well with excellent forward runs into the channels, a sequence that especially enabled Marcos Llorente to thrive and consistently get involved in goals. Having already understood the positioning of the forwards with respect to space creation for the wing-back, we shall now go into the specifics of how this benefits the central midfielder as well.

While Figure 46 neatly visualises this, it is important to understand how the forwards are more or less the final piece of this particular manoeuvre, with the rest of the players having already played their parts to perfection. For example, the centre-backs have spread out to allow the right wing-back to receive the ball wider down the flanks and draw the opposition out, while two central midfielders have shifted over as well to cause an overload, with one of them providing a passing option to the feet and the other looking to attack the channel.

The forward who moves wider now completes the overload by becoming the fourth Atlético player down the flank, and his movement has also pinned the opposition full-back to the wider zone. The gap between this full-back and the closest centre-back is now widened and, to prevent the centre-back from closing it off too much, the second forward does just about enough to keep him busy while also creating some uncertainty between the two centre-backs with his positioning. As a result of this, the gap created in the back line is significantly big enough for the central midfielder to attack, leaving him with just his opposition counterpart to shake off before finding a relatively free run into the channels.

Once this is done, the wider forward can even overlap and provide a passing option should the central midfielder need it, or they can move centrally towards the penalty area to receive a pass and get closer to the goal. The more central forward can simply look to make the most of the situation to find himself some time and space in and around the area either to get on the end of a cross or a pass and get the ball in the net. This way, both the forwards can still be goal threats after initially starting the sequence with their movement and allowing the side to break through the opposition defence.

Now, creating space for others is one thing, but how do the forwards operate in space themselves? After all, Atlético now have a structure that can facilitate a more patient build-up, which would naturally require the forwards to be able to receive from the back as the side steadily progresses and, in this next segment, we shall take a look at this.

If we once again recall what we have seen with the wing-backs and the centre-backs, we know that first of all, using the wing-backs, Atlético can stretch the opposition and open up central spaces. After this, the centre-backs not only have more time on the ball to pass it out, but they also have better passing lanes through the middle as well, and in this specific case, shown in Figure 47, we will consider their passes out to the forwards.

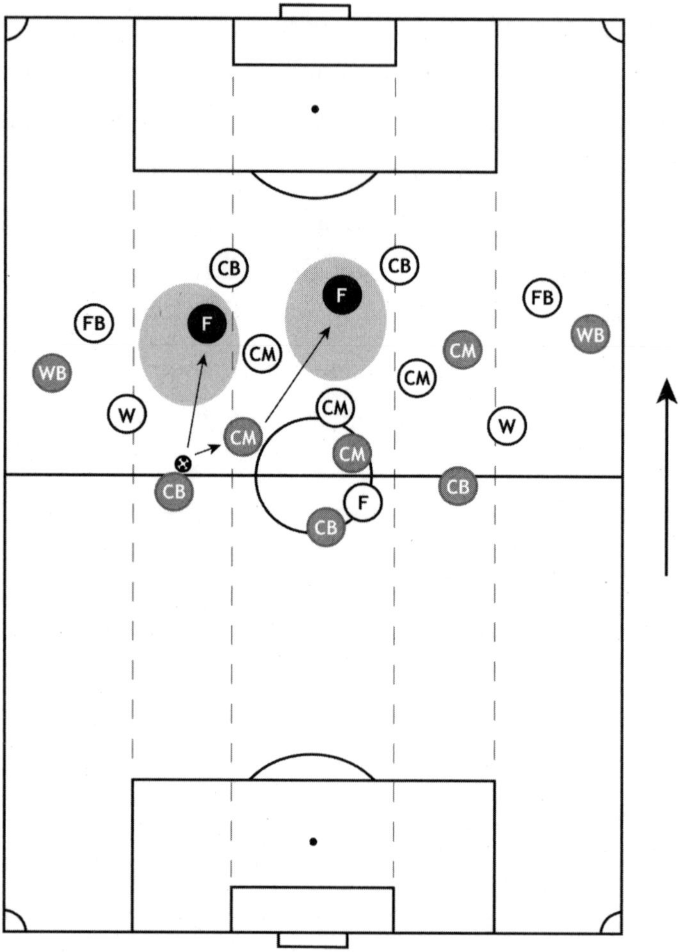

***Fig. 47** Forwards making use of space created for them in the build-up*

In this situation, as Simeone's side looks to build up, rather than the forwards creating space for others, space has been created for them instead in order for them to receive directly from the centre-backs. While this does have its similarities to the earlier pass in the 4-4-2, it is also in a sense a very different pass since the centre-back is playing the ball into the feet of the forward rather than aerially or in behind. Not only does it have a higher chance of succeeding, but it also allows the forward to do more on the ball after receiving, instead of simply looking to head it on or chase after it.

This would, in fact, be a very important means of ball progression as it provides an excellent alternative to the switch pass out to the wing-backs in case the opposition looks to shield that off and, in general, this allows Atlético to break opposition lines and slice through them centrally. As can be seen from Figure 47, both the forwards have space in the middle of the pitch, and while one can remain central, the other can move into the channels and provide a relatively simple, yet effective, passing option. Moreover, by shifting into the channel, this forward can also attempt to attack the space in between the opposition full-back and centre-back. We have spread the defence across quite leniently here in order to better explain the situation, but such gaps will still exist in some capacity and can be exploited.

Another benefit of having the two forwards is also the fact that, should one be covered, the ball can still be worked to the other. Referring to our specific case in point, if the opposition central midfielder moves to block out the forward in the channel, the centre-back can simply play the ball to the central midfielder ahead of him, who in turn can play to the more central forward instead. Should the opposition central midfielder cover off this forward and have the winger cover for the forward in the channel, the pass out to the wing-back becomes available instead and, even though it might be a less threatening option, it still serves as a good means of progression.

Apart from this, the fact that Atlético in general like to have two of their midfielders drop deeper in the build-up phase, while the other is ready to attack the channels, means that progression through the middle might not be as effective as it can be, and having the forwards drop deeper and move accordingly helps to mitigate this by either bringing them into midfield or effectively bypassing it instead. As a result, they now do so much more in possession as compared to earlier and can better use their wide range of skills to benefit this Atlético side in attack.

This, of course, does not mean that their defensive duties will ever take a back seat and, though it does have certain similarities to the line-ups before, it does have some interesting tweaks as well.

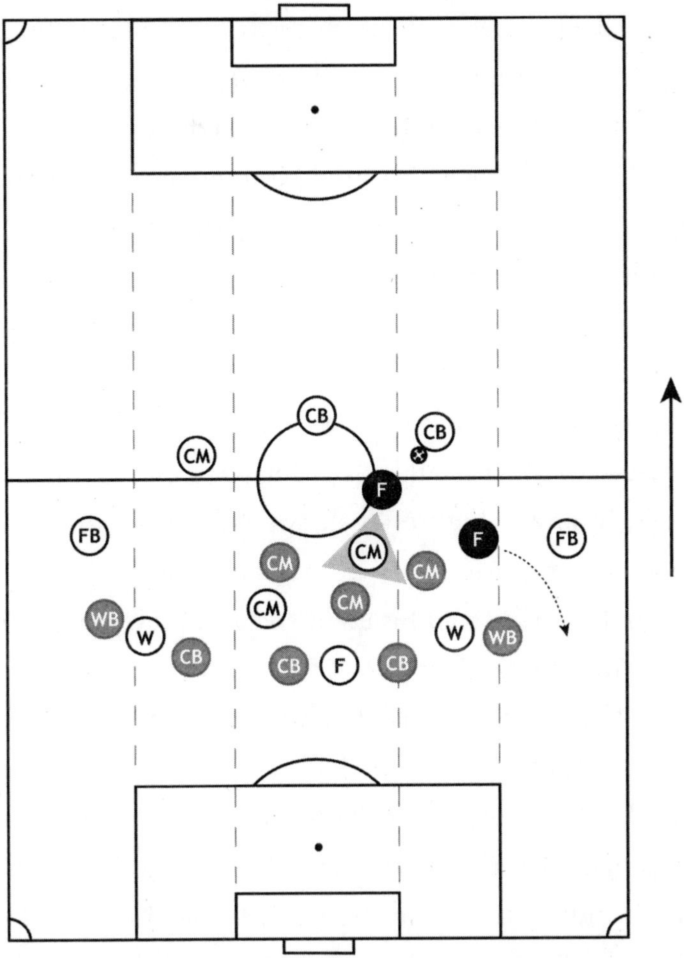

***Fig. 48** Forwards contributing to the compact defensive shape with different positioning*

In terms of similarities, this is basically with respect to the fundamental roles of the forwards itself and much like in the 4-4-2, one takes up a more static role while the other is given greater responsibility in covering ground. However, with just three players in the midfield line rather than the four from before, there is a change in how they go about their individual duties.

The first change is in the positioning of the more static forward, and where this was often not too specific earlier on, it is now of greater significance. When in the 4-4-2, this forward mainly had to stay central and apply some level of pressure higher up before ensuring that he dropped back suitably in order to keep himself stationed as a useful outlet should possession be recovered. In this case, however, Figure 48 shows us how the forward now has to ensure that he has kept the opposition central midfielder in his cover shadow, preventing the pass and stunting the opposition's central progression. Additionally, this forward also has to coordinate with the midfield since, as we had seen earlier, the three midfielders along with the forward have to create a pyramidal (or to be more precise, tetrahedral) shape surrounding the opposition midfielder in order to quickly close in and engage should the pass still be played.

The static forward essentially leads this block and, while still being the outlet, this extra responsibility now has him more involved out of possession. As for the other forward, dropping into midfield remains a priority, especially considering the fact that Atlético are now a man short there in this new formation. Moreover, when playing with three central midfielders, spaces can open up on either side of the midfield for the opposition to exploit, meaning that the forward needs to drop back in order to allow the side to spread out a bit more and cover these spaces as well. Though not crucial, this forward can also join in the shape created by the midfielders and the other forward as well and, with this, a 5-4-1 shape can be created effectively.

This first part is largely in line with the forward's role in the 4-4-2, but the next bit is where the responsibilities change. Owing to a lot of moving parts in the 5-3-2 formation, for example the wing-backs stepping up and the midfielders shifting across, there are multiple ways of shifting formations accordingly even without the movement of the forward. This is not to say that the forward is redundant, but instead this means that he is not entirely fixed to any position, and now has much more freedom to move between lines, considering that the primary purpose is to add numbers in deeper positions. As a result, looking at Figure 48, it is not entirely unnatural to see the forward even drop into the back line, taking on the role of a wing-back and essentially creating a 6-3-1 structure out of possession.

Such a shape is an extreme one, even by Simeone's standards, but its ingenuity certainly cannot be faulted.

Naturally this occurs when the opposition has forced Atlético deeper, but by moving into a six-man defence the side is then extremely compact and can comfortably defend in numbers, suffocating the opposition with this alone. In addition, it also provides more freedom to each individual in the back line in the sense that they can now step out of position to engage if they need to, promoting a more assertive style of defending since there is more than enough cover at the back should they step out.

Of course, a forward defending like a wing-back will certainly raise eyebrows, but since this forward has anyway been used like a winger and has the experience of defending in the wide areas, it is still an entirely viable move and gives Atlético that added option of pretty much retreating into their shell and playing their infamous 'park the bus' football. It may not be pretty, but beauty does lie in the eyes of the beholder and, considering its effectiveness, it might just be attractive enough to draw you in. Simeone certainly thinks so, and not only has he managed to get the best out of his forwards in possession with the new structure, he has also stayed true to character and found a way to get even more from them defensively as well.

While there might have been scope for an argument in the early years to say that Atlético's forwards may have been inhibited despite their effectiveness, it has definitely become harder to put this case forward in recent times. It is also important to understand the standing of the club itself when Simeone took over, and that the style of football played throughout that period clearly defined a team that were looking to punch above their weight, naturally requiring a more fixed set of roles as opposed to greater freedom. Though such a style of football is still visible now, Atlético's evolution is undeniable and their game in possession has certainly undergone a massive change, with the side now being far more patient and controlling in possession than they have ever been. This is not just down to the change in formation either, and even in the later years of the 4-4-2, conscious efforts were made to accommodate the changing player profiles that were present in the team.

The major beneficiaries of this have been the forwards and, contrary to popular belief, even if there is not a direct improvement on their goalscoring numbers (largely due to how effective the previous style was), they now have a more holistic development. After all, there are not many young strikers who can say that they have had to work consistently on their heading, finishing, movement and dribbling while also undergoing a significant improvement in their defensive work, meaning that they can almost suit any type of forward role in a top side. Of course, this does not apply to all the forwards who have played under Simeone, but there are enough examples to prove that it works, with Félix being the latest in line to go through this development, eventually coming good after some (natural) initial struggles.

If he keeps going, there is every chance that he ends up as successful as those before him, if not more, and he would certainly add to the list of stars that now follow.

* * * *

Radamel Falcao

There is no better player to kick us off than the talismanic Falcao, who was perhaps only second to Simeone himself as the face of a rising Atlético side back in early 2012. At his peak, Falcao was undoubtedly one of the deadliest forwards on the planet, with a goalscoring record that even the best might struggle to match. However, his story could have been the biggest case of what might have been had his father not encouraged him to become a forward, a move that came about after Radamel Sr's own experiences.

Radamel Enrique García King had been a defender himself, playing for Colombia at the 1980 Olympic Games, while also having a club career that saw him feature for eight different sides in Colombia and

Venezuela. Throughout his travels, a wide-eyed Falcao had followed him and, having spent time in dressing rooms and growing up in the footballing world, the young child needed little nudging to take up the game himself. Feeling that forwards have more fun than the players in his position, Radamel Sr would push his son to the opposite end of the pitch and there began his path to professional football.

In truth it was not really a long path, because in 1999, at the youthful age of 13 years and 199 days, Falcao became the youngest-ever player to debut in Colombian football after coming on as a substitute for second-division Lanceros Boyacá. There had been a rule which meant that clubs at the time had to field players under 16, even if it was for just a minute, and with most of the other under-16 players unavailable Falcao made history in this rather unplanned fashion. He was not even entirely out of his depth though, and any concerns over his age were quickly set aside as his talent shone through. Even if his opportunities to play were somewhat limited, it became clear within a couple of seasons that this 16-year-old was destined for greener pastures and he eventually signed for Argentinian side River Plate in 2001.

Working his way up through the ranks, starting in the eighth division with the youth side, it would be more than four years later that Falcao would make his senior debut with River, quickly making use of this opportunity to become a regular in the side. However, ligament tears in his right knee in November that year would see the forward sidelined, and after further damage to it before a full recovery, he would find himself out for nearly a year. Though he returned towards the end of 2006, his breakthrough season would arrive a year later, with Falcao netting 19 times in 39 games at the age of 21, before following it up with 16 goals in 38 games in the season after that. This would in fact be the first time that the Colombian linked up with Simeone as well, though the manager would leave towards the end of the second season, with River at the bottom of the table just a year after winning the championship.

Falcao would also leave just a few months later, and European clubs had begun to take notice of his goalscoring abilities. Portuguese side Benfica failed to cough up an extra €700,000, which allowed their rivals Porto to seal Falcao's services in the summer of 2009. Now aged 23, his first big move did little to faze him and, at the end of his first season, Falcao had bagged 34 goals in just 43 appearances before taking it up a notch in his second, scoring 38 in 42 at a rate of almost a goal a game. Add to this the fact that Porto won a treble in that second season in 2010/11, securing the Primeira Liga, the

Taça de Portugal and the Europa League, and Falcao's dominance was clear. He would even set a Europa League record during this run, with his 17 goals from 14 games being the highest number scored in a single campaign.

It is, therefore, no wonder that Atlético made him their most expensive signing at over €40m at the start of the 2011/12 season, and though it may seem impossible, Falcao managed to find yet another gear. Despite scoring six in his first three appearances for *Los Rojiblancos*, the initial months were difficult for the club and it would take a reunion with former boss Simeone to really get them going again. Atlético were now a counter-attacking team that needed a clinical forward to convert whatever chances they got, and Falcao filled this role perfectly. After spearheading the side to the Europa League in 2012, he became the first player to win the competition consecutively with two different clubs. Once again, he picked up where he left off in his second season, scoring a fantastic first-half hat-trick against Chelsea in the UEFA Super Cup to start the season with a trophy. He would end it with yet another, this time the Copa del Rey, beating rivals Real Madrid for the first time in over a decade in what would prove to be his final game in red and white.

Though he himself did not seem too interested in a move, after 70 goals in 92 appearances Falcao would head to France with Monaco, under new ownership, willing to spend around €60m on the then 27-year-old, starting a rather poor period for the Colombian before a rise back to the top. Injuries would plague the forward, the biggest of which came in the first season for Monaco in a relatively straightforward cup tie that saw him taken out in a rough challenge and tearing his ACL.

One of Colombia's greatest-ever players would unfortunately miss out on the 2014 World Cup, and after his return to football he would secure a loan to Manchester United in September 2014.

Of course, by this time he could have been a Spanish champion with Atlético, but the player who left Madrid was still there, or so most believed. Despite arriving to much fanfare and with a club looking to spring back to the top of English football, Falcao's time there could not have gone much worse, scoring just four goals in 29 appearances in a season where Dutch manager Louis van Gaal made him play in an Under-21 game in which he would be taken off on the hour mark. While the intention had not been to humiliate this once great forward, Falcao's form had simply been that poor and after the 2014/15 season United would opt to forgo their right to sign him permanently, sending him back to Monaco instead.

That was not where he would play the next season though, and Falcao returned to England immediately, with José Mourinho hoping to bring him back to his best at Chelsea. The move did not help, however, and where Falcao had managed to better his performances year after year, he was now on a downward slope as he managed to score just once in 12 games in a second consecutive poor season. He promptly found himself back at Monaco at the start of 2016, and it was here that his fortunes would finally change for the better. Upon his return, he found a club that was different to the one he first joined, with the French outfit now favouring a more youthful side. Manager Leonardo Jardim, however, felt that Falcao would be a fitting leader, and made him the captain even though he was no longer the sole star of the show.

With Kylian Mbappé, Bernardo Silva, Fabinho and Thomas Lemar as some of his team-mates, the now 30-year-old would reinvent himself, scoring 30 goals in 43 appearances that season as Monaco went on to lift the league title for the first time in 17 years and reached the semi-finals of the Champions League. Falcao contributed 21 and seven goals respectively to these successes and, while bigger European sides picked apart the rest of the cast, Falcao would remain at Monaco for a couple of seasons more before moving to

Galatasaray in Turkey. This spell would prove to be yet another poor one though, and his two years there would largely be spent on the sidelines as he faced further injury struggles, the worst of which was a facial fracture after a collision in training.

Nevertheless, there is always redemption in some form as Falcao has shown and he would return to Madrid in 2021, this time with the more modest Rayo Vallecano. It probably is not the likeliest of places to find a forward of Falcao's calibre, but conversations with ex-Atlético and current Rayo team-mate Mario Suárez would see him return to the Spanish capital, where he announced his arrival with a goal within ten and a half minutes of his debut. Aged 36, it was a whole 23 years since Falcao made his professional debut, going on to become his country's top goalscorer while spearheading many successful attacks in Europe. He is still remembered fondly among the Atlético faithful for his priceless contributions to kickstart this unforeseen period of excellence for the club, and his legend will certainly live on.

El Tigre, he is dubbed, quite literally translating as 'The Tiger', and though his stripes were in the colours of red and white, whenever Simeone needed someone to pounce in those precious moments Falcao proved to be the ideal predator.

Diego Costa

'I had no respect for the opposition, I thought I had to kill them,' Costa said in an interview with Spanish newspaper *El País* back in 2012, and for someone who scored goals by the truckload, his fiery personality on the pitch is usually what stood out. Costa could perhaps pick a fight with anyone, and even take on an entire opposition on his own, but the fact that he could do this with the ball as much as he did without it made him all the more intriguing.

Born in the small town of Lagarto, Brazil with a population of around 100,000, Costa would be named after the great Diego Maradona himself, with his father having been an avid fan of the sport. In fact, he along with his older brother (Jair, after Brazilian winger Jairzinho) were named in such a manner since his father hoped that one of them might eventually make it as a professional, though this did not even look likely as the pair grew up. Jair was apparently the better player but never followed through, opting to work instead and, as for Costa, he would tear it up at the local pitches without ever considering the fact that it could lead to something more. After all, the 'academies' in his town were not the biggest and his coaching was not really formal either, a reason why his playing style would become so rash and aggressive. 'Boys who grew up playing in academies are taught to control themselves and respect others, but no one ever told me otherwise. I didn't have a school to teach me that. I was used to seeing players elbowing each other in the face and thought it was normal,' he would later admit.

Moreover, seeing his brother earn a wage and have the freedom to party, Costa too was far more interested in that life and eventually, just as he was turning 15, he would leave his hometown for the big city of São Paulo, where his uncle worked in a shop selling goods brought from Paraguay. The original idea had been for him to work there, and so it panned out at least initially, but when his uncle managed to secure a trial through one of his contacts, Costa's life would change dramatically. Funnily enough, the teenager was not the least bit interested in the trial and would arrive an hour late without any gear, requiring the club, Barcelona Esportivo Capela, to provide him with some and leaving his uncle resigned to an inevitable rejection. However, as fate would have it, Barcelona Capela were in immediate need of a striker and, as Costa quickly started putting the ball in the net, he was signed despite not having played for any recognised team before.

There began his footballing career, though it would nearly immediately come to a halt. With his club situated on the other side of the city, the travel and finances involved were always in Costa's head and on quite a few occasions he would simply quit, stating that he wanted to work instead, only to be persuaded to get back on the pitch. His talent was never in doubt, but he himself was not cooperating and Costa would nearly miss his ticket to Europe after picking up a red card for an altercation which saw him banned for a period of around four to six months. This meant that he would miss a game which a leading agent and a friend of the famous Jorge Mendes was due to attend, but as fate would have it, a persuasive appeal from Barcelona Capela allowed Costa to feature. The forward would only come on as a substitute, but his performance was enough to catch the eye of the agent who would take him to Portugal in 2006, at the age of 17.

For once, it was Costa who wanted to move, despite his mother not being entirely sure, but the young forward would sign for Braga and, since they did not have a youth team, he would play for Penafiel in the country's second division. Impressively, this kid who had only started playing football properly a couple of years earlier, would catch the eye of Atlético Madrid at the end of 2006, and the Spanish side would sign Costa before loaning him back to Braga. He would officially be presented as a *Rojiblanco* in the summer of 2007, but he would have to wait three years before really making a mark on the first team. These three years would be spent out on loan as Costa travelled around with Celta Vigo, Albacete and then Real Valladolid, before earning a run for Atlético in the 2010/11 season as manager Quique Sánchez Flores fell out with star striker Diego Forlán.

His association with the club might have ended at the end of that season though, as Costa agreed a move to Turkish side Beşiktaş only for a knee injury in pre-season to stop him from passing his medical. By the time he was back playing, Gregorio Manzano had departed and Simeone had entered, the latter sending him out on loan to Rayo Vallecano in January 2012 for some game time until the end of the season. This meant that Costa missed the Europa League triumph that year, but on his return, he would find himself thrust into the first team alongside Falcao, finally playing regularly for Atlético as he turned 24, after joining them nearly five years earlier. Anywhere else and his disciplinary record that season would probably have seen him dropped as the forward picked up cards, both yellow and red, for various incidents, but such was Costa's fit in this side that Simeone continued to select him whenever available.

Though not the most elegant of players, Costa operated with impressive pace and power, making him perfect for *Cholo*'s counter-attacking philosophy, with the forward often taking on opponents on his own during transitions without needing his team to get forward in numbers alongside him. His impressive performances in 2012/13 would culminate in a crucial equalising goal in the famous Copa del Rey final, forcing the game into extra time where Miranda nodded home the winner. That goal would also see him edge Cristiano Ronaldo as the top scorer in that season's tournament, but Costa was just getting started. His tally of 27 league goals the next season would see him fall just short of Lionel Messi (28) and Ronaldo (31) in the race to be the top scorer, though it would power Atlético towards their first league title in nearly two decades and his performances would also take the side to the Champions League final as well. Unfortunately, Costa would have to be taken off early in both the final and the famous last-day draw against Barcelona owing to a muscle injury, and how differently the former might have played out had he continued.

At the end of that campaign, Chelsea promptly met his release clause as they also picked up Filipe Luís on top of recalling Thibaut Courtois. Costa's three years in London would have their fair share of ups and downs, first of all breaking the record for most goals scored in a player's first four games as he netted seven times, forming an excellent partnership with Cesc Fàbregas and eventually ending on 20 in his first year, which saw him finish as the third-highest scorer in the league in a season where Chelsea won both the League Cup as well as the Premier League. The following campaign, however, Costa had an incredibly tough time after a rumoured fallout with José Mourinho meant that he was not playing as much and, with fans siding with the manager who would eventually face the sack after poor results, his relationship with the supporters deteriorated too. His form did improve under interim manager Guus Hiddink, but most of his season was marred by more fights on the pitch and the English media branding him as one of football's biggest-ever villains.

Costa would rise back up just as rapidly though in the 2016/17 season under Antonio Conte, and despite another falling out in January 2017, he would once again score 20 goals in the league to bring the title back to Chelsea. Conte, though, decided that Costa was no longer necessary and made this clear to the forward, allowing him to return to Atlético in September 2017. It would be a happy reunion, with Costa winning the Europa League in his first year back and scoring twice as they defeated Real Madrid in the UEFA Super Cup just as he was approaching his 30th birthday. The following years, however, would be a period of decline for the once-terrorising forward, and with fights and arguments still popping up every now and then, he was no longer the undroppable player that he had once been; his contract was essentially terminated upon mutual agreement in December 2020. He then entered the football wilderness, with a six-month stint at Atlético Mineiro being the only bit of professional football that he has played in about two years having been a free agent either side of that period.

He has also fallen off the radar of Spain's national team post-2018, and his decision to swap the yellow of Brazil did come under fire from the country of his birth. Having only appeared in a couple of friendlies for them though, he was within his right to play for his adopted nation when he received citizenship starting in 2014, playing 24 times for Spain in the four-year span and scoring ten times.

'A helpless Bambi up against a roaring panther' was how Spanish news outlet *AS* once described a match-up between Costa and an opposition defender, and this predator was sure to torment opponents, not even needing the ball to do so.

* * *

Antoine Griezmann

Griezmann's inclusion over Fernando Torres might raise a few eyebrows but it is important to remember that we are looking at players who have become a force under Simeone, and it can be argued that for Torres, Atlético's beloved *El Niño*, his best performances in red and white came alongside Simeone in the early 2000s rather than under his management. Torres, of course, still remains one of Atlético's finest ever, but for now, our focus shifts to a Frenchman who, despite not having the same level of admiration, has certainly been one of *Cholo*'s most trusted players.

Born in Mâcon, France, Griezmann is also of Portuguese (maternal) and German (paternal) descent, and has football in his blood, with his maternal grandfather having played for Portuguese side Paços de Ferreira and his father, who was also a town councillor, the coach of a local team. Professional football would be his dream and in fact, it was at this local side, UF Mâconnais, where little Griezmann's career would begin as the young kid attempted to find a path to the top. However, at a time when French football had been overly preoccupied with athletic and physical abilities, his smaller size meant that despite attending trials at a host of clubs, he failed to find any success, with one even cancelling a trial at the last minute due to his size even though they had invited him over initially. His father naturally became sceptical of any further approaches, but this did not deter Griezmann from trying and he would find himself at the training ground of Paris Saint-Germain as part of a trial with Montpellier.

The then 14-year-old would not play for either of those clubs though, and despite playing well at the tournament that was organised, most of the French scouts would overlook him once again, only for a scout from Real Sociedad to offer him the chance to trial in Spain. Funnily enough, this scout was only present as he had decided to visit some friends while on vacation, but seeing Griezmann's technicality, he would clear it with the clubs that were present and proceed to make his offer. A couple of weeks with Sociedad was enough to make the deal permanent, and so began the Frenchman's first foray into professional football. It was a new culture and a new language, which was naturally hard for Griezmann to adapt to, but his determination to succeed was enought to overcome any obstacle.

Within a couple of years he would move up into the reserve team, impressing coach Martín Lasarte, and when Lasarte took on the role of first team manager in 2009 Griezmann would move up too, with the side playing in the second division at the time. They would immediately secure promotion to the top flight and, as an academy product at a Basque club, he was quickly becoming a fan favourite and helping his side secure Champions League football by the time 2013 came around. During Atlético's famous title-winning campaign in 2013/14, 22-year-old Griezmann kept going and he had 16 league goals out of a total of 20 in all competitions, making him the highest scorer outside the top three teams that season. The champions would immediately pay his release clause of about €30m, bringing the Frenchman to Madrid for the first time.

Adaptation, once again, was not easy and the promising youngster that arrived with all his attacking flair struggled initially to adapt to Simeone's more rigid structure. This is not to say that *Cholo* himself would go easy on Griezmann, and the manager would sometimes even publicly ask for more from his new forward. By January, though, he had picked up the Player of the Month award and had sprung to life in Atlético's system, eventually netting 22 times, the third-highest tally in the league and a number that saw him overtake Karim Benzema to become the highest-scoring French player in a single Spanish top-flight season. He would go on to be even more influential in the 2015/16 campaign, scoring in the quarter-finals against Barcelona and bagging the decisive away goal in the semi-finals against Bayern Munich to send Atlético into the final of the Champions League for the second time in three years. Unfortunately, he would miss a penalty in normal time, with his side trailing by a goal and despite the game eventually going to penalties, where he would convert his kick, they would ultimately fall to rivals Real Madrid.

Still, Griezmann earned himself a Ballon d'Or nomination for his exploits and, only 25 at this time, he continued on season after season. The turning point, though, would arrive at the end of the 2017/18 season when, after leading Atlético to a Europa League triumph, he would release a controversial documentary surrounding his decision to move to Barcelona, eventually announcing that he would be extending his contract in Madrid anyway. Naturally this did not sit too well with either fanbase, but he would still pick up the UEFA Super Cup in 2018 and finish the 2018/19 season in second place, while also becoming Atlético's fifth-highest scorer in their history. This time, though, Barcelona would activate his €120m release clause, after much controversy over the actual amount, and it seemed like the Frenchman had burnt his bridges with *Los Rojiblancos*.

Griezmann was 28 at the time, but adapting to Barcelona would prove difficult as he was often played as a winger rather than as a second striker, where he had thrived. Add to this the fact that his popularity with the fans was low and that first season would pass by him with a mere nine league goals out of a total of

15. He would seemingly find his stride in 2020/21, though, playing a crucial role in winning the Copa del Rey and increasing his goal tally to 13 in the league and 20 overall, but with Barcelona in a financial crisis, Atlético would extend a helping hand, both to the club and to Griezmann, to take him back on loan for a year with the option of an extension, following which an obligatory €40m purchase clause would be activated.

This move was not too popular back in Madrid, but Griezmann was still a player that Simeone liked and despite his turning 31 midway through the 2021/22 season he started most games for which he was available. The forward took until the end of September to reopen his account with Atlético, but a goalscoring streak after that gave the impression that the once prolific player was back only for his form to fade away once again. His work rate and intensity have certainly returned though and have been useful for a side with a largely inconsistent season, but with the forward not contributing much to goals like he used to, how his future pans out beyond this loan period remains to be seen.

A player like him does not simply disappear as, after all, Griezmann is a successful international with loads of experience and is currently on the way to his third World Cup in 2022. For France, he has played for the Under-19, Under-20 and under-21 teams, winning the

2010 Under-19 World Cup and featuring in the 2011 Under-20 World Cup as well. Though a year-long ban from all of their national teams for disciplinary reasons due to a late night out meant that Griezmann nearly considered switching allegiance to Portugal, he eventually debuted for the French senior team in 2014. The forward would play in the 2014 World Cup later that year, but his biggest performances on the national stage were yet to come, with Griezmann being named as the player of the tournament at Euro 2016 on home soil, having been the top scorer with six goals in seven games, a record second only to Michel Platini's tally of nine at Euro 1984. France would suffer a heartbreaking defeat in extra time to Portugal in the final, but they would make no mistake at the FIFA World Cup, finishing as winners with Griezmann voted the third-best player at the tournament.

For the moment at least, the Frenchman has certainly managed to build back at least some of the broken bridges with the fans since his return, largely due to the changed mentality that he has shown upon returning, being unselfish and putting in a shift for his team-mates to profit from, and perhaps a few more goals may have seen him fully accepted back at the place where he really made his mark. When he signed all the way back in 2014 it signalled a change in how Atlético were to be viewed around the world; they were now seen as a team capable of cultivating some of the biggest stars in the game and, even tactically, it showed how under Simeone they could slowly develop a more expansive and intricate style of play for these stars to shine.

Where his size was once a concern, Griezmann has certainly grown in stature, and he now excels in the air and on the ground with his quick feet and pace giving him the versatility to play anywhere across the attacking line. Add his relentless stamina to the mix and beneath his usual cheerful facade lies one of football's most complete attackers, with a predatory instinct that is up there with the very best.

* * *

'You need to know which one precise second to train for, and to understand that moment. That's something that comes with instinct, with the intelligence or experience of a player.'

Simeone is back to talking about moments, and for someone who lives every second of the game he truly knows how important each one is. After all, everything he does is centred around these moments, whichever end of the pitch it may be, because he realises that it is in these moments that games are won and, unfortunately, lost. Formations and tactics are nothing but numbers and squiggles once you set foot on the pitch and, when it is time to strike, you simply need to take your chances.

As Atlético bide their time on the pitch, they know that their moments are forthcoming. For now they might be the prey, but there is never any doubt that their time will come because, ultimately, that is what they have been preparing for, to ruin the opponents' moments while creating and making use of their own. It is only a matter of when and not if, and when the moment does arrive, Atlético are more than ready.

The hunter becomes the hunted, and out come the forwards, the perfect predators.

9

Silent Guardians: Goalkeepers

'Order is a way of life'

IT WAS the first week of October 2019 and in those last few months before Covid-19 was a thing, the Champions League was back for its second round of group stage fixtures that season. The first round had served up some excellent fixtures, with Chelsea losing 1-0 at home to Valencia, Napoli scoring two unanswered goals to beat holders Liverpool and Paris Saint-Germain hitting three past Real Madrid as fans rejoiced at the return of Europe's premier club competition. The second round, though, piled on the action as Barcelona came from behind to beat Inter Milan after Bayern Munich smashed seven past Tottenham earlier on, with Liverpool involved in an entertaining 4-3 victory over RB Leipzig as well.

All these games would grab the headlines in one way or another, and deservedly so owing to the size of the clubs involved and the sheer entertainment that the matches had provided, but there would be another moment from a rather unassuming fixture that would go viral as well. Atlético Madrid travelled to Russia to face Lokomotiv Moscow, after a 2-2 draw with Juventus in the first round, to face what was generally assumed to be a fixture that *Los Rojiblancos* should win comfortably. Most of the general viewers had naturally tuned in to the more enticing games on air, and two goals within 15 minutes after half-time effectively put the tie to bed, confirming the public consensus on the result. However, those that did decide to watch the game would notice a particular incident seconds before the interval and, within minutes, this would be shared across the world.

It was the second and final minute of stoppage time at the end of the first half and, with the scores level, Atlético were awarded a free kick just inside the opposition half. The ball would be floated in towards the penalty area to make something out of what was possibly their last chance of the half, but the goalkeeper's failed catch would fall kindly to his team-mate, who even under considerable pressure, would work the ball away and start a transition. Fifteen seconds remained, and Atlético had just two men back.

What followed would closely resemble an Olympic 100m dash, with six Atlético players sprinting back alongside each other to get back into position – centre-backs, midfielders and even forwards among the bunch. By the time the opposition got to the box, the seven players they had sent forward found themselves a man short of Atlético's eight who were now between them and the goal. Seven seconds remained and, try as they might, there was no way past, with a rushed shot blazing high over the goal (just as the clock ticked over two minutes) being all that the opposition could fashion. After all the initial panic, order had been restored.

Did Atlético need that many players to sprint back the way they did? Probably not, and Diego Simeone would call it 'emotional', saying, 'They come back desperately, so you can't score against them. It's an emotional gesture, a different gift, because not everyone feels the same way.' The incident was not entirely born out of necessity; rather it was a gift from one player to the others, putting in their own effort to reduce the burden on the next, who would carry it forward. Ultimately, the final player in this chain would have little to do and, in this case, it was the goalkeeper, Jan Oblak, who calmly watched the ball sail into the stands. It is a gift that he was more than happy to receive.

Just two years earlier, he himself had been the bearer of gifts in the same competition, as Atlético welcomed Bayer Leverkusen to Madrid for the second leg of a round of 16 tie. Simeone's side carried a 4-2 lead into the home leg, knowing that they had to lose by three goals if they were to be knocked out owing to the away goals rule in operation at the time. As you would expect, it was a game in which Leverkusen searched for goals to mount some sort of challenge but as the minutes ticked on, none were forthcoming.

Goalless at half-time, the German side finally thought that they had their chance eight minutes after the hour when Julian Brandt found himself through on goal after picking up on a poor pass and firing a shot that should have begun a fightback. His shot would ricochet off Oblak's chest only to land at the feet of Kevin Volland, who now had the goal at his mercy, or so he thought. At full stretch Oblak would block this too, but the ball would fall kindly for Volland once again and surely it had to be third time lucky for the visitors. A third successive save, diving back across, would deny him again though, only for the ball to fall for Javier 'Chicharito' Hernández instead, and this time the shot would go wide. '*Qué paradón de Oblak, Qué paradón de Oblak, QUÉ PARADÓN DE OBLAK*,' yelled the Spanish commentator each time, and what a save indeed. This sequence was the fault of the defence and, this time, Oblak answered with not one, but three gifts to keep the scores level. Once again, order was restored.

These two sequences paint a fitting picture of Atlético's goalkeeper situation, for to assume that a shot-stopper is an island on his own would be nothing short of a complete misunderstanding, even if it is the keeper that we notice pulling off stunning saves in front of our eyes. Of course, in the modern era, most goalkeepers are now more involved in possession and rely on communication and coordination in attack as much as they do in defence, but in a team like Atlético where they expect the ball to be in and around their area, this relationship between the keeper and the outfield players is all the more crucial. After all, the prevention of goals is a team effort, and not the sole responsibility of the keeper, so as the side repel attacks that come their way, it is the duty of each one to pass on their gift to the next.

Moreover, it all points towards the order and discipline that Simeone demands from his players. These may not be the first words to come to your mind and, in fact, they might be the exact opposite of the often loud and aggressive side that we see on the field, but when it comes to fulfilling their duties, order and discipline are key characteristics that are the basis of Atlético's defensive principles. Every single member of the outfield line knows their role and it is their responsibility to carry it out with total commitment and discipline to maintain the order on the pitch. The attack shields the midfield, the midfield shields the defence and finally the defence shields the keeper, who has the last chance to restore order to the game whenever the ball finds its way past those ahead of him. Though Simeone would like it not to be a foregone conclusion, a shot is bound to find the target at some point, be it in that game or the next, and when it does, the goalkeeper needs to be ready to stop it.

This is where things become difficult for a goalkeeper, and not just because they are finally called into action. Iker Casillas, the legendary Real Madrid custodian, would phrase it best, saying, 'Being a good person is like being a goalkeeper, no matter how many goals you save, some people will only remember the one you missed.' There is certainly truth to this, and while the ordinary saves pulled off by keepers are hardly remembered beyond a few days, the slightest of blunders may even go on to define their careers.

The reasons for this are fairly obvious and can be attributed to the fact that the goalkeeper position itself is one of low visibility, especially in a sport where attack takes precedence. A keeper is often taken for granted, almost expected to make a save most times, and even when they kick the ball out, be it long or short, the pass is simply expected to reach its target. Not many really give a second thought as to what exactly it is that these players do and even when they are required to perform their duties, the attention of the viewer is naturally on the player striking the ball rather than this player attempting to stop it, and only when the ball is stopped in dramatic fashion do they get noticed.

In fact, even with respect to advanced statistics, goalkeeper actions have only recently been quantified beyond surface level in order to truly understand how good an individual is. For a long time, clean sheets (games without conceding) and save percentages were the main metrics by which goalkeepers were judged and, considering how most of their actions are reactive rather than proactive, it was not easy to properly compare and quantify their wider involvement. However, neither of these metrics properly describe how good a goalkeeper is simply because both are based on how the team performs rather than the keeper's performance itself. For example, a goalkeeper in a more defensively stable side will by default keep more clean sheets even if they are not the best in their own position owing to the lower quality of shots faced and, in this case, they have a higher chance of boosting their save percentage. Inversely though, if a keeper was to face more shots from better goalscoring positions owing to a poor defence, there is only so much that they can do to prevent a goal, meaning that despite their ability they could lose their clean sheet and have a lower save percentage as well.

As a result, such metrics quickly became secondary measures in the modern era as teams placed a greater emphasis on fully understanding everything that a goalkeeper does. Moreover, they had to consider more than just volume metrics, for example the number of saves a keeper was making, as this would once again be a factor of the team rather than the keepers themselves and quality metrics, such as the xG (expected goal probability) of the shots faced, would come to the fore. In the scope of this book we will not dive into the intricacies of these metrics, but rather our takeaway is to understand how the keeper position has been increasingly scrutinised and tracked, and to identify the broad areas under which they are now assessed.

So, what are these areas? After much deliberation, there is now a general agreement that a modern goalkeeper has to do more than just stop shots, though that is still their primary duty. Possession-based sides now prefer to build up from the back and, by having a goalkeeper involved in this sequence, they can get an extra player in possession to better navigate through an opposition's press or defensive structure. Apart from this, teams that look to play a high line also need their goalkeepers to leave their line consistently to sweep up any passes played in behind to thwart attacks and cover for their defenders, giving them greater support in a setup which does leave them slightly vulnerable. This is not the only case in which goalkeepers need to leave their lines though, and for sides that force opponents into crosses or end up conceding set pieces, keepers need to be comfortable enough to take control of their area and punch or claim the ball to effectively end the attack and relieve the pressure on their sides. Broadly classifying all these duties, the ideal modern goalkeeper needs to be adept at stopping shots, claiming crosses or exiting their line, and last but not least, comfortable with the ball at their feet.

You may be wondering what any of this has to do with Atlético, but it is with these three broad categories that we will analyse the goalkeeping position under Simeone. This chapter will differ largely from the previous ones in that it is much shorter due to the fact that there are no outright tactics or sequences for us to view, and rather we will discuss the duties of the goalkeepers and how they compare with those of the template modern goalkeeper we saw earlier. Before we begin, though, it is important to once again go over Atlético's style of play to understand the requirements of a goalkeeper in this system.

We know that Atlético's tactics have undergone a massive overhaul in recent times owing to a change in structure, but starting with the 4-4-2 formation, we see that they prefer to defend deeper before springing quick attacks and catching opponents out with their directness and incisiveness. Gradually, as the years went by, the style of football played in this structure would also shift to a slightly more possession-based one, with Atlético still looking to be the same incisive side but also playing higher up and seeing more of the ball.

In this setup, the job of a goalkeeper is limited only to the out-of-possession phase, when the side is defending, as the build-up is far more basic and direct even when Atlético operate higher up the pitch. We have already seen how the centre-backs are responsible for ball progression, with the midfielders offering them some support in this regard in the later years, but this is something that the goalkeepers need not be involved in. The only progression that they need to be involved in is from goal kicks, most of which would be played long and into the opposition half for team-mates to contest, with there also being enough players around to win the second ball. Apart from this, starting counter attacks once they receive possession, either after a save or a claim, is the only other task that they have when the side is in possession, hence they require a good kicking and throwing ability but not anything more advanced in terms of playing with their feet.

Instead, it is these saves and claims that they are more involved in considering the overall defensive structure of the side, and these duties prove to be far more important than their distribution. Especially in the 'bigger' games against opposition expected to control possession, Atlético know that they will have to regularly face attacks, which means more shots against them. While the primary duty of the outfield players is to make these shots as difficult as possible for the opposition, no defensive structure can be so airtight as to prevent a good chance from ever seeping through, hence shot stopping becomes an extremely important ability for a goalkeeper in this setup.

Breaking down shot stopping into individual attributes, a goalkeeper in this Atlético side needs to have good reflexes, positioning and diving ability, and while all of these seem like the most basic traits that a keeper should have, it is imperative that Atlético have someone who is proficient in all these abilities. For a team that defends deeper, there is a considerable chance that opponents shoot from closer to goal, requiring the keeper to make good reaction saves, either by quickly closing them down or by sticking an arm or a leg out to stop the shot. Positioning also plays its part in this allowing the keeper to effectively cut out angles and get in the line of the shot, and this is also important when saving shots from distance to ensure that the goal area is well covered and that a long shot can be saved with relative ease. Of course, in the case of the shot simply being too good, a keeper would need to put in an equally good dive to get across and push the ball to safety.

Claiming is also important in such a side because Atlético do force opponents to the wide areas and invite crosses, and if it was only the duty of the defenders to head the ball away, the side might risk consistently conceding possession and getting caught up in this cycle. By stepping out to claim or punch the ball away, the keeper not only helps his team-mates deal with the balls in, but he can also relieve pressure by making a catch, allowing Atlético to regroup and start their own attack, especially since a quick counter is on with a pass out from the keeper as well.

Added to this, when Atlético did look to play higher, they also required the keeper to cover space, and while not exactly needing to sweep like Manuel Neuer would, defending in one-v-one situations would also be important. In pursuit of a more attacking setup, the defence was not something Simeone was willing to compromise, but even with centre-backs who could cover space and defend in a higher line, balls in behind could still penetrate the back line and create good chances for the opposition. While this was quite uncharacteristic of Atlético in the initial stages, it has slowly become a more prominent feature, and hence the goalkeeper has had to evolve to suit this and add one-v-one defending to the armoury.

Much like when leaving the line to claim a cross, awareness is crucial here as well to ensure that the keeper leaves the line at the right time and engages the opponent at an optimal point of their run, and they would be required to cover this ground with good speed as well to close down the opponent quickly. Moreover, it all boils down to cutting down the angles that the opponent has to shoot, and covering as much of the goal as possible, so the keeper's ability to make himself as big as possible also adds to his effectiveness in this situation.

This would become even more important when Atlético shifted to a 5-3-2 formation as, even though there was an extra centre-back for cover, the side now wanted to play in a much more controlled manner in possession, operating a higher line than they had before. We have already seen how the outfield players act in such a structure and, most importantly, how the centre-backs especially have been given greater freedom in possession to even carry the ball into midfield. Moreover, just as Atlético's press had become higher throughout the evolution of the 4-4-2, they would be even more comfortable pressing higher in the 5-3-2 as they had the necessary cover at the back with the three centre-backs. However, despite the numerical advantage, a high press does still leave some scope for opponents to play the ball in behind if they manage to bypass the initial press, meaning that the keeper now has to be all the more proactive in covering the space behind the defence.

With more advanced statistics now available to track such scenarios, we can quantify this change in the figure overleaf.

With the help of StatsBomb, via FBref, we can see how Atlético's keeper fares in two metrics, the number of defensive actions outside the penalty area (taken on a per 90-minute basis rather than a total to accommodate for varying minutes in a season) and the average distance of defensive actions from the goal line. Now, by using these two metrics, we are aiming to understand not only the frequency with which the keeper steps out of his area to cover for the defence (sweeping), but also the

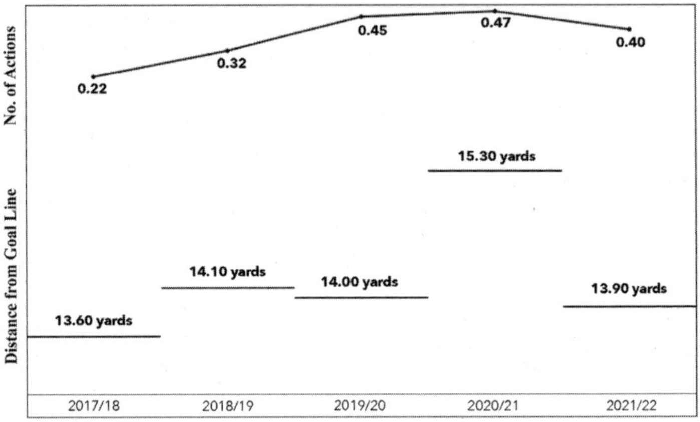

Fig 49 *Number of Defensive Actions Outside Penalty Area per 90 minutes and Average Distance of Defensive Actions from Goal Line from the 2017/18 season to the 2021/22 season*

general distance that he covers off his goal line for all his actions, be it inside the box or out of it. Since the shift to become more proactive in this manner started sometime during the 2017/18 season, we will look at how these statistics have changed since then.

Right up until the 2019/20 campaign there has been a steady increase in terms of the number of defensive actions outside the penalty area, with the value increasing from 0.22 per 90 in 2017/18 to 0.32 per 90 in 2018/19 before another increase to 0.45 per 90 in 2019/20. Remember that for most of these three seasons, Atlético were still operating with a 4-4-2 formation, but as we said earlier, there was a clear shift in terms of how the side wanted to advance in possession, leading to the keeper having to defend more space in behind. This is also evident from the average distance from the goal line, and while this also includes how far the keeper steps out for claims or to block one-v-ones, there is a clear increase from the 13.60 yards in 2017/18 to 14.10 yards in 2018/19 after which it is fairly consistent in 2019/20, with an average of 14 yards. This may go against the increase in actions outside the penalty area, but it can be attributed to the simple fact that Atlético conceded fewer crosses that season, meaning that the keeper stepped out less often to claim these balls into the area.

The general increase does, however, confirm what we have said about the keeper being more proactive and, with the complete shift to a 5-3-2 in the 2020/21 season, we see a marked difference in the average distance of actions from the goal line, with the value going up to 15.30 yards. The increase in actions outside the area is marginal, which suggests that the keeper is covering more ground within the box this season and stepping closer to the edge in order to engage opponents. It is also interesting to note that, with the change in formation, Atlético actually conceded even fewer crosses into the box, but since their higher line did get exposed with opponents looking to hit them on the break, the keeper was still required to leave the line and step out further than usual in order to effectively prevent the concession of goals from one-v-one situations.

This too confirms what we said earlier about the keeper having to cover even more ground with the change to the 5-3-2, but the significant drop in the 2021/22 season does seem to go against this despite Atlético sticking with the same formation. The explanation for this is largely circumstantial though, as in what was a rather poor and inconsistent season, especially defensively, Atlético were regularly exposed at the back when trying to play with a high line, leading to Simeone having to switch things up continuously and even drop the line deeper at times. Add to this the dip in form of Oblak himself, who was the number one between the sticks throughout all the previous seasons as well, and the confidence of both the player and coach to cover larger spaces behind the defence lessened, leading to the significant change in the values. With time off after the season to rework the tactics and come up with a permanent fix to the structure, we can expect these values to increase once again in future seasons.

As for the distribution aspect, the only thing that would change with the new formation was that the keeper would now play shorter passes more often than before, considering that Atlético have become more patient in the build-up. The keeper himself does not actively participate in this build-up but is now more comfortable recycling possession and passing the ball out to the centre-backs for them to start attacks, while continuing to play longer passes forwards whenever necessary. This is quite understandable as well, considering the fact that the three centre-backs can easily spread across the pitch and do not require the keeper to split them when playing out from the back.

However, the fact remains that this is one of the areas that Simeone has not looked to actively modernise, sticking to his tried and tested method of opting for a better shot stopper as opposed to a keeper that is good with his feet and instead finding other ways to play out from the back. This in turn has resulted in stability in defence, and it is clear that *Cholo* likes what he sees and would rather not attempt to add on additional responsibilities. In fact, throughout Simeone's tenure, the goalkeeper is possibly the only position on the pitch that has been immune to the axe, barring the 2014/15 season, which was perhaps the only time that there were two genuine contenders for the number one spot.

A testament to this is the fact that throughout Simeone's tenure of over a decade, out of the nine keepers who have featured for Atlético, only four have made over ten appearances. The disparity between these four is massive as well. The one with the highest number of appearances, Oblak, has made more than 350 (and counting) which is more than double the next best, Thibaut Courtois, with 154. Third and fourth are even further back, with Miguel Ángel Moyà featuring 67 times, followed by Sergio Asenjo who, despite making 41 appearances in total, only featured 15 times for Simeone.

The faith and trust placed in the man between the sticks has certainly brought results, making Atlético one of the best defensive teams in the world by ensuring that there is always at least one constant at the back to provide the solidity and continuity in terms of defensive partnerships. Moreover, the clarity of the role itself allows the keeper to focus on what he does best, paving the way for confidence in his own abilities, which is then followed by consistent performances.

This is especially true for the top two on the appearance list who, even now, are widely considered to be among the best keepers in the world. Both of them have starred in La Liga title wins as well as runs to the Champions League final and have an enviable trophy cabinet along with a long list of stunning saves to match, meaning that it is only right that we make them our standout players for this chapter.

* * *

Jan Oblak

Born in the small town of Škofja Loka, Slovenia, Oblak grew up in a sporty household, with his father having been a goalkeeper for the local side, while his mother had played handball for a bit as well. His elder sister, too, would go on to play for the national basketball team and it was always clear that Oblak was no different, he also enjoyed picking up the ball in his hands. Living under the same roof as his role model, Oblak would travel to games with his father, standing behind the goal and diving along with him to pull off saves even though it was only one of them that actually touched the ball.

No one was forcing him to become a goalkeeper, but his heart was set on it and at the age of five the young boy would join local side Ločan, though this was not where he would first be noticed. Oblak was still going to his father's games and, at half-time, he would often stand in goal while his sister, who was good at football herself, fired shots at him and it was during one such instance that Olimpija Ljubljana noticed him, and decided to sign him up. At this point, Oblak was just turning ten and, in spite of having to cycle over 20km just to get to training, he would snatch at the chance to turn his footballing dream into reality.

Around five years later, in 2008, Oblak started to train with the first team who were now in the second division as a result of financial difficulties, but his talent had become evident and even before his senior debut for the side, he would reject a contract from Italian side Empoli and even have a week-long trial at English side Fulham, though he eventually extended his contract at Olympija until 2011. His debut came along soon after when he was aged 16, towards the end of that 2008/09 season, as the side earned promotion to the first division and it was in the top division that Oblak would get his big break. The keeper hardly missed a game in his first full season as his side finished fourth in their first year back up, but even with a year left on his contract, his performances made it clear that he was destined for bigger things.

Portuguese giants Benfica came calling in the summer of 2010 and, even though he had only just started to play regularly, Oblak had found his ticket to the top and was not willing to pass up on such an opportunity. The move, however, was anything but easy and, on top of having to settle into a new culture, the keeper immediately found himself sent out on two unsuccessful loans to Beira-Mar and then Olhanense, where he was often out of the line-up and failed to feature regularly for either side. Regular playing time would only come in 2011 when União de Leiria took him on loan and gave him 17 appearances that season, but Oblak was still not quite ready for Benfica and another loan would follow in the 2012/13 season, this time in the first division itself, as Oblak made 31 appearances for Nuno Espírito Santo's Rio Ave. The Slovenian had now completed three seasons in Portugal and, going into his fourth, the 20-year-old would finally be recalled to Benfica's first team.

The start of the 2013/14 season was rather anticlimactic, though, as Oblak played second fiddle to first-choice keeper Artur, and he would have to wait until about midway to finally have his break. A series of errors and niggles plagued Artur, leading to manager Jorge Jesus dropping him in favour of Oblak and handing him his first start for the club that he had signed for over three years earlier. The chance had arrived and Oblak would not look back. Starting 24 games that season, he would concede just six times and even go on a run of 12 games in which he let in just one, winning the domestic treble with Benfica and also winning the award for best keeper in the league. Oblak had well and truly made the most of his opportunity and, aged just 21 at the end of the season, he had become one of the hottest goalkeeping prospects in football.

Atlético Madrid would make him the most expensive keeper in La Liga history when they signed him for €16m in July 2014, during a window that involved a lot of goalkeeping moves, with Keylor Navas heading to Real Madrid and Marc-André ter Stegen joining Barcelona along with Claudio Bravo. Naturally, Oblak was expected to fill the boots of Courtois, who had just been a crucial part of Atlético's title victory, but much like his time in Portugal the keeper's time in Madrid would get off to a shaky start.

The more experienced Moyà got the nod in goal and a knock in pre-season did not help Oblak's chances either, but rumours that he had been offered back to Benfica even before his debut did little to help him settle. His first appearance would damage his reputation more than help it though, and his first start for the club against Olympiacos in the Champions League ended in a 3-2 defeat, with Oblak making key errors contributing to goals.

He would have to wait three months for his next start, which came about in the Copa del Rey against L'Hospitalet away from home, with Oblak keeping his first clean sheet. This would prompt Simeone to give him a run in the cup while Moyà remained the first choice in the league, but a fine performance in the home leg of the round of 16 tie against Real Madrid, which saw Atlético win 2-0, meant that Oblak was starting to settle in nicely. However, another bump on the road was on its way when by the end of January Atlético were out of the cup, losing to Barcelona in the quarter-finals. It would be nearly two months before Oblak played again, but this time there was no going back to the bench.

With Atlético trailing 1-0 on aggregate to Bayer Leverkusen in the round of 16 of the Champions League, Moyà walked off injured just 23 minutes into the second leg in Madrid. Oblak would come on and put in what was a career-defining performance, keeping the Germans at bay and taking the tie to penalties, where he would save Hakan Çalhanoğlu's effort to make up for Raúl García's earlier miss and give his side a 3-2 victory in the shoot-out. Without much competition, Oblak would finally start regularly and fully showcase his quality, with another stunning display against Real Madrid in the quarter-finals of the same competition sealing his place in the side, so much so that even when Moyà returned from injury he was not to be displaced.

It is easy to forget that Oblak was just 22 years old at the end of that 2014/15 season, and the Slovenian stopper would only go from strength to strength, finishing the 2015/16 season having conceded just 18 goals in 38 league games. He would also save a crucial Thomas Müller penalty against Bayern Munich in the semi-finals of the Champions League, sending his side to the final, though his heroics could not be repeated there. Nonetheless, he won the Zamora Trophy back home for having the lowest goals-to-games ratio among all the keepers in La Liga and also featured in the Champions League's team of the season. The Zamora Trophy was one that he would retain for four consecutive seasons, equalling Víctor Valdés's record for the most consecutive prizes won as Oblak continued notching up clean sheets and making crucial stops, including that spectacular triple save against Leverkusen in 2017.

Some may argue that clean sheets are a team effort, but with saves such as those, it is hard to deny his exceptional quality and, on his 178th appearance for Atlético, Oblak kept his 100th clean sheet in a 2-0 victory over Borussia Dortmund in the group stages of the 2018/19 Champions League. By this time he was already a Europa League and UEFA Super Cup winner as well, the first trophies that he majorly contributed to in Madrid. At the start of the 2019/20 season, he would be named as the vice-captain and, in December 2019, he would break the club record for the most clean sheets in La Liga, surpassing Abel Resino's tally of 95 on only his 169th league appearance.

Oblak's stunning performances would continue, and in March 2020 he would make nine saves to deny Liverpool at Anfield as Atlético mounted an exceptional comeback in the Champions League round of 16, before breaking yet another record for becoming the fastest keeper to achieve 100 clean sheets in La Liga history, doing so in his 182nd game, 40 fewer than previous holder Miguel Reina. In that same game, he would also become the first non-Spanish keeper to keep 100 clean sheets, but the best was yet to come and in 2020/21 Oblak secured his first league title with Atlético, playing an extremely crucial role as they switched to the 5-3-2 formation. Unfortunately for him, his performances would drop for the first time in over half a decade in the 2021/22 season, but Oblak still overtook Abel Resino to become the goalkeeper with the most appearances in Atlético's history.

He is still only 29, which is relatively young in terms of a goalkeeper's prime, and if anything he has only ever shown that he has the drive and determination to consistently overcome adversity of any kind. His career has been all about finding the window of opportunity, and when it has been presented to him, Oblak has shown a clinical nature that Simeone's forwards would be proud of, providing a sense of stability that has defined this Atlético Madrid defence.

* * *

Thibaut Courtois

Much like Oblak, Courtois's family was a sporty one too, except that his parents played volleyball. His sister would take up the sport professionally as well, going on to represent that national team, and while Courtois spent a lot of his childhood on the beaches with a volleyball it would be football that truly caught his eye. The diving around did not immediately translate to him becoming a goalkeeper, however, and it was in the left-back position that the young Belgian would begin his career.

Starting out at local side Bilzen V.V., Courtois would join the youth academy of Genk at the age of seven, still playing outfield. It would take about two years before he eventually made the switch to become a full-time keeper when the coaches, who had watched Courtois train as a keeper at times, realised that his athleticism and calmness suited the role perfectly, hence kickstarting what would become a very successful career. He would continue to climb up the ranks at Genk alongside fellow Belgian Koen Casteels and, even though it was the latter who was better regarded in those early years, a goalkeeping crisis driven by injury and suspension saw Courtois make his debut in April 2009, at the age of just 16.

Though it was a foot in the door, this was not yet Courtois's big break and he, along with Casteels, would continue training with the senior side for little over a year as they remained backup options to the first choice, László Köteles. It was at this point that Hoffenheim attempted to take him to the Bundesliga, but with his parents unwilling to allow a transfer before he had graduated from school, Courtois would turn down this move and with the 2010/11 season looming large he would become the regular starting keeper at Genk. Having just turned 18, this would prove to be his breakthrough season and, by keeping 14 clean sheets while conceding only 32 goals in 40 games, Courtois would be pivotal in the side's title victory that year, also winning individual awards for being the Goalkeeper of the Year and Genk's Player of the Year. Hoffenheim would come back, but by then Courtois was on his way to Chelsea and the German club would pick up Casteels instead.

Within weeks of his €8m transfer to Chelsea, Courtois had his bags packed and headed to Atlético on loan, landing in the Spanish capital in the summer of 2011. David de Gea had just left for Manchester United and, while Sergio Asenjo and Joel Robles were at the club, it was Courtois who became the first choice, getting off to an impressive start and keeping four clean sheets in his first six league games. A dismissal towards the end of November in a Madrid derby that would see Real comfortably win 4-1 would be the only major bump in those early months for Courtois, but Atlético were inching closer to the relegation zone. Along with Simeone came the results, and with his promising showings in goal, Courtois managed to win his second major trophy at the age of 20, keeping a clean sheet in the Europa League final as Atlético triumphed 3-0 against Athletic Bilbao.

The loan would be extended for another season and, in his first game after the extension, Courtois would win the UEFA Super Cup against his parent club Chelsea, making it his second trophy with Atlético in just about a year. He was not slowing down either and, after setting a club record of going 820 minutes without conceding during the 2012/13 season, the Belgian would reach yet another final, this time in the Copa del Rey against Real Madrid. As the heavyweights with the likes of Cristiano Ronaldo, Karim Benzema, Luka Modrić and Mesut Özil in their ranks peppered his goal with shots, Courtois pulled off save after save to deny them and keep his side in the game, eventually being named man of the match as Atlético not only ran out 2-1 winners after extra time, but also ended a 14-year winless streak against their city rivals.

Petr Čech was still the first-choice keeper at Chelsea though, so Courtois would have his loan extended by another year – which would prove to be the best of them all. Conceding just 26 goals in 38 games, the Belgian was just turning 22 when Atlético went on to clinch the La Liga title and with his exceptional goals-to-games ratio, he would win the Zamora Trophy to add to his personal accolades. For the second time in his career he was a league champion, and his contributions would extend into Europe as well, where he played a crucial role in helping Atlético reach the final of the Champions League after notably knocking Chelsea out in the semi-finals. Interestingly, Chelsea had initially insisted that the Belgian could not play against them, but with UEFA eventually intervening and siding with the Spanish outfit, he was cleared to feature. Unfortunately, though, despite a valiant performance in the final a week after the title celebrations, Courtois and Atlético could not repeat the heroics of the Copa del Rey, finishing runners-up but still rounding off what was an extremely successful season for both player and club. By now, his performances were catching the eye of teams all across the continent, and Atlético were resigned to letting him go when Chelsea decided it was time to take him back for good.

With the familiar faces of Filipe Luís and Diego Costa also following, Courtois settled in fairly well in London, displacing Čech and becoming the first choice as Chelsea won the Premier League title in what was, at last, his first season in London. He would also win the League Cup, though his minutes were shared with Čech, and complete a nice double upon his return. The 2015/16 season, however, was a more tumultuous time for Chelsea and for Courtois as well, as he would be sent off in the opening game. The club struggled and, after suffering an injury in September, the Belgian was sidelined for about three months before becoming only the sixth goalkeeper to be sent off twice in the same league season after a foul against Manchester City in the middle of April. The less said about that season the better, but with Antonio Conte coming in the following year Courtois was once again on the up.

It is easy to forget that he was still only 24 by the time 2016/17 came around and Courtois once again showed why he was now one of the top keepers in the world, keeping 16 clean sheets in the league and winning the Golden Glove award as Chelsea were crowned champions for the second time in three years. By this time, he was already a key player for Belgium in a national team that was labelled as a golden generation and expected to achieve some form of success on the international stage. After all, they boasted the likes of Eden Hazard, Kevin De Bruyne, Yannick Carrasco and Romelu Lukaku, and Courtois himself was the pick of the bunch between the sticks, making his debut back in November 2011 and becoming the youngest keeper to play for his country. Unfortunately there would be no solid success with the national team as Courtois formed the core of the sides that would play in the 2014 and 2018 World Cup as well as Euro 2016 and 2020, getting knocked out in the quarter-finals each time other than in 2018, when they reached the semi-finals. The only consolation was that they had three times lost to eventual finalists (Argentina 2014, France 2018, Italy 2020), with two of them going on to win the tournament (France and Italy), but the defeat to Wales in 2016 remains one of the biggest upsets Belgium have faced.

Back at club level and skipping ahead slightly to the end of the 2017/18 season, Courtois had now played as many games for Chelsea as he had for Atlético but would soon burn bridges with both clubs when he expressed his intent to move on. While this was not so much the issue, the manner in which this panned out and the eventual destination would sour things as Courtois opted not to show up for training to force a move when Chelsea stated that they could not let him go until a replacement was found, and he eventually joined Real Madrid.

It did not help that he would later state, upon joining the club, that stepping on to the pitch in Real colours was a childhood dream, following up on it nearly three years later before a match against Chelsea when he said once again said that that winning a Champions League trophy with Real was a childhood dream, effectively ensuring that despite his contributions to both his previous clubs, he will not be remembered all too fondly at either. In fact, while Chelsea fans whistled and jeered him upon his return, Atlético fans went a step further and threw toy rats at him in his first game at the Wanda Metropolitano for Real Madrid, though Courtois no longer seems to mind. His hunt to achieve that dream of winning the final with Real Madrid finally ended, however, with Real Madrid triumphant against Liverpool in the 2022 final.

Though *Los Colchoneros* may no longer care for him, it is difficult to ignore Courtois's contributions in those initial years of Atlético success, during a period where *Los Rojiblancos* staked their claim to be among Europe's best, when his all-round capabilities proved to be a perfect cover for the side's rugged defence, shutting out the best of the best along the way. In the end, those three years can be remembered as a mutual partnership between Courtois and Atlético, as both relied on each other during their respective rises to the top.

* * *

Order. Simeone craves it, but he knows that he cannot simply demand it. That is not how his Atlético works, and no matter how loudly he yells from the touchline, that will never be how his Atlético works. Simeone's Atlético is the one that showed itself on that Champions League night in Moscow, with players sprinting back to cover for their team-mates and keep their goalkeeper safe. Simeone's Atlético is the one that ensured Leverkusen would not find a way back, with the goalkeeper this time ensuring that the rest of his team were safe. Simeone's Atlético is all about gifts, ensuring that the work that one puts in serves as the best gift for the others, with the assurance that the favour would be returned in due time.

He knows that he is not exempt from this gift-giving culture either, and for the only position in his XI that does not have another of its kind, Simeone reserves his biggest gift of all. Where all the other positions have needed flexibility, the goalkeeper is instead given stability and even with the rest of the team adapting to modern times in a complete formational change, Simeone has ensured that the keeper's role has largely remained the same. It is then no wonder that these goalkeepers give him exactly what he needs, with his faith and trust allowing them to perform at a top level over a substantial period of time as they throw themselves about between the posts to deny anything that is about to cross the line.

Atlético's goalkeepers are fully capable of the spectacular, so much so that it soon becomes the normal, and you would be unwise to take for granted that you have altered the balance of the game with a strike on goal. For just as you wheel away in celebration, the arm comes out, denying what seemed inevitable just a second before.

Order, once again, restored.

10
Conclusion

WALKING DOWN the Paseo de los Melancólicos, or the Way of the Melancholic, the south-west bank of the River Manzanares is certainly a little quieter these days. The scenery has changed and where there was once a football stadium drawing crowds that made the area almost uninhabitable on matchdays, the general mood now could not be better described by the very road that had led to the ground. Construction crews fill the void, having taken over the grassy stage upon which *Colchoneros* had witnessed captivating performances, with the memories of over 50 years having been steadily sown into the ground. The roots of those seeds remain, and even with the M-30 motorway (which had passed under the main stand) being given an extension to cut right through the pitch, the sanctity lingers.

The beloved Estadio Vicente Calderón is no more, but the sound of machines pounding and whirring is nothing compared to the roars of over 50,000 who flocked to this great venue, and once the parks and residential blocks finally take over the landscape, the neighbourhood will only get quieter, achieving a sense of tranquillity that has not been present for half a century. Times have changed and, even if the river remains the only constant, the banks will never be the same. Atlético Madrid have departed for bigger things, moving into the Wanda Metropolitano about 15km away, quickly filling the additional 15,000 seats and carrying over the undying passion and memories of old. Their new home is now this stunning stadium with facilities that rival the best in Europe, a symbol of their growth and transformation over the years to be right up among the continent's elite, despite coming from the less extravagant side of Madrid.

The real beauty, however, is that none of this matters. After all, Atlético's residence is not in any physical establishment, but rather it is in the heart of its *Colchoneros*, and that will always be their home. It is a home in which a special room will always be reserved for Diego Simeone, the man who has become synonymous with their successes and who has been almost solely responsible for all these drastic changes. With the Europa League and UEFA Super Cup triumphs in his first half season, Simeone had nearly doubled the club's tally of three trophies in the 15 years from 1996 to 2011, one of which was the Segunda División triumph in 2002, and out of nowhere Atlético were suddenly back on the footballing map as a serious side.

Had you taken a look at how the club was being run, you might not have deduced this state of affairs, but Simeone's ability to consistently get results on the pitch did more than just mask this and, before you knew it, *Los Rojiblancos* were champions of Spain, and the frequency of visits to the Plaza de Neptuno had increased. The powerful Neptune is depicted upon his chariot with a trident in his arm, pulled by the seahorses symbolising storms and the agitated sea, and Atlético too had ridden their own storms only to now bask in all their glory, a moment that seemed surreal.

Simeone is their most successful manager ever, but, above all, he is one of them. The scrappy South American who landed in the Calderón all those years ago could not have been more Atlético if he tried, and in him the stands found someone that they could trust. Commitment, passion and the fighting spirit, this is Atlético, and this is Simeone, and no other arranged marriage could ever lead to such a big love affair, which has never wavered over the years, and will remain the same until eternity.

Perhaps this is Simeone's biggest achievement, to have transformed the club while essentially keeping it the same. He has often been criticised for being too rigid and sticking to his defensive principles when the squad at his disposal is up there among the best in terms of talent alone. Surely Atlético could play football that was more eye-catching, and surely Atlético could play 'good' football, a phrase that seemingly suggests that there are right and wrong ways to play the game. Further criticisms suggest that Player X certainly cannot be happy playing in a team like this, or that fans certainly cannot enjoy watching a team that plays this way, and the opinion that Atlético are simply a club that is a shame to modern football has been increasingly propagated, even by people that are paid for their opinions on the sport.

Anyone who suggests this makes a mockery not just of themselves, but of football itself, for the beauty of it lies in the fact that there are infinite ways to play the game. If anything, the sole aim is to win, a goal that has only become more important in modern times but also a goal that Atlético have increasingly achieved over the last decade. To say that Simeone's football is not to your liking is fair, but for the idea of it being bad or wrong to gain momentum is a reflection of how shallow and skewed the modern perception of the game is, where top teams with extraordinary budgets have separated themselves from the rest of the pack and have the freedom to operate as they wish. Atlético themselves have now evolved to fall into a rare grey area, having developed a budget bigger than most but one that is still well short of the big guns that they are often clubbed in with. They have got here with their footballing success, playing how they do in order to punch above their weight and no matter how big they get, this will always be their tradition, and this will always be what the club aspires to.

The very foundations of Atlético are built upon a tradition of suffering, and for Simeone to fully understand this and mould a team accordingly while also achieving consistent success is, no matter how you put it, nothing short of footballing greatness. 'Football is passion,' *Cholo* says, and everything he does is based around this passion. A style that harnesses the passion of the fans, a system that evokes the passion of each and every single player, and performances that marry the two to bring about the best possible result for Atlético. He is a tactician, man-manager and even crowd conductor, all rolled into one.

Simeone just sees the game differently, and this is what makes him so unique as a manager. Even his trademark runs down the tunnel right after the final whistle show how much thought he puts into every single action, as what is often criticised as a lack of sportsmanship is just his own way of settling down, before seeking out the opposition manager later on and thanking them for the game. He studies every single matchday situation and knows when to be reactive and when to be proactive, and even his defensive structure differs from most others simply because it has the right blend of aggressiveness drilled into it. His ability to combine rigidity and fluidity, alternating between both at the snap of a finger, only serves to provide us with further insight into the intricacies of his tactics, with ample thought given to every minute detail.

All this would all be tough for anyone who is not Simeone because, apart from all these traits, he also has the exterior to match, coolly tackling all the constant criticism and persisting with his methods, showing a sense of self-belief that you find in the greatest of leaders. His hardness allows him to smile in the face of adversity, giving him the strength to battle and win in the toughest of circumstances and, even if he does lose, he is able to quickly dust himself off and focus on the next challenge.

Simply put, he is a mentality monster, and he has tuned himself so perfectly to the demands of his role that he is almost always a step ahead with a special knack of understanding and dealing with situations far better than most.

This is not to say that Simeone is without his flaws, and the raw emotions of the game do get to him at times, culminating in outbursts and sideline scuffles. It does not help that he presents himself as the game's biggest antagonist either, and it is easy to see why most people do not take an immediate liking to the man, whose aura gives off vibes similar to that of a superhero villain. But it is in these instances that Atlético supporters see Simeone as what he is, a human and a fan just like them, bringing him down momentarily from the god-like status to which he has been elevated.

Indeed, he is probably best described as an anti-hero, someone who may never quite fit the conventional characteristics that are often associated with regular heroes, a complex character with a dark side but well and truly one of the best and most important figures in the modern game.

He has not only shown that the path to success is not a straight line, but that it is not even a single line, and that as long as you are willing to put in the effort and commit to finding it, then success can be achieved in many ways. It is highly probable that in an age gone by, Simeone might just have found himself being one of the world's most revolutionary thinkers.

So, what next for Atlético Madrid? Well, they say that the more things change, the more they stay the same and, despite their development, Atlético will not be judged on their trophies but rather on their performances regardless of the result. They remain the pride of the fans and, as long as the fans are able to see their commitment on the pitch, the support will never waver. Instead, their frustrations will always be directed at the board who, in their view, have been trying to take their club away from them, with many an argument arising over the years.

A revamp of the club crest in 2017, for example, saw an alteration to *El Oso y el Madroño* (The Bear and the Strawberry Tree) which has long been a symbol of Madrid and a part of Atlético history for nearly a century, and the move naturally did not sit well with the fans.

The change had clearly been made for corporate purposes, to allow for more straightforward reproduction of the logo across a variety of media by simplifying the colour scheme and individual components, but it was viewed as an attack on the club's identity, with protests going on to this day whenever a jersey is released with the new crest. Some sort of compromise might slowly be reached on this issue, however, and Atlético rolled out a fourth kit featuring the old logo for the 2021/22 season, with rumours that it could feature on some of the 2022/23 kits as well. What is certain, though, is that the lack of trust that the fans have in the board will continue, and this remains a fractured relationship.

This is not to say that the club is being ran nearly as bad as it was under Jesús Gil, whose son and current CEO, Miguel Ángel Gil Marín, and current president Enrique Cerezo have managed to somehow provide a sense of stability in this period of success despite their own differences. The pair of them barely talk, but Atlético currently have one of the most efficient wage bills in Europe and, along with the money from their transfer activity, they have managed to consistently compete with more financially fortunate clubs. This may seem bewildering on the face of it, considering the number of transfers and comments from the pair of them that have raised an eyebrow or two, and a large part of the success is probably down to Simeone's ability to churn out results with whatever tools he has and generate sums based on sporting merit, but without calling them hidden geniuses it is possible to acknowledge that at least something is being done right, even if not all of it is.

They still have some way to go before they are fully accepted by the fanbase and they are yet to show that they are truly the best people to drive Atlético forward, but for now, they remain at the top of a truly intriguing football club.

Where Atlético go from here, though, remains to be seen, but their performances over the past decade have seen them create an excellent platform for them to push on and aim for greater heights. In ten full seasons under Simeone, *Los Rojiblancos* have never finished outside the top three in La Liga, cementing their status as Spain's third-best club, and while they have kept Real Madrid and Barcelona honest over the past decade and picked up their own fair share of trophies in that span, it does seem ever so tantalising that they could soon hop on to that top step and not just be outside hopes anymore.

'We want to win, the club's objective is to enter the Champions League, but ours is to become champions,' Simeone said ahead of the final game of the 2021/22, season and this is a very different statement of intent coming from a manager that has consistently prided his side on being the underdogs. Atlético's mentality is slowly shifting and they have the talent pool to match, giving them the platform to genuinely take the step to become clear challengers and, dare we say favourites, for the league title. Spain's top division has been a two-horse race for so long, with Real Madrid and Barcelona having benefitted massively as a result of La Liga's direct support, especially in the modern era, such that it needs both of them to have poor seasons for there to even be a consideration of the possibility that someone else can win the league. Maybe, just maybe, Atlético have done enough to prove otherwise.

Remember, we are only talking about the future of Atlético as a club here and hard as it may be to separate it from Simeone, it does look like the path forward is a good one. They might have never got this far without him, but thanks to his efforts, Atlético might now just be able to survive without him. There is, of course, a reason why we say survive and not thrive, and that is due to the fact that Atlético have become so attached to Simeone that they still have some way to go before they can be considered a sufficiently good side on their own. In fact, there have even been some nearly blasphemous claims recently that Atlético can (or even will) take that final step without him, but in truth, such statements only serve to compliment Simeone even more because for people to even suggest this shows how far he has brought the club forward in the last decade.

There will come a time when *Cholo* leaves the pitch for good, but for the next manager to understand this club and balance every aspect of the job the way he does will certainly be a major challenge in itself. Manchester United, for example, are yet to fill in the void left by Sir Alex Ferguson close to a decade on, and for Atlético, the fear is that the same could happen to them as well.

This is not to say that they will plunge into total darkness though, but even if there is someone out there able to take up the reins and steer Atlético to success, it is difficult to picture anyone having such a strong connection with the club unless it turns out to be another former player. Whether this is sustainable or not is a huge question, but another manager may have a playing style that goes against what Atlético have grown to love, and another might not be able to deal with the board for instance. With more questions than answers at the moment, it is clear that the immediate future of the club is one that includes Simeone and perhaps just as he answered those questions all those years ago when he took on the job, he might answer these as well and leave Atlético in a position where the doubts are no longer relevant.

For Simeone, this works out fine because, loyalties aside, he is only 52 and still has many years left in his managerial career unless he abruptly decides otherwise. With his impulsiveness this is honestly not entirely out of the question, but with his passion for football it is certainly hard to see him walking away from the game entirely when he still has so much to give. In the same way, it is hard to imagine him walking away from Atlético either, having stayed through thick and thin and for him to leave a club that he loves so dearly with a project that he has been the architect of for so long would be nothing short of a huge surprise. He did, of course, admit that he once considered this after the second Champions League Final loss to Real Madrid in 2016, though he stated at the time that it was down to him doubting his ability to motivate his side again rather than any other offers or him simply feeling he was done.

The latter might never happen, but Simeone has certainly been on the radar of the likes of Manchester United, Manchester City, Chelsea, Arsenal, Tottenham and Paris Saint-Germain, though it has only ever been another of his former clubs, Inter Milan, who have ever caught his eye. 'As I have always said, and I have no fear of saying it again now, one day I will return,' he confidently stated, and for someone with so much conviction in his words, it does seem like this will become an eventuality. This is certainly no slight against Atlético though, and despite the Italian outfit's advances in the past, Simeone has stayed in Madrid and continuously shown his commitment and loyalty to the project at hand. However, when the time finally arrives, *Cholo* will once again trade the red and white stripes for blue and black, and be assured that it will come with the blessings of *Colchoneros* everywhere.

For now, Simeone remains the longest-serving manager at a single club out of the current crop in La Liga, as well as across the top European leagues, and his association with *Los Rojiblancos* is certainly not over just yet.

The elusive Champions League trophy will forever be in his sights and, closer to home, Simeone appears fresh as ever despite a rather weak title defence in the 2021/22 season. You would think that would demoralise most, but for *Cholo* it is a clean slate with no expectations and a perfect setting for him to hatch perhaps the biggest heist of them all.

Having had to swim against the tide for so long, he senses the opportunity to turn his underdogs into the top dogs and is moving ever so slyly towards doing the unthinkable, which is to have control over a league that once looked like it could never be theirs. He has had a taste of it, twice, and he continues sniffing, knowing that when the time comes to turn bark to bite he will be ready to leave yet another mark, this one being the biggest and deepest of them all. For when *Cholo* senses an opportunity, you can be assured that he does not need a second invitation.

Knives between teeth, Diego Simeone and Atlético Madrid are always ready to go hunting.

Partido a partido.

Appendix, Figure references

About the author

Ashwin Reuben Ballal hails from Chennai, India, and has worked in the football industry as an analyst and scout for clubs and organisations across the globe. He has published numerous articles that dive into tactics and data for *Total Football Analysis* magazine. His chapter on Manchester United was part of the *English Premier League: Preseason Prospectus 2020/21*, published in 2020. This is his debut book.